EXPLORING CONCEPTS OF CHILD WELL-BEING

Implications for children's services

Nick Axford

First published in Great Britain in 2008 by

The Policy Press
University of Bristol
Fourth Floor
Beacon House
Queen's Road
Bristol BS8 1QU
UK

Tel +44 (0)117 331 4054
Fax +44 (0)117 331 4093
e-mail tpp-info@bristol.ac.uk
www.policypress.org.uk

© Nick Axford 2008

British Library Cataloguing in Publication Data
A catalogue record for this book is available from the British Library.

Library of Congress Cataloging-in-Publication Data
A catalog record for this book has been requested.

ISBN 978 1 84742 065 7 hardcover

Cover design by Kevin Mount
Front cover: photograph kindly supplied by Chris Cockram
Printed and bound in Great Britain by MPG Books, Bodmin

Contents

List of tables

Acknowledgements

This book would not have been completed without the input of many people. In particular I owe a great deal to colleagues past and present at Dartington. Some helped me develop the measures for the study and most have at some point pushed a relevant article across my desk, or helped with technical problems, or contributed ideas in discussions. For enriching the study (and me) in many ways, and for helping to make Dartington such a vibrant and supportive place in which to work I am extremely grateful.

I would especially like to thank Michael Little, who guided me throughout my PhD (which this book is based on). He was instrumental in the early formulation of the ideas and his advice was invaluable in helping to clarify arguments. The written drafts benefited greatly from comments by Roger Bullock, Bill Jordan and Roy Parker, and I am extremely grateful to them for their time, interest and insights (and the occasional joke). Louise Morpeth and Vashti Berry have been a source of encouragement and banter throughout and, with others, generously enabled me to have the time to finish editing the book. I have received critical and stimulating comments from Ian Gough and Gordon Jack, my PhD examiners, and two anonymous reviewers, all of which I hope have improved the end-product. Lastly, I would like to thank my parents for their ongoing support and Chloe, my wife, for being interested in and excited about what I get up to.

It goes without saying that I alone am responsible for what is written and therefore for any errors or omissions.

ONE

Introduction

The concept of well-being has entered public policy rhetoric in the UK and other western developed countries as a companion to other buzzwords of recent years. It is linked with the new science of well-being and happiness, also referred to as 'hedonic psychology' – which studies self-evaluated overall life satisfaction – its components, causes and correlates. Recent years have seen a flurry of academic and popular publications in this area (eg Kahneman et al, 1999; Huppert et al, 2005; Layard, 2005; Martin, 2005; Nettle, 2005; Haidt, 2006; Offer, 2006; Schoch, 2006). This shift has arguably been fuelled by macroeconomic and social trends:

> With the collapse of Soviet state socialism and the triumph of market individualism, it appeared that the links between private property, capitalism, democracy and economic growth on the one hand and human well-being on the other, were unchallengeable. Now there are serious doubts over whether material prosperity leads to greater happiness, and whether individual freedom and consensual government supply the best institutional framework for well-being. (Jordan, 2006a, p 42)

However, the well-being approach has not yet been systematically applied to children. There is a growing body of research charting patterns of and trends in aspects of child well-being (Bradshaw and Mayhew, 2005; Ben-Arieh and Goerge, 2006; Bradshaw et al, 2007a, 2007b) and suddenly it seems that everyone involved in children's services in the UK and several other western developed countries is talking the language of 'outcomes' and 'well-being' (see Scott and Ward, 2005; McAuley et al, 2006). But it is easy to jump on bandwagons, and some caution is required. It is not yet clear if findings from adult populations can easily be transposed to child populations (Jordan, 2006a), and there could be a danger of discarding valuable perspectives in favour of a new one simply because they are unfashionable.

In any society there have always been children and young people whose well-being is viewed with concern. Among the different terms used to describe their predicament are need, violated rights, poverty, poor quality of life (QoL)[1] and social exclusion. All are different ways of considering well-being. Sometimes, of course, these concepts are elided or used interchangeably, as in 'poverty and social exclusion'. Different professions or disciplines are more likely to use one term than another, for instance medical practitioners speak about 'QoL' more than lawyers and children's advocates, who are more comfortable with 'rights'. There is also evidence of past fashions for certain concepts, so that whereas the use of the term 'need' might have been in favour with government in the UK in the 1990s, at least in children's services, it has since been overtaken (first by social exclusion, now by 'well-being').

Often the implication is that the same predicaments, or at least the same children, are being described using different words. But is this true? Certainly figures from the UK indicate a varied situation. Successive publications have put the proportion of children in need in England at about 5% (DH, 2001a; DfES and National Statistics, 2006). Experts often imply that *all* children have their rights violated by virtue of being a minority social group (eg Franklin, 2002; Mayall, 2002). National statistics suggest that over a quarter of children (27%) in Britain live below the poverty line (DWP, 2006). In 2004 4% of children aged 5–16 years in Britain had an emotional disorder (anxiety or depression) – one proxy indicator for a poor QoL (Green et al, 2005). And although there is no national figure for children, just 2% of the population aged over 15 years are socially excluded (eg Burchardt et al, 1999, p 236). A related question is: are the terms used in a way that is helpful from a service perspective; for example, do they enrich our understanding of children's circumstances and how best to improve them? Or is it better to draw everything together under the umbrella of 'well-being'? There is a danger that disparate terminology gives vulnerable children and families better vocabularies but not better services.

What this book is about

The study described in this book set out to explore such questions. It had three main aims. The first was to identify the defining characteristics of the five concepts of child well-being – need, rights, poverty, QoL and social exclusion – and to explore the relationships between them. A number of questions were investigated. For example, what is the difference between being in need and having one's rights violated? Is social exclusion another word for poverty? Does QoL serve as an overarching concept that embraces the other four? Based on the above figures and research into vulnerable children by the Dartington Social Research Unit (where the author works), the hypothesis was that the concepts are related but not as closely as is widely assumed.

The second aim was to measure the prevalence of the conditions to which the concepts refer for a population of children representative of a particular community, and to compare the overlap between them. (The term 'condition' is convenient shorthand for the empirical formulation of the concepts.) Again, there were several questions to be answered. For instance, how does the prevalence of need compare with official estimates? Is the proportion of socially excluded children similar to that of adults? Can a child have a decent QoL even though their family is in poverty? It was hypothesised that the prevalence of the conditions varies considerably, and that although there is greater overlap between some conditions than others, none subsumes another.

The third aim was to consider the implications of the findings for policy and practice in children's services, defined here as those interventions organised and provided on behalf of children by agencies such as social services, health, education, youth justice, the benefits agency, housing, leisure providers and the voluntary sector. Questions included: Do services informed by need tend to have a different emphasis to those underpinned by a concern to protect children's rights? Are efforts to combat social exclusion likely to help or hinder anti-poverty initiatives? And, practically, what steps might be taken towards implementing a more cohesive service mix? The hypothesis was that services aimed at addressing some conditions can be ineffective in relation to others, and that while contradictions exist they can be minimised by a better understanding of the concepts.

In order to address these aims, the study drew on theoretical literature, empirical studies and the original analysis of existing data in approximately equal amounts. The latter involved reanalysing data collected for a separate study on 234 children living on a fairly deprived and ethnically diverse inner-city London housing estate. Dichotomous tests were devised for each of the five concepts of child well-being and applied to the dataset. The book is targeted at researchers, senior managers and policy-makers working in children's services, in particular those concerned with the design, implementation and evaluation of services. It introduces insights from diverse fields concerning the understanding of well-being, shows how these may be applied in relation to children and encourages reflection on the implications for research, policy and practice.

Child well-being in policy and practice

The aims just outlined are particularly relevant in the present policy and practice context in the UK and other western developed countries. The five approaches to conceptualising child well-being are all recognised policy objectives in children's services, and there is evidence of connections between them being recognised and promoted. At the same time, tensions have surfaced between them, perhaps because one perspective is perceived to supersede another in policy discourse, or as initiatives orientated towards one concept appear to counteract programmes informed by another. These points are illustrated in the discussion that follows.

Starting with need, the government's vision for children's services in England and Wales, *Every Child Matters* (DfES, 2003), and the ensuing 2004 Children Act are concerned with early intervention to improve children's health (physical and mental) and safety (being protected from harm and neglect). They also talk about children with 'additional needs', defined as those at risk of poor outcomes, while subsequent guidance encourages local agencies to measure the level of need locally and use the results as the basis for planning services. This builds on and reinforces the requirement in the 1989 Children Act for local authorities to assist 'children in need', defined as those whose health or development is actually impaired or likely to become so without remedial help (Part III, s 17(10)).

This latter piece of legislation attempted to recalibrate the balance of rights and responsibilities between the state, parents and children. This followed concerns about the unnecessary removal of children from their parents but also several scandals in which abused children were failed by the system (Parton, 1991). More significantly, as signatories to the 1989 UN Convention on Children's Rights (CRC) the UK and all countries in the world bar the US and Somalia (who are not signatories) have their progress in implementing each Article monitored by an independent body, and the 1998 Human Rights Act incorporates into UK law the European Convention on Human Rights. Arguably the climate created by such developments has contributed to the attention paid in the 2004 Children Act and ensuing guidance to making services more accountable – for example, via lead professionals, a Children's Commissioner and a Common Assessment Framework – and taking action on behalf of children who are deemed not to be adequately parented – for example via Parenting Orders. Indeed, these developments are symptomatic of the *Zeitgeist*; from being considered the eccentric preserve of activists, human rights has fast become the language both of international diplomacy (Kennedy, 2000) and also of policy-making and management in children's services. There is now an acceptance in policy that children are entitled to participate in the planning, delivery and evaluation of services. In terms of links with other concepts, the promotion of children's rights to participation is predicated partly on the argument that involving service users helps with meeting their needs (eg Sinclair, 1996), although robust evidence for this link is scant (Kirby et al, 2003).

Poverty is also firmly on the global and national agendas. No G8 summit now passes without mass protests about world poverty by church members, trade union activists, pop stars and a myriad of non-governmental organisations, galvanised most recently by the worldwide 'Make Poverty History' campaign. And in the UK, a mixture of area-based initiatives and tax and benefit measures have been introduced to help fulfil the government's pledge to eradicate child poverty by the year 2020 (Blair, 1999), albeit with mixed success to date (eg Bradshaw, 2005; Evans and Scarborough, 2006; Hirsch, 2006; Palmer et al, 2006), while the 2004 Children Act expressly requires services to improve children's economic well-being. For many this goal is a rights issue, underpinned by Article 27 of the CRC concerning the entitlement to adequate living standards, but potential tensions with measures aimed at combating social exclusion have also been highlighted (eg Levitas, 1998).

The current UK government also has an explicit if little-known strategy for improving people's QoL, together with a series of indicators for tracking progress on topics such as fear of crime, air and water quality, urban regeneration and access to services and leisure facilities (DETR, 1999a, 1999b; DEFRA, 2004). It is also looking to expand psychological services within the NHS in the light of evidence that depression and chronic anxiety are the biggest causes of misery in Britain today (Bell et al, 2006); indeed, health has been explicitly concerned with patients' QoL for some time now (Bowling, 1997). Again, the 2004 Children Act and associated documents are interesting for the prominence they give to children enjoying and getting the most out of life, one manifestation of which, arguably, is an emphasis on culture, sport and play (DCMS, 2006). As before, there are links with other policy objectives, for example sport and summer holiday clubs are often used as diversionary activities to tackle antisocial behaviour and so reduce social exclusion.

The term 'social exclusion' entered UK policy discourse with the birth in 1997 of the Social Exclusion Unit – a cross-departmental body to research solutions to linked problems such as unemployment, poor housing, bad health and family breakdown. Since then it has underpinned measures concerning teenage motherhood, truancy and the education of children in care, and it has driven various childcare, health and education initiatives in deprived neighbourhoods – Sure Start, Health Action Zones, Education Action Zones and so forth. Proposals in *Every Child Matters* demonstrate a concern to combat social exclusion, for example the desire to encourage children to make a positive contribution by being involved with the community and society and not engaging in antisocial or offending behaviour. Similarly, the emphasis on multidisciplinary teams, the use of universal services as a location for specialist help and the co-location of several services reflect the mantra 'joined-up solutions to joined-up problems' (eg HM Treasury, 2002; HM Government, 2006; Buchanan, 2007; Social Exclusion Task Force, 2007). As an example of the way that policy objectives jostle for position, children 'at risk of social exclusion' rather than those 'in need' increasingly became the explicit target of national policy, although the difference between them is rarely articulated.

The study of childhood

There are numerous factors that have contributed to the five concepts of child well-being becoming popular policy objectives today (see Axford, 2003). One factor worthy of particular mention is the growth of 'childhood sociology', a body of work in which children are portrayed as active participants in society rather than as passive subjects waiting to become adults (eg Qvortrup, 1994; Corsaro, 1996; James and Prout, 1997; James et al, 1998; Mayall, 2002). This perspective has contributed to a greater interest in studying childhood per se, with at least three themes particularly salient here.

The first is that children are viewed as 'a minority social group, whose wrongs need righting' (Mayall, 2002, p 9). This perspective is informed in part by feminist thinking, with generation replacing gender as the axis of distinction in an unequal power relationship; compared to older people, children require more protection, since they know less, have less maturity and less strength, and as such they have moral inferiority. This view of children as a minority group is also related to the perceived low status of children in society, as indicated by the poor quality of some services for children, the continued prevalence of child poverty and constraints on children's opportunity to take part in decision-making about any aspect of their school experience. A further reason for viewing children in this way is that, in school at least, their own accounts suggest that 'they see themselves as a group vis-à-vis the adult group, and as a group whose rights are both neglected and rejected' (Mayall, 2002, p 21). This relationship is recognised even by five-year-olds and continues into adolescence, and the 'commonalities override detail of gender, ethnicity and age' (p 136).

A second theme is that children should be viewed as social actors and moral agents in their own right who are embedded in society and who both have and fulfil socially ascribed responsibilities. This view of children as active and constructive members of society counters the view that having been removed from paid work they are precious but burdensome, no longer valued for their direct economic contribution to family and the labour market and instead dependants being socialised, with school activity considered to be preparatory. Children are clearly *social actors* in that from early on they take part in family relationships by expressing wishes, demonstrating strong attachments and feelings, and seeking justice. They are also *agents*, though, implying a further dimension: 'negotiation with others, with the effect that the interaction makes a difference – to a relationship or to a decision, to the workings of a set of social assumptions of constraints' (Mayall, 2002, p 21). Again, this is supported by empirical evidence. Even in infancy children respond to and initiate interaction with parents and others, for example imitating actions and interacting playfully, angrily or aggressively. Children also participate in necessary activities – including paid and unpaid work in the family (domestic labour), school and labour market – as well as in economically useful activity (for example buying their own clothes). And they are *moral* agents; in their daily interactions they also 'confront issues of justice, equal distribution and sharing. They respond to each other's actions and feelings, and meet approval or disapproval in their own actions' (Mayall, 2002, p 88). If children are conceptualised as participants in society, it follows that they have needs that must be fulfilled to allow them to participate and that they can also be excluded.

A third theme in the literature is that the boundary between childhood and adulthood is disappearing, 'making children stressed and rushing them too fast through what should be a carefree and innocent period of life' (Mayall, 2002, p 3). This is apparent in the amount of activity demanded by schools, in their access to sex and drugs, and in cultural and fashion taste, and raises important questions about their QoL.

Taken together, these themes have contributed to childhood being at the forefront of political and academic agendas. It is noticeable, for instance, that there is a concerted effort to study childhood, in particular through children's own accounts (eg Mizen et al, 1999; Morrow, 2000), and to recognise that there is a child standpoint: 'those inhabiting childhood have a particular take or standpoint on their status in relation to adult status ... a child standpoint (analogous to a woman's standpoint) is important for contributing to a proper account of the social order' (Mayall, 2002, p 8). There is also a broader move towards a more child-centred approach to social policy analysis (eg Hendrick, 2005; Ridge, 2005) – one within which this book seeks to position itself.

Research on the five concepts

It is clear from the previous sections that the aims of the present research were timely. However, executing them was complicated by three factors. The first of these is the contested nature of each concept. The different approaches to defining each concept are explored in greater depth in Chapters Two to Six, but here the debates are introduced, starting with need. Bradshaw (1994) described need as 'too imprecise, too complex, too contentious to be a target for policy ... [it] leaves a lot to be desired both as an epidemiological identifier and also as a basis for evaluating the performance of policies' (p 45). Commentators have interpreted it variously as dressed-up preferences and wants manufactured by capitalism, although others have argued robustly for it being the universal basis for distributing welfare (Chapter 1 in Doyal and Gough, 1991). Indeed, the concept has an enduring quality in policy and practice that demands it be better understood.

Most research on rights has comprised philosophical discussions about what rights people have and attempts to interpret national and international legislation. There have been fierce debates between libertarians, who argue that freedoms are the only bona fide rights (eg Nozick, 1974), and defenders of socioeconomic rights (eg Plant, 1991). The children's rights movement added a crusading tone to the academic debate, and stirred up discussions about the extent to which children can have rights, and, if so, if they include self-determination as well as protection (eg Holt, 1974). Such debates continue today, if only as an echo, with a more modest path being advocated between the extremes of 'caretaking' (children should not be free to make autonomous decisions) and 'liberation' (children are entitled to all rights enjoyed by adults) (Fox-Harding, 1991; Archard, 2004).

Since Rowntree's (1901) seminal study in York, poverty has become an area of sophisticated scientific scrutiny. Even so, its discussion remains coloured by normative and political judgements. There have been heated debates over whether it refers to a subsistence minimum (Joseph and Sumption, 1979) or rather an unacceptably low standard of living in a given society (Townsend, 1993). Others have queried whether it concerns a lack of resources per se or the inability to enjoy certain activities and goods (eg Ringen, 1995). International comparisons complicate matters further, with different yardsticks being applied depending on a country's relative affluence: this raises the possibility that a person may be poor in one country but not in another.

QoL is a complex concept because it is studied in a range of disciplines, including philosophy, medicine, economics and ecology. All approach it from a different angle. There are also widely contrasting views about the ingredients of 'a good life' and how it might be measured. Some commentators place great emphasis on feeling happy and satisfied, on having one's desires and preferences fulfilled (in the tradition of utilitarians like Jeremy Bentham). Others focus on the goods and conditions that routinely make life better; for example, food, shelter and friendship (eg Sen, 1999). Connected with this is the tension between objective and subjective perspectives, and discussions about *who* can judge an individual's QoL: must it be the person whose life it is?

The study of social exclusion is a relatively recent development. There is no standard definition, indeed the plasticity of the term 'exclusion' means that it is invoked indiscriminately (Sen, 2000). Thus, one commentator found the term used to describe 30 different conditions, from unemployment to being sexually abused (Silver, 1994), and another observed that it was applied variously to unemployment, a moral underclass and economic hardship (Levitas, 1998). Others reserve it for chronic, multidimensional disadvantage resulting in a catastrophic detachment from society (eg Room, 1999).

The result of these observations is that different people mean different things by each of the terms. What a researcher means by 'need' may be at odds with a professional's understanding of the same concept. Policy-makers define poverty in ways that often make little sense to a service user desperate for money to pay for food and electricity bills. A practitioner in Liverpool will think of social exclusion differently than will a colleague in London. And so on. In short, there is no common understanding of what the concepts mean and what the conditions they refer to look like. This represents a significant barrier to achieving a more congruent pattern of children's services; that is, one that is informed by agreement concerning desired outcomes, by consistent thresholds regarding who receives what kind of intervention and why, and by an appreciation of the potential conflicts between different approaches.

The second complication affecting the study was that multiple measures are used to measure each way of conceptualising child well-being. This reflects the ongoing debates about definition. In some cases empirical analysis is relatively scant, in part because of theoretical ambiguity, whereas in others – and for similar reasons – a plethora of measures is employed. So, there is much research into need, but no single reliable figure for the proportion of children in need in the UK. There is a plethora of need audits at a local level (Axford, 2007) and attempts have been made nationally to calculate children's 'need for services' (eg DH, 2001a; DfES and National Statistics, 2006). However, much of the research has conceptual weaknesses (see Chapter Two) and each measure has its own idiosyncrasies.

Empirical research on rights, by contrast, is very underdeveloped, largely because there are conflicting perspectives about when a right is violated. Understandably, from a humanitarian perspective, many studies focus on children suffering extreme hardship or exploitation (for example sex workers) or those in contexts associated with abusive relationships (for example prison). This approach may fulfil an important political function but there is no sense in which such research operationalises rights. Other studies latch onto characteristics that make children disproportionately susceptible to unfair treatment – having a disability, belonging to a minority ethnic group and so on. There are audits within countries of the extent to which national policy and practice uphold rights, invariably including indicators relating to specific entitlements, but no attempt, it appears, to calculate the number of children with violated rights in a given population.

Poverty has been measured in a number of ways, from the proportion of children in families that receive basic social assistance to those unable to afford socially perceived necessities. Much of this work is extremely rigorous, although from a policy perspective it can become somewhat confusing (if convenient at times) when an individual is poor on one measure but not on another. Moreover, there has been a tendency to take the household as the unit of analysis and to assume that children living there share the same living standards; yet some non-poor households contain poor children, and vice versa (Middleton et al, 1997), and the nature of research undertaken is changing accordingly.

QoL, meanwhile, is measured at various levels, including countries (for example life expectancy), geographic areas (for example recreational facilities) and individuals (for example health). Most research into individuals' QoL takes place in medicine where, again, there are different approaches, from assessing the degree of basic functionality to ascertaining the quality of individuals' conscious experience (Bowling, 1997). Consequently, each measure generates a different perspective of QoL. In relation to children, where comparatively little empirical work has been done (Jordan, 2006a; Skevington and Gillison, 2006), studies tend to focus on select groups – the chronically ill, or those whose predicament is dire by any standard, such as sweatshop workers.

Empirical work on social exclusion has grown considerably in recent years and mostly takes the form of national indicators (for example, unemployment, divorce, school exclusions), studies of discrete groups of people displaying particular social characteristics or fitting into specified administrative categories (for example those with disabilities) or the identification of deprived areas. In recent years more studies have looked at the condition per se rather than at its components (eg Paugam, 1996a; Burchardt et al, 1999; Gordon et al, 2000; Pantazis et al, 2006) but few look at children under 16 years of age.

It is apparent from this brief survey that for each of the five concepts examined in the study there are numerous different measures, that in some cases it is rare for any to be applied to children, and that where children *are* included in research they may only be a select – usually profoundly disadvantaged – group. These observations are noted here because in the absence of further data they constrain comparisons between the associated conditions.

This leads to the third barrier to undertaking the study, namely the lack of similar work conducted previously. Few studies have examined explicitly the links between the concepts/conditions, even less their implications for policy. There has been work on the relationship between need and rights (eg Plant et al, 1980; Doyal and Gough, 1991), and the conceptual and empirical differences between poverty and social exclusion have received attention (eg Room, 1995; Bradshaw et al, 2000). As noted earlier in the chapter, many studies refer to the impact of poverty on aspects of need and QoL – health, relationships, recreational activities and so on. Research using an ecological framework highlights the connections between poverty, social isolation and poor-quality neighbourhoods and suggests how policy might be orientated accordingly (eg Jack, 2000). However, a literature search suggests that for various reasons (see Axford, 2003) no previous study has focused on how all five concepts are related theoretically, analysed their prevalence and overlap among children in the community, and considered the implications for service provision.

The contribution of this book

This book seeks to make three contributions to this policy and research context. Part One is mainly conceptual. Chapters Two to Six endeavour to advance understanding within the children's services field of how the five concepts of child well-being are conventionally defined and measured. There is an attempt to outline key perspectives and debates and to organise the different ways of operationalising the concepts (with examples). The aim is to draw lessons concerning the content, form and practicability of measures used in previous studies in order to explain the approach used in the study described here (and accepting the parameters of the data available). Inevitably, given the complexity of the concepts examined, there is considerable simplification (hopefully avoiding superficiality) and the review of literature is by no means exhaustive; rather, it sets the scene for what follows and serves as a gateway to sources where the ideas are elaborated in greater depth. Chapter Seven draws on this material and other research to summarise the distinguishing features of each concept and how they are related. (Those readers who are already familiar with the five concepts may wish to turn straight to Chapter Seven and refer back as necessary.)

Part Two presents empirical findings. It starts by describing briefly the method for the empirical part of the study and sets out the prevalence of the five conditions among children in an inner-London community (Chapter Eight). It draws out the distinguishing features of the conditions and summarises important messages about the different kinds of children affected. Chapter Nine explores the relationships between the conditions using quantitative and qualitative methods. Particular attention is paid to relationships that are especially poignant given current policy debates; for example, why some children whose rights are intact may be in need, or how it is possible to be socially excluded but not poor.

Part Three considers what the study means for children's services. Chapter Ten looks at the implications of the study's findings for service provision in terms of the style of service required for treating each condition, and the number and kinds of children who would miss out if services were targeted at some conditions but not others. Chapter Eleven highlights possible contradictions between different service responses, and suggests how these might be minimised. It sets out a theoretical framework and some practical steps aimed at helping different stakeholders in children's services to use the findings to improve the fit or 'congruence' of children's services. This is particularly salient given the twin dangers identified in this opening chapter of policy-makers either speaking with a forked tongue by bolting together several potentially incompatible initiatives or discarding a perfectly useful perspective in favour of one that is shiny and new. Chapter 12 summarises the main findings of the study and presents overall conclusions.

Note

[1] This chapter and the remainder of the book employ the standard abbreviation of quality of life (QoL) used in most texts on the subject.

Part One
Defining child well-being

TWO

Need

Recent years have witnessed a revival in the popularity of measuring need as a precursor to distributing services, particularly in health, housing, social care and children's services (Percy-Smith, 1996; Axford, 2007). There are several reasons for this, starting with new legislation: the England and Wales 1989 Children Act, for example, requires every local authority to identify the needs of children living in their catchment area and to provide services accordingly (subsequently reinforced by the 2004 Children Act). Another factor is the growing expectation that agencies will achieve maximum benefit from minimum expenditure; this increases the pressure to chart the need terrain before allocating resources. There is also the growing realisation among academics, practitioners and policy-makers that children's problems are best understood if viewed from several angles; need as a concept permits this holistic perspective. And public disquiet about social inequalities, notably the way in which people with similar needs are treated differently, has prompted more attention to service consistency.

Notwithstanding this trend, philosophers and social scientists have long argued about the meaning and usefulness of need as a concept. Opinions range from those who think that need provides a rigorous moral basis for the distribution of welfare goods, to those who consider it so ambiguous as to be useless (Plant, 1991). Some would like it to underpin the activities of government, filling the gap left by the collapse of theological and metaphysical convictions. Others argue that this would impose one set of values on a morally pluralistic society.

Concept

Need is a slippery concept that resists definition. It is used diversely in everyday speech without much distinction between the qualitative nature of statements such as 'I need a burger' or 'she needs to get better'. Therapists, social workers, educational psychologists and other professional groups all interpret need differently. What a person is considered to need also varies with age, activity, physical and mental capacity and outlook. Bowlby (1951) looked at infants and stressed the need for intimacy and opportunities for forming close, loving relationships with responsive people. Maslow (1943) examined successful people and suggested that children's needs for nourishment and safety are superseded in adulthood by the need to achieve fulfilment through creativity and relationships. Miller (1976) argued that some needs are instrumental in that they facilitate certain pursuits, for example the need for running shoes to compete in a marathon; the implication is that need constitutes the gap between a person's current state and a desired state such as good health or happiness. Others have distinguished between those needs relevant to everyone, for instance food and shelter, and those specific to some, for example young children being carried or extra help with writing for those with special educational needs (Hill and Tisdall, 1997). Yet surprisingly few people have tried to identify the fundamental requirements of a healthy childhood; one exception notes 'the very most basic needs, the kinds of care without which children cannot grow, learn, and thrive' (Berry Brazelton and Greenspan, 2000, p ix), including physical protection, safety and regulation, and developmentally appropriate experiences. Their list of 'irreducible needs' is based on analysis of what happens when children lack certain items, for instance how residents of Romanian orphanages who were denied warm, nurturing or appropriate social and intellectual interactions developed severe physical, intellectual and social deficits.

It is evident from these approaches that the epistemology drives the definition of need; that is, different sets of values and methodological approaches are likely to produce contrasting ideas about what need is. Inevitably this makes some of the conclusions controversial, and everything can seem very subjective. Indeed, attempts to define need often create as many questions as they answer. Distinguishing between *thick* and *thin* interpretations of need can bring some clarity.

Thick and thin definitions of need

A *thick* notion of need is culturally determined (Soper, 1993; Tao and Drover, 1997) and relative to at least four things. First are an individual's aspirations and ideals. Miller (1976), for example, suggests that a person's needs can only be determined in relation to a life plan. 'Harm' to that individual results when anything interferes with the activities essential to this plan, and correspondingly needs comprise whatever is necessary for these activities to be carried out. Second is the period of history in question. Illich (1999) argues that needs are manufactured by economic development and essentially a mutation of desires. So whereas a lengthy trek to the market or spending a day washing clothes by hand were once endured unthinkingly, today cars and washing machines are regarded as necessities in most western societies. The social and geographic context is a third standard against which relative needs are defined. An individual's physical circumstances are important insofar as one has no need for a fur coat in Havana or a bikini in Antarctica (Goodin, 1990). This is known as the *weak* sense of relativism. But the quantity and kinds of food and clothes a person needs depend not just on the local climate and geography but also on what others in that society are eating and wearing. This, then, is the fourth factor – the modus operandi of society (which includes the possessions and activities of other people in that society). It is known as the *strong* form of relativism; to be in need is to be unable to act as a full agent in society (Ware and Goodin, 1990). The social construction of need is shaped by the shifting moral and legal consensus of a society, professionals' pragmatic concerns, scientific evidence concerning the consequences of certain deficits and the efficacy of different services, and the views of consumers (see Chapter One).

By contrast, a *thin* notion of need is abstract, objective and universal. It opens up the possibility that an expert is best placed to define an individual's needs, and rests on several criticisms of the relativist case. One is that the 'A needs X in order to do Y' formulation can result in almost anything being defined as a need, from a fast car (to enhance enjoyment of driving) to food (to provide nutrition). This leaves no basis for discriminating between what is needed because it is indispensable to life, and what is desirable because it is life-enhancing (Soper, 1993). It is surely the universality of X that renders X a need, and not the strategic efficacy of X for achieving some specified goal (Doyal and Gough, 1991). In a variation on the instrumental argument, Miller (1976) suggests that need defined in relation to a specified goal is legitimate if the goal (or life plan) has been adjudicated as intelligible and valuable; thus the pyromaniac's claim to need matches and wood would be illegitimate. However, this is still a relative judgement since the moral significance of satisfying need X becomes predicated on prior acceptance of the moral value of plan Y (Doyal and Gough, 1991).

Another weakness of the relative perspective is that it ignores the fact that if certain human purposes are not fulfilled, harm nearly always ensues; an individual's relative circumstances are irrelevant (Plant, 1991). For example, the need for food is pretty much absolute and fixed by nature; minimum calorific intake is the same for everybody, and not at all relative to the society or how much food others are eating (Goodin, 1990). Put another way, a society where everyone is starving – nobody has needs relative to anybody else – is not one where everyone's needs are met. The argument here is that if need is relative in the *strong* sense, there are two ways of meeting it: increase supply to the relatively more needy, or decrease supply to the relatively less needy. The latter option is almost always regarded as unacceptable; thus, continuing the food example, few would advocate throwing food into the sea as a strategy for combating famine.

A further rejoinder to the relativist case is that certain things are not only essential to avoiding harm, they are also necessary for human agency of any kind. Basic needs relate to the capacity of individuals to choose and live out a course of action, whatever its morality, in any society and in any period of history. These needs can be summarised as *autonomy* and *well-being* (Gewirth, 1978, 1982). The mode of satisfaction will vary with time and space, but this does not detract from the central point that the general nature of need can be elucidated (philosophically and empirically) and holds firm regardless of one's ideological or moral standpoint.

Linking the thick and thin definitions

One way of connecting thick and thin theories of need would be to say that human needs are *absolute* insofar as they facilitate agency (the ability to act in any society), and *relative* insofar as they enable participation in particular societies. This takes account of cultural and geographical diversity while acknowledging that there are some objective and universal standards. These ideas are elaborated helpfully in *A Theory of Human Need* (Doyal and Gough, 1991), which offers a clear set of criteria for demarcating between what is fundamental to human well-being and what may only be claimed as a condition of further flourishing.

Doyal and Gough base their argument on the contention that welfare states should enable individuals to achieve minimally impaired participation, in other words the freedom and ability to pursue goals and engage in activities that they deem of value and thereby to gain a sense of fulfilment. They begin by distinguishing need from wants, the latter deriving from individual preference ('I need a beer') or the cultural environment ('I need to buy a Christmas tree'). They also separate need (universalisable goals) from biological drives with which we have little choice but to conform. This is justified on the grounds that drives are not necessarily needs (the desire to eat chocolate) and needs are not necessarily drives (the need to exercise).

The failure to reach certain goals causes an individual to suffer harm. These *basic* needs are identified as *physical health* and *personal autonomy* since they constitute the preconditions for any individual action, irrespective of its morality or the cultural, geographical or historical context in which it takes place. Poor physical health usually interferes with the manual, mental and emotional abilities required to complete a range of practical tasks in daily life. The Doyal–Gough theory defines physical health in negative and biomedical terms as the absence of serious disease. This allows for cross-cultural understanding of ill-health: not only will the individual feel unwell, but also they will be incapacitated and their illness will have a medically identifiable cause. Autonomy is defined as an individual's ability to make informed choices about what should be done and how, and comprises three elements: understanding oneself and one's environment and culture; cognitive and emotional capacity – the ability to formulate options for oneself; and opportunities for new and significant action.

Physical health and autonomy are, in turn, dependent on *intermediate* needs, those properties of goods, services, activities and relationships that enhance physical health and human autonomy everywhere and at any time. Doyal and Gough list 11 of these:

- adequate nutritional food and water;
- adequate protective housing;
- a non-hazardous work environment;
- a non-hazardous physical environment;
- appropriate healthcare;
- security in childhood;
- significant primary relationships;
- physical security;
- economic security;

- safe birth control and child-bearing; and
- basic education.

While all of these needs are universal, the goods and services required to satisfy them are culturally, geographically and historically variable. For example, the need for nutrition and protection from the elements can be met from a potentially infinite variety of cuisines and forms of dwelling. Doyal and Gough use the term *satisfiers* to denote all objects, activities and relationships that satisfy basic and intermediate needs. As regards the level of need satisfaction required to secure minimally disabled social participation, they advocate the 'constrained optimum', namely the best level presently achieved in the world or a feasible better level.

The Doyal–Gough theory has five strengths that are particularly relevant here. First, it bridges the thin–thick divide by welding together philosophical insights on need with empirical observations. Soper (1993) observes that theories of need veer between being so abstract and uncontroversial as to be interesting but ultimately uninformative, and so culturally relative that firm universalisable statements become impossible. *A Theory of Human Need* avoids these pitfalls. It sets out a list of universal and objectively identifiable needs that lend themselves to being measured, and it recognises that often the same needs may be met in various ways. This broad perspective underpins recent approaches to need assessment in children's services, most of which require the measurement of specified aspects of children's development, care and environment followed by the design or selection of an appropriate intervention to meet the needs identified (eg DH et al, 2000; DfES, 2006a, 2006b).

A second strength is that the theory distinguishes between need and want. A person can need something that they do not want – food in the case of an anorexic teenager – and want something that they do not need – a millionaire's umpteenth car (Ware and Goodin, 1990). The difference is that whereas a person is always impoverished when their needs are not met, the denial of subjective preferences rarely has such a drastic effect. This is because needs depend on the way the world is whereas wants depend on the workings of the mind (Wiggins, 1985). Thus, a person can need what they want, and want or not want what they need, but they cannot consistently *not* need what is required in order to avoid serious harm (Doyal and Gough, 1991). This is why any discussion of children's needs should properly focus on the requirements for healthy development (Berry Brazelton and Greenspan, 2000).

Third, it is implicit in the Doyal–Gough theory that needs exist alongside each other rather than forming a progression across the life span. Even a rudimentary understanding of child development indicates the truth of this perspective (see Kellmer-Pringle, 1974). Thus, autonomy, which some may consider does not apply to children, works in the sense of being an evolving capacity to make informed choices about what should be done and how to go about doing it. So, for a five-year-old it might mean deciding which toys to play with or contributing to a family discussion about where to go for a day out, whereas for a teenager it might involve choosing a college course or set of friends.

Fourth, the theory covers needs in all aspects of an individual's life, including health, significant primary relationships and housing. In that sense it dovetails well with the ecological insight that an individual's developmental needs are affected by family and environmental factors (Jack, 2002). A fifth feature is that the theory is supported by empirical evidence; path analysis on data from 120 countries demonstrated causal linkages between intermediate need variables and levels of basic need satisfaction (Gough and Thomas, 1994).

At the same time, there are critiques of the Doyal–Gough approach. Some argue that it is more ethnocentric than it purports to be. Soper (1993), for instance, suggests that intermediate needs, like economic security and significant primary relationships, are redolent of western perceptions of 'the good'. She claims that meeting basic and intermediate needs would probably be ecologically unsustainable in the context of current developed world expectations of living standards; the country that Doyal and Gough identified as having the highest levels of need satisfaction (Sweden) also had one of the highest levels of per capita energy consumption in the world at the time. Tao and Drover (1997), meanwhile, contend that a Chinese-Confucian worldview would pay less attention to individual autonomy and focus more on the way that met need allows individuals to fulfil caring obligations. The view expressed in the book *A Theory of Human Need* that harm can be objectively identified also comes under fire. Plant's (1991) work is broadly in line with that of Doyal and Gough but he cites the observation that, for example, physical disability, such as blindness, can bring out other gifts in a person.

It is not possible to discuss these critiques here at any length (see Gough, 2000, for a lengthier rebuttal), but their implication is that harm and need are innately value-laden concepts. In response, it might be argued that Soper's concerns are less about the *content* of the needs than about the volume and nature of satisfiers that people expect. Concerning the other points, no one can pursue *any* life plan successfully without some modicum of physical health and autonomy. These 'goods' are universally required for people to become fully functioning agents in society, and in that respect the Doyal–Gough theory is not tied to any specific morality.

Conclusion (1)

This study defines a child as 'in need' if their health or development is actually impaired or likely to become so without some remedial intervention. Impairment refers to the absence of normal healthy development; that is, when a condition *usually* interferes with daily social functioning and performance (Hill, 2002) (this is based on the definition in the ICD-10 international classification of diseases [WHO, 1993]). This definition of 'in need' is informed by the preceding discussion, in which need is linked explicitly to the existence or likelihood of harm, which in turn is connected, critically, to the ability (or inability) to act in society. It is thus dependent on seven points of context.

First, need is related to agency. The universal needs that must be satisfied to enable individuals to choose and live out a course of action can be reduced to well-being (or physical health) and autonomy. These apply as much to children as they do to adults, although autonomy should be developmentally appropriate. Thus, for a preschool infant it entails being able to express choices about food and sleep, and having learning experiences; for adolescents it encompasses the freedom to pursue chosen educational or social interests, and to critique and shape the wider world (eg Dworetzky, 1996; DeHart et al, 2004).

Second, need is a scientifically identifiable phenomenon that should be measured in terms of an individual's health and development rather than the services that they receive or the policies and procedures that affect them; it is related to outcomes, not to outputs. No child needs foster care, but for some children the need for physical security and basic education might best be met by being cared for by substitute parents.

Third, people have needs in all areas of their lives. In particular, unmet need is not necessarily related to a lack of economic resources, an unwitting assumption that appears to permeate some discussions (eg Bennett, 2005). Impaired development for children takes on different forms, including physical (for example obesity), behavioural (for example persistent offending) and emotional (for example separation anxiety in adolescence) (Little et al, 2003). The likelihood of such impairment is affected by the quality of parenting/care and by the child's family situation and the wider environment (DH et al, 2000).

Fourth, need claims are ultimately based on guaranteeing people's survival and a minimally adequate life (Wiggins, 1985). In some respects, therefore, the quality or desirability of the need-satisfier is immaterial; ideally it should be acceptable to the person concerned, but unappetising food can satisfy hunger, and security in childhood is promoted as much by discipline as by emotional warmth and stimulation.

Fifth, needs are objectively identifiable but need-satisfiers are contextual. Put another way, the need-satisfier may vary geographically, over time or with a person's age, but the need does not. For instance, the need for clothing is universal and timeless, but sombreros are only suitable in certain climes, chimney-sweeps' smocks were from another historical period, and only very young children wear romper suits. So-called *felt* needs (see later discussion) are arguably only wants; real need – need which, if not satisfied, invariably results in harm – is not limited by individual perceptions or by knowledge about the availability of particular services (Bradshaw, 1972).

Sixth, need is best determined following a rounded appraisal of an individual's situation. For example, it might be argued that violence towards a child may not constitute an unmet need for protection per se; the likelihood of harm ensuing depends on the severity, frequency and duration of such treatment and whether it occurred in a nurturing or abusive environment (DH, 1995).

Seventh, the antecedents of a situation have no bearing on the *existence* or otherwise of need. A child who falls off their bike and breaks their leg needs medical treatment irrespective of the cause of their accident, and a homeless adolescent needs adequate housing whether they have been kicked out by their family or have chosen to run away. Administrative regulations may render certain people ineligible for assistance, for example because they have made themselves deliberately homeless, but this is about recognising and responding to need, rather than the presence of need per se. The individual still needs support.

Measurement

The complications associated with defining need make it a difficult concept to operationalise. Attempts to measure need in relation to children have variously looked at the cause or context of need, the manifestation or symptoms of need, the response of a service provider to need, and what individuals think they need (Sinclair and Carr-Hill, 1996; Sinclair, 1999). Ironically, 'need' often gets lost amidst these impostors. This section seeks to disentangle the different elements of the measurement of need and looks at how they are incorporated in various empirical studies.

There are at least four aspects to the measurement of need. The first concerns the *kind* of need that is being identified. Research that purports to concern need does not necessarily measure need in the sense elaborated earlier in this chapter. Rather, need is identified by asking individuals what they want (*felt* need), or by calculating the demand for services (*expressed* need), or by extrapolating the sociodemographic characteristics of service users for the whole community (*comparative* need), or by ascertaining levels of expert-defined need (*normative* need) (Bradshaw, 1972). The overlap between these different kinds of need is imperfect, so it is important to know which one is being measured. The *type* of need is a second measurement dimension. This refers to the aspect of a person's life that is in question, such as their housing, their relationships, their behaviour and health, or their education and employment. The third element is the *seriousness* of need and the criteria by which this is judged. Primarily this concerns the threshold at which some kind of problem or deficit is deemed to constitute a need, and it therefore affects the volume of need that is identified. The matter of *whose* needs are being measured is the fourth aspect: need can be measured for individuals, population groups, administrative groups, and even geographical areas – housing estates, countries and so on.

Although there are studies that incorporate the measurement of some of these elements, few include all four. This will be apparent from the strengths and weaknesses of the studies on which this research draws. It is convenient to review them under the four categories used in Bradshaw's typology.

Felt need

Ascertaining felt need involves enabling individuals to articulate their own needs. At a clinical level in services for the under-eights, for example, practitioners often communicate with children using techniques that are concrete and tactile, such as art and games, rather than abstract and verbal (Thomas and O'Kane, 2000). At a planning level, methods increasingly used to find out how children and families perceive their needs and whether they think they are being met include focus groups and opinion-poll-style surveys (eg Braye, 2000). Community audits are another approach. A good example of one such study identified felt need in a district of a large city in the UK (Percy-Smith and Sanderson, 1992). Residents were asked to evaluate their needs against headings such as housing, healthcare and employment opportunities.

Three features of that particular study are especially salient here. First, it sought to identify the needs of *all* people living in a clearly defined geographical area. Of 4,600 randomly selected adults, one third responded to a survey, giving a sample of 10% of the overall adult population of the area (ca. 16,000). Second, it operationalised the 13 basic and intermediate needs of the Doyal–Gough theory. For example, there were questions about the incidence of illness (concerning the need for physical health), about stress and depression (autonomy), about damp and noise levels (adequate protective housing) and about the quality of diets (adequate nutritional food and water). Third, the study combined a measure of felt need with information about normative need. For instance, respondents' assessments of whether they ate healthily (*felt* need) were complemented with data on the incidence of food poisoning and doctors' evaluations of levels of cholesterol in patients' diets (*normative* need). Joining together information about several kinds of need in this way is a trademark of many studies of need. To rely solely on respondents' subjective views of their situation would be a weakness because it is difficult to know if the identified need is approximately of a similar level of seriousness. For instance, what one person considers a health need another person with identical ailments may not; individuals have different pain thresholds. An objective yardstick is required for comparative purposes.

Expressed need

The measurement of expressed need involves adding together the number of individuals either receiving or waiting for a service. Effectively, it captures demand. Thus, Packman (1968) calculated what she called the 'total childcare problem' by adding together for one day in 1960 the numbers of children receiving specified forms of social care provision. This included children who were:

• awaiting adoption;
• in residential care or approved schools;

- supervised under child protection legislation (in private foster homes and nurseries); and
- maintained in local authority boarding schools or hostels on account of maladjustment.

Social services departments in England and Wales often calculate the local extent of child need by summing the numbers of children at risk of maltreatment, with special needs, in care, or locked up. Indeed, the official estimate of the proportion of children in need in England is based on the number known to social services departments at any one time (DH, 2000; DfES and National Statistics, 2006).

A broader view is taken by Preston-Shoot and Wigley (2005), who conducted an interagency (social care, health, education) audit of the needs of children in receipt of or waiting to be allocated services in a calendar month in one locality. Proformas were completed for each child on caseloads during the calendar month, with 7% children in the area found to be 'in need'. Other tried-and-tested methods for doing this involve gathering quantitative (Little et al, 2002) and qualitative (Little et al, 1999) data from case files and grouping the children together according to the similarity of their needs (Little and Madge, 1998; Tunnard, 2002; Melamid and Brodbar, 2003; Johnson and Sawbridge, 2004; Taylor, 2005; Dartington-i, 2007; for alternative approaches see Colton et al, 1995; Ward and Peel, 2002).

The main drawback with this general approach to measuring need is that it ties need to service receipt. Yet not every child who receives a service is in need (defined in the legal sense of actual or likely impairment to health or development), just as some children will be in need without coming into contact with a service provider. For example, data from a study of children in an inner-London community show that a fifth (21%) of children with actual or likely *significant* impairment to their health or development – that is, extreme on the spectrum and/or likely to result in enduring damage – were *not* receiving help from services (Little et al, 2003).

This mismatch between need and services arises because factors other than need determine who receives assistance – legal requirements, fads and fashions, demographic changes, the resources available, whether or not individuals request or accept help and so on. Particularly relevant is the exercise of professional discretion; flexibility in relation to satisfiers is a frequent complaint of recipients of needs-led as opposed to rights-based interventions, particularly in the context of disability studies (eg Oliver and Barnes, 1998). The expressed need approach is also vulnerable to administrative bias. In individual assessments of children's needs, professionals are prone to focus on the reason for referral or their specific area of expertise. For example, one study in a rural district in England found that the small percentage of children in a geographical area who were in contact with all four of the main service agencies (social services, education, health and the police) received a separate and sometimes contradictory assessment of their need from each provider (Little and Madge, 1998). Yet, for instance, most maltreated children referred for help also have educational needs, just as some healthy children have behavioural needs (Little et al, 1999).

Comparative need

This approach measures levels of need by ascertaining the prevalence in the wider community of the sociodemographic characteristics of service recipients. Bebbington and Miles (1989) conducted a survey of 2,500 children entering care in 13 local authorities over a six-month period, recording family background information using factors widely associated with being 'in need' – benefit-dependency, mother under 21 years of age, minority ethnic group status and so forth. (Children scoring on any of these need indicators were disproportionately likely to become cared for away from home, and where all factors held the probability of that child entering care was one in 10 [compared to one in 7,000 where none applied].) They constructed an index from the selected variables and used it to rank electoral wards by severity of need. In a similar vein, Gordon and Loughran (1997) used child deprivation indices to guide the allocation of resources among social services childcare teams in a rural English county. The method was based on the empirical assumption that children's services' clients originate predominantly from families in poverty (see Bennett, 2005).

A similar child need index has also been used as part of the formula for determining how central government in the UK allocates funding to local authorities (Carr-Hill et al, 1997). It comprises four risk factors associated with relatively intensive interventions or being at risk of maltreatment: lone-parent household, rented accommodation, household receiving basic social assistance, and household with priority housing need. At a more local level, Brown and Smith (1997) measured child need in an English county using factors connected with children who were separated from their families. These included overcrowding, receipt of state benefit, and coming from a lone-parent family or a family with four or more children. A composite index was developed using Census and local authority data and applied to each district.

The main strength of the comparative need approach is that it looks beyond service recipients or other expressed need. However, several weaknesses remain. The first is that instead of measuring the seriousness or volume of need (pure threshold), it measures the *likelihood* of a person getting help from various agencies (process threshold). Estimates of need that are based on existing provision are intrinsically conservative, especially since they invariably focus on a subset of services. For example, at the time this study was conducted the formula in England and Wales for determining the level of central government grants to local authorities took less than one fifth (18%) of children receiving services into account (Rowlands, 1997).

A second weakness is that the patterns of need that emerge using this method are based on geographical areas rather than aggregated individuals. This can easily lead to the assumption that *all* children in a deprived area are in need; the indices capture increased risk but mask variation between individuals.

The third shortcoming with the comparative need approach is that it employs sociodemographic indicators as proxies for need, despite the relationship being far from clear-cut. For instance, although there is a link between low household income and children having disabilities or emotional, conduct or hyperkinetic disorders, most deprived children develop reasonably well (Little and Mount, 1999; Gordon, 2000b; ONS, 2000). Moreover, taking a children's services perspective, estimates of area need are often based on indicators such as economic development and may not give due weight to other factors associated with child need (Hall, 2000). This raises doubts about the ability of deprivation indices to capture the volume of need among children in any community.

Normative need

Studies of normative need frequently focus on *basic needs*, measuring the extent to which people enjoy a minimally decent life defined in terms of health (life expectancy and infant mortality), nutrition (child malnutrition) and education (literacy). A major strength of this approach is that, in contrast with studies of expressed and comparative need, it focuses on individual well-being, not on service use: it uses *outcome* indicators. It also has a strong theoretical foundation, since the three main dimensions – health, nutrition and education – are widely acknowledged to be essential preconditions for any activity (Stewart, 1996).

In order to measure levels of overall need-satisfaction, this type of study often combines basic need items to form a composite index. For example, Gough and Thomas (1994) used two composite indices – the *Physical Quality of Life Index* (PQLI) and the *Human Development Index* (HDI) – to measure levels of need-satisfaction in 128 countries. The benefits of using composite indices in this way are, first, that they allow an assessment of overall need-satisfaction and, second, that they often encompass elements of both physical health and autonomy. So, the two scales referred to here include the variables life expectancy at birth, infant mortality, literacy, mean years of schooling and per capita income. However, composite indices are less successful at discriminating between developed societies, most of which have high scores. It is also hard to say if indices capture need-satisfaction accurately because the component indicators are arguably weighted arbitrarily (Streeten et al, 1981).

More elaborate than the basic needs method is Doyal and Gough's (1991) attempt to operationalise their theory and conduct a global cross-national comparison of levels of need-satisfaction. Drawing on official statistics, they attached indicators to all 13 basic and intermediate needs; these included mortality (physical health), illiteracy (autonomy), deaths and injuries from work-related accidents (non-hazardous work environment) and doctors, nurses and hospital beds per population head (appropriate healthcare). The major advantage of this approach is its theoretical underpinning; while the focus is on the basic needs and thus *actual* harm or impairment, by gathering evidence on intermediate needs it helps with measuring *likely* impairment to physical health or autonomy. It also demonstrates that distinguishing between degrees of need–satisfaction can be relatively straightforward.

A further approach to capturing normative need is represented by the audits of children conducted by numerous children's services agencies in the UK and abroad using the practice tools *Matching Needs and Services* (Little et al, 1999) and *Aggregating Data* (Little et al, 2002). Researchers and professionals elicit evidence of expert-defined need from case notes on referred families. Each child's situation is summarised on a special form in terms of living situation, family and social relationships, behaviour, health, education and employment, either qualitatively (*Matching Needs and Services*) or quantitatively (*Aggregating Data*). A decision is then made following a clear process (Little et al, 2003) about whether or not the needs in question are impairing, or likely to impair, the child's health and development. A child whose needs cross this threshold is regarded as 'in need'.

Although restricted to service populations, this audit approach has four obvious strengths. First, it embraces a multidimensional perspective of need. Second, it sets out clear, objective criteria in the form of a structured decision-making process for distinguishing between children who are in need and those who are not. Third, it aggregates the needs of individuals and thereby draws out important connections between different needs. Fourth, it allows needs to be articulated without inferring potential solutions. The natural temptation is to describe need in terms of the interventions that would benefit an individual, for example 'this child needs family therapy'. No child needs family therapy: in this instance the *underlying* need could be for parents to understand how their behaviour affects their children, or for children and parents to communicate better; the need–satisfier might involve family therapy but, equally, some other service could fulfil the same function. Generally, interventions reveal little about a person's need, a rule that applies at the aggregate level also. This becomes apparent when data on different kinds of need are combined in the same piece of research, as in a study that used data from agency need audits, community surveys and administrative records to chart the pattern of need and service use among children and families among a child population of 23,000 in a district with 121,000 residents (Axford et al, 2004). This exposed wide disparities in estimates of the number of children 'in need', particularly between those based on service receipt (expressed) and child health and development (normative) respectively.

Conclusion (2)

The empirical part of this study required a measure of need commensurate with the theoretical discussion in the first half of this chapter. The method was devised to avoid the shortcomings of the various approaches discussed earlier and, wherever possible, to reflect their strengths.

The situation of each child in the sample was captured in relation to all areas of their life – their living situation, family and social relationships, behaviour, health, and education and employment. In this way, information was assembled about aspects of child development, the quality of parenting, and the child's wider family and environmental context. This approach also ensured that the Doyal–Gough criterion of connecting intermediate and basic needs was met. The data were gathered primarily by asking parents/carers to describe their child's circumstances against scientific measures, so providing a normative/felt need hybrid. No reference was made to potential solutions to any child's predicament in the form of services; the focus was on the child.

Based on this summary of the child's situation, an assessment was made of the extent to which the child's health or development was actually impaired or likely to become so without remedial services. Sociodemographic characteristics such as age, gender and family income were used to help judge the risk presented by the child's circumstances; they were not, however, used as evidence of need per se. (For example, certain difficulties can be impairing at some ages but not others; toddlers are particularly vulnerable to separation experiences because their attachments are in the process of being established, whereas older children are protected in relation to the same experience by their ability to maintain relationships over time and space [Rutter, 1989].) The assessments were then aggregated to provide a prevalence rate of children 'in need' in the selected community (this goes beyond children who are in contact with a children's service agency).

THREE

Rights

There is a general consensus that some individual interests and liberties are so basic that all states and human beings should respect them. Calling them rights means that they should take precedence over the private interests of those in power and the pursuit of other social goals and aspirations, and that societies should seek to secure them, irrespective of traditions, history or levels of economic development (Waldron, 1984, 1993). This belief is expressed in international law, for example in the 1948 UN Declaration of Human Rights, and many countries have a bill of rights designed to prevent government interference with free speech, religious liberty, equal access to the law and so forth. In the UK, this function is fulfilled by the 1998 Human Rights Act – a higher law with which all other laws, policies, practices and procedures must comply (Klug, 2000). National legislation and associated guidance set out in more concrete terms the goods and freedoms to which citizens are entitled.

The seductive language of rights has also seeped into children's services, as discussed in Chapter One. However, as with need, rights is a controversial and complex concept, a fact often masked by its liberal and somewhat indiscriminate use. There is much rhetoric about rights: the complaint of the scorned, angry shopper; the indignant claim to protection by advocates of torture victims; claims to welfare provision made through various advocacy organisations; and so on. This chapter sketches out some of the key points of agreement and debate concerning rights. It examines different approaches to measuring rights, but first it looks at what rights are and why they are important, how they become violated, what they cover (their substance) and what makes something a right (or how one obtains a right). It is important to note that the chapter does not focus on children's rights per se, although it touches on this (for an extended discussion on this topic see Archard, 2004). Rather, it takes a broader perspective on the concept.

Concept

The nature of rights

A right is a claim to be treated in a certain way. The content of the claim is justified on the basis that every person has inherent worth, irrespective of their virtues, abilities or value to others: this is the 'Y' in the formula 'A has a right to Q against B in virtue of Y'. The 'B' in the formula refers to the organisations and individuals obliged to assist and forbear as required in order to respect the right-holder's recognised interests and liberties. The state should protect this agreement. This means that rights theorists are interested in the rules that constrain behaviour

(Plant, 1991); thus, relating this back to the previous chapter, need is related to the *good* whereas rights are about what is *right* (Ware and Goodin, 1990). Put another way, need refers to the content of a claim, and a right is the *normative form* in which the claim is couched; to suggest – as some do in a children's services context – that there should be a greater focus on need at the expense of rights is like saying that we should concentrate less on duties and more on truth-telling; the languages of need and rights are perfectly compatible (Waldron, 1993). Rights are therefore arguably more of a legal or moral concept than a scientific one.

Rights claims usually 'trump' other considerations (Dworkin, 1978, p xi). This means that, generally speaking, rights should prevail over concerns such as the promotion of national prosperity, administrative convenience and what individuals are judged to deserve (Waldron, 1984). They protect a person against any interference that another person has judged necessary to increase the sum of utility, that is, the satisfaction of preferences in society more widely, and free the right-holder to do or have things that are not deemed to be needs (Miller, 1976). In that respect, rights tie the right-holder and the person or body responsible for upholding the claim into a binding contract. They enable a person not only to demand what is their due – without having to beg, or express gratitude when it is given – but also to express indignation if their claim is not honoured (Fox-Harding, 1991). Thus, a child in a foster or residential placement who wishes to contribute to decisions about their care is not required first to explain the value of their opinions: it is their right to express them. Even when states or individuals fail to uphold claims, the fact that they have agreed to perform certain duties is valuable moral coinage for the affronted (Hill and Tisdall, 1997).

Viewed in this way, rights are de facto violable. They are not a perfect guarantee. There may be other claims (some of which may be competing rights). For example, in international law, children have the right to protection from abuse (Article 19 of the UN Convention on the Rights of the Child [CRC]), but decisions about removing victims of maltreatment from their homes must be balanced with the parents' right to raise their offspring (Article 18) and the child's own views about where he or she would like to live (Article 12). In addition, the costs of such intervention should be weighed against the resources required to fulfil other claims that could be made by children, for example to leisure and cultural activities (Article 31).

A complication arises, however, in that since rights are often defined in abstract terms, this means that the actions required to comply with the demand are often subject to some discretion. What is the legitimate content of the claim? And when has that claim been fulfilled? Specificity can be improved by enshrining the right in legislation. A *legal* right is an officially recognised entitlement such as an amount of social assistance, a complaints procedure or a particular service. *Moral* rights are aspirations or beliefs about what people *ought* to have – free speech, adequate nutrition, a safe environment and so forth. Nickel (1987) notes that sharply defined legal rights evolve from high moral aspirations when parallel duties are specified and the measures to enforce these liabilities are put in place. Strong guarantees demand specificity in each element of the statement 'P has a right to X': who ascribes the right; who holds the right; the content of the right claim; the conditions in which the claim applies; and who is charged with upholding the claim. Of course, moral rights do not necessarily become rights under law: 'law and morality do not always perfectly coincide' (Archard, 2004, p 56).

Critics argue that talk of moral rights is politically dangerous and ultimately unintelligible because exaggerated claims are made that cannot be realised (Warnock, 1998). This is based on the principle that something *cannot* be a right if making it a reality requires resources that do not exist or interference with the freedom and possessions of others; it would contravene the 'ought implies can' maxim (Plant, 1991; Waldron, 1993). Put another way, to say that someone has a duty (corresponding to another person's right) presumes that they are able to fulfil that duty. So, for example, is it helpful to proclaim that children have a right to adequate nutrition in countries where acute poverty renders that aspiration little more than fantasy? This question is addressed later in this chapter.

The violation of rights

The formula 'P has a right to X' means that third parties have a duty not to prevent P from doing or enjoying X, and that the point of that duty is to promote or protect some interest of P's. By implication, therefore, 'rights are *correlative* to duties, so that talking about rights *is* a way of talking about people's responsibilities' (Waldron, 1993, p 576; emphasis in original). Duties of forbearance (not preventing) and assistance (promoting and protecting) may be held by the state in which the right-holder lives and by other human beings (in which case the state usually has a duty to guarantee compliance).

Sometimes, of course, these rules designed to constrain the behaviour of individuals or organisations are broken and the right-holder is treated inappropriately. Their rights are then said to be 'violated' or 'infringed' (the words tend to be used interchangeably), and the responsible third party is said to have defaulted. Usually this is because whoever is responsible for executing or underwriting the corresponding duty has been negligent. There are two important points to make here. First, individuals cannot violate their own rights. In other words, a difficulty that arises because of a personal deficiency can never constitute a rights infringement. Second, whether or not the right-holder has suffered or is likely to suffer harm or impairment – central to the concept of need – is inconsequential in determining if their rights have been breached. So, it would be nonsensical for me to say 'My right to protection has been infringed' if I drive carelessly, wrap my car around a lamppost and end up in hospital with a broken leg; by contrast, we do not wait to assess the long-term damage suffered by a child who is beaten before acknowledging the violation of their right to protection.

The content of rights claims

The different content of rights claims is captured in the distinction between negative and positive rights. Liberty or *negative* rights – traditional liberties such as free speech, religious tolerance and being able to vote – oblige third parties to refrain from obstructing an individual's action or interfering with their choice. Welfare or *positive* rights – claims to free medical care, elementary education, decent living standards and so on – emphasise duties to provide assistance (Waldron, 1984). While negative rights have largely been accepted as a given, notwithstanding gross violations of the kind charted by Amnesty International, positive rights have come in for sustained criticism. Three such criticisms are mentioned here.

First, it is argued that positive rights are role based and therefore cannot be universalisable. In other words, they are only relevant to some people in some situations; so, for instance, the right to basic social assistance is the preserve of the less well off, just as only the employed can claim paid holiday. The counter-argument is that the same thing holds for negative rights; for example the right to fair trial is only for the accused or arrested. Therefore both kinds of rights are universal because they are concerned with how an individual ought to be treated in circumstances in which any person could find themselves (Plant, 1991).

A second criticism of positive rights is that upholding them requires invading the autonomy of individuals that negative rights are designed to protect. Nozick (1974), for example, questions the legitimacy of socioeconomic rights on the grounds that, logically, the act of fulfilling them would require property to be removed forcibly from the rich and redistributed to the poor. The flaw in his argument, however, is that it overlooks the way that autonomy is restricted by deprivation as much as it is by interference; in order to enjoy the fundamental freedoms that may be couched in terms of 'negative' rights one must also enjoy a modicum of the material well-being protected by 'positive rights'. Put another way, since the essentials for a healthy life are a prerequisite for enjoying *any* rights, malnutrition and disease can debilitate the human faculties that autonomy involves (Waldron, 1993): the starving child is hardly free.

The third criticism is that positive rights tend to make vague and impossible demands on limited resources. For example, Cranston (1967) argues that since most developing countries lack the wherewithal to guarantee all inhabitants basic living standards, let alone holidays with pay, it is absurd to denote these things as rights. Negative rights, by contrast, are considered to be more clear-cut and to require less effort: it is easy to refrain from killing someone (the right to life) and to not tamper with their mail (the right to privacy). One problem with this argument is that securing negative rights can be costly, for instance forbearance has to be imposed through a legal framework and publicly funded police and judicial services (Plant, 1991). Another difficulty, which picks up the question posed at the end of the section 'The nature of rights', is the implicit assumption that the existing distribution of resources should remain undisturbed: as Waldron (1993) puts it, 'the '*ought*' of human rights is being frustrated less by the '*can't*' of impracticability, than by the '*won't*' of selfishness and greed' (p 580). Moreover, an individual's duty is surely to support the institutions that exist to meet social need, rather than trying to help everyone personally (Plant, 1991). It means paying tax to fund health services and not, for example, working around the clock to alleviate illness.

Drawing these threads together, it might be concluded that positive rights are neither conceptually distinct from nor inferior to negative rights; the two stand or fall together. Any individual interest that should be protected or promoted can be expressed as a right. But does this apply to children?

The rights of children

Children's rights throw up special challenges because of the contested nature of childhood. To simplify, protagonists fall broadly into two camps (Fox-Harding, 1991; Franklin, 2002; Archard, 2004). The *protectionist* view is that children are vulnerable and immature and therefore need nurture and protection first and foremost. Also referred to as the 'caretaker thesis', it holds that children should not be free to take autonomous decisions but rather that their caretakers should take this responsibility, and that only by so denying children the rights of self-determination now will children acquire them in the future (eg Purdy, 1992). According to the *liberationist* perspective, children are oppressed rather than inherently dependent and should enjoy full adult rights; age should be no more a ground for discrimination than gender or ethnicity. For proponents of the view, practically this means entitling children to vote, have sex, travel, direct their education and so forth (Holt, 1974; Farson, 1978); in other words, it goes beyond children's traditionally recognised rights to protection and treatment, for example with regard to health, education and freedom from violence and cruelty, and instead extends to those rights that children themselves choose whether to exercise. Underpinning the difference between the two camps are competing theories of what it is to hold a right. *Interest theory* maintains that 'a right is the protection of an important interest' whereas *will theory* holds that 'a right is the protected exercise of a choice' (Archard, 2004, p 54). Those who argue that children are incapable of exercising choice will therefore conclude that children do not have rights.

Needless to say, both the protectionist and liberationist views have been criticised. The former, on its own, is now considered to be anachronistic; most people today acknowledge that children should have some say in decisions that concern them. Indeed, such a right is enshrined in the CRC (Article 12), which codifies a recognisable canon of thought about the rights of children in what Archard (2004) calls 'western liberal democratic post-Enlightenment societies' (p 58). Equally, unfettered autonomy can put children in danger and take precedence over the complementary aspects of citizenship, namely *duties* (Fox-Harding, 1991). Indeed, there is arguably a balance to be struck: psychological evidence shows that young children require special care and stimulation (Freeman,

1983) and that self-determination is a capacity that develops as much as a right to be expressed.

Consequently, most western developed nations have steered a sometimes inconsistent path between these two perspectives. The England and Wales 1989 Children Act, for example, requires service providers both to make children's welfare a paramount consideration in all matters concerning their upbringing but also to strive to accommodate children's wishes and feelings (Lyon and Parton, 1995). The concern with making children's welfare a paramount consideration (s 1) is reinforced by the requirement for children's services agencies to identify children in need locally and provide appropriate services for them (s 17 and Schedule II). Accommodating children's opinions is dealt with in the legislation by making provision for children to have their own advocates (s 41), to complain about how they are being treated (s 26) and to challenge an agency's decision to remove them from their family (s 45). In addition, the views of a child cared for by the state must be ascertained before case reviews (s 26), and older teenagers may refer themselves into local authority accommodation if their welfare would otherwise be seriously prejudiced (s 20(3)).

International law also opts for a happy medium, balancing children's autonomy with their best interests – what Freeman (1983) calls a kind of moderate liberal paternalism. Thus, the CRC obliges states to make children's best interests a primary consideration and to ensure that due weight is given to children's opinions in matters concerning their upbringing (Articles 3 and 12). It portrays children as people who need protection while also deserving to be brought up in a spirit of dignity, freedom and equality (Verhellen, 1999).

Conclusion (1)

Rights are the interests and liberties to which humans are entitled. Violated rights are therefore identified by establishing, first, the freedoms and resources to which an individual is entitled and, second, how that individual has been treated by the third party (person or body/organisation) with the corresponding duty to forbear or assist. The following points, drawn from the preceding discussion, underpin this understanding.

First, rights are claims that derive from and reinforce a person's status. They are unconditional, not earned, based on individuals' inherent human worth; entitlements to collective state provision tend to require minimal parallel duties, usually military or jury service and paying tax (Stewart, 1995). Rights preserve individuals' dignity and security by enabling them to claim something as their due, knowing that their entitlement outweighs competing claims to the item in question (Nickel, 1987).

Second, because rights concern how an individual is treated, they are more about outputs – the existence of structures and procedures – than about outcomes. In other words, whereas impairment to a child's health or development signifies the presence of need, it does not necessarily denote a violation of the child's rights;

equally, rights may be infringed but not cause harm. Put plainly, the effect of an incident on an individual's health and development does not, or at least should not, affect judgements about rights violations; the presence or absence of any ensuing harm is of no consequence (see Chapter Seven).

Third, rights claims are attached to a range of topics. The entitlements enshrined in international charters are as disparate as adequate housing and health on the one hand, and freedom of speech or protection from abuse on the other. Arguments in favour of recognising negative rights only have been found wanting; positive rights are equally valid.

Fourth, rights claims are generally concerned with minimum standards. *Legal* entitlements are usually fairly conservative because of the argument that only *enforceable* claims warrant being called rights. *Moral* rights are more ambiguous; international charters appear on the one hand to stipulate basic minimum standards but on the other to set out ideals to which individuals and states should aspire. For example, some commentators have described the CRC as a vision of what a child's life should be like, whereas others have argued that it sets out what no child should be without. In reality it is probably a combination – an aspiration for all children to enjoy basic standards of provision, protection and participation.

Fifth, a person's subjective view does not affect whether or not their rights have been infringed. It is true that the rights perspective *does* assign considerable weight to ascertaining an individual's opinions, both in relation to everyday activities and in particular settings such as a court of law (Eekelaar and Dingwall, 1990; Waldron, 1993; Lyon and Parton, 1995). However, so long as subjects have had a reasonable chance to express themselves, it must be considered that their right to participate has been respected; how they *feel* about either the process or the outcome is irrelevant.

Sixth, it should be relatively straightforward to determine if a violation of rights has occurred, but this is conditional on there being clarity about a person's entitlements, the nature of attendant duties, and events leading up to the pertaining situation. Rules are rules, and there is little room for discretion. This can make rights a fairly sensitive concept such that incidents regarded on another yardstick as relatively unimportant, even innocuous, register as significant and worthy of redress. For example, it is arguable that *any* violence towards children breaches their right to physical integrity, irrespective of the severity of the attack or the context in which it occurred. Viewing the same scenario with a view to identifying the child's needs would entail greater consideration of both the context and sequelae of any incident.

Seventh, the antecedents of a situation *do* affect whether or not it involved the breach of an individual's rights. The judgement must be 'no' if an individual's predicament is self-inflicted, genetically related or the product of misfortune. However, it is another matter altogether if the state or other responsible persons cause or perpetuate the difficulty by neglecting their duties. For example, if a child falls off their bike and cuts their leg, their rights are potentially still intact. They may have been riding dangerously, or had a fit and lost control, or hit a pothole. But if they were knocked down by a drunken driver, or if a passer-by delayed calling an ambulance, their rights *have* been violated.

Measurement

The rights tradition generally does not have a strong empirical track record, and certainly in the area of *children's* rights much work is based on philosophical conjecture and anecdote (Fox-Harding, 1991). Often the implicit assumption in both academic and advocacy circles is that all children's rights are de facto violated; to caricature (but only slightly), not only are children disenfranchised, economically disadvantaged and subject to degrading punishment (Franklin, 1989; John, 1996a), but also their modern dependence contrasts with the past when they behaved and were treated as adults (Freeman, 1983; John, 2003; Mason and Fattore, 2005).

Although widespread, this perspective lacks the rigour to determine that those responsible for delivering specific entitlements have defaulted; for example not all children are hit. It often adopts a narrow interpretation of particular rights, for instance focusing on voting as a measure of participation when children may be involved in various forms of decision-making. It sets the baseline too low to make any useful distinction between different degrees of rights infringements. Any hardship experienced by a child is assumed to be the fault of someone or some body or organisation: apparently no account is taken of alternative explanations, for instance accidents or natural conditions. And presumably at some point rights cease to be violated; that is, things move on – for example, the situation of the victim changes or the defaulter makes amends. This too is often overlooked.

No proven off-the-shelf model for measuring rights violations in a community context existed at the time of the study reported in this book, however, so it was necessary to search the literature in order to identify key principles on which to base a new approach. This suggested that there are three logical stages to the measurement of rights:

(1) deciding if a person's rights have been breached;
(2) codifying a breached right, that is, marking it in a public and recognisable way; and
(3) aggregating these codified judgements in order to state the proportion of people whose rights have been breached.

This section of the chapter considers each stage in turn before outlining how they were linked in the inner-London study on which this book is based.

Stage 1: Deciding if someone's rights have been violated

As a rule, children in the literature are deemed to have had their rights violated on one of three grounds. The first is a difficulty experienced in various areas of life. For example, in relation to housing the focus would be on inhabitants of properties that require substantial repair. Much attention is paid to fairly blatant examples of the products of exploitation and oppression – street children, child soldiers, sex workers, unaccompanied refugees and so on (John, 1996a, 1996b, 1997; Ennew, 2002; Schimmel, 2006). However, with less extreme cases there is little consideration of relevant matters such as how the situation arose or who is responsible for addressing it.

The second approach to determining rights violations involves identifying a characteristic that makes children disproportionately susceptible to discrimination or maltreatment and then assuming that everyone with that characteristic suffers violated rights. For example, children with disabilities may be segregated from their peers in education or find their mobility restricted by poorly designed buildings (Jones and Basser-Marks, 1997; Lansdown, 1998). This method tends not to be stated explicitly but it underlies much campaigning work in the rights arena. The problem with it is that some children with the characteristics in question are treated well.

Contexts that might be regarded as oppressive in some way constitute the third ground for judging that a child's rights have been violated. The focus is on subjects of systems that lack the necessary infrastructure for upholding rights – legislation, policy, procedures, organisational structures and so forth. Some schools use punitive punishment techniques or deny children opportunities to influence decision-making, and the care and justice systems harbour various abuses (Franklin, 1989; Fox-Harding, 1991; Jeffs, 2002). The advantage of this approach is that instead of focusing on harm it concentrates on how third parties act towards children; this is appropriate given the emphasis in a rights perspective on how individuals are treated. The drawback is that children can be treated well even if the legislation does not require it, just as exacting procedures are not necessarily followed. For this reason it is important to examine each case on its merits.

Notwithstanding their weaknesses, all three of these approaches are helpful. However, it is important that any attempt to measure rights violations makes explicit its underlying assumptions. A more sophisticated approach to determining if someone's rights have been violated would therefore involve working through a structured series of considerations.

One consideration concerns what rights are recognised; if something is not recognised as a right in the first place it makes no sense to ask whether or not it has been violated. It is important, therefore, to be clear about three things. First, do socioeconomic *and* civil-political rights count? Some international treaties, for example the European Convention on Human Rights (ECHR), contain only civil-political rights such as freedom of speech and respect for privacy. Judged by these rules extreme material hardship could not infringe anyone's rights. Second, can both commission and omission cause a violation? Although rights can be violated as much by the state's failure to intervene as by its interference, attention is often focused on the latter, so that not taking positive steps to facilitate freedom of speech is treated more leniently than concerted efforts to suppress it. In interpreting the ECHR, for instance, the European Court of Human Rights

(ECtHR) has taken the view that both forbearance and affirmative action are relevant in determining whether or not a person's rights have been infringed. For instance, upholding Article 8 'Respect for Family Life' requires both recognition that the child is part of a family *and* tangible steps to reunite children and parents who have been separated (Kilkelly, 1999). Third, are legal or moral rights being considered? If only the former are being considered, the failure to reach standards prescribed by an international law that a country is not bound by *cannot* constitute an infringement.

Another consideration affecting judgements about whether or not a person's rights have been infringed is *who* or *what* can violate rights. This, too, is therefore part of the series of questions to consider. A person whose predicament results from the action or omission of someone or something that is incapable – in legal terms – of violating rights cannot claim that their rights have been violated. Generally speaking, people think in terms of the state rather than individuals in connection with rights being upheld or infringed. Yet it seems counterintuitive to say that children abused by their parents have *not* had their rights violated. One approach therefore is to hold the state responsible both for what it does to prevent such events and also for how it responds when abusive events do occur. For example, one of the principles guiding how the ECHR is interpreted – 'effective protection' – means that even if a breached right is attributable to an individual, responsibility may be deemed to lie with the state for its failure either to protect the claimant or to do anything about the issue in question (Kilkelly, 1999).

A further consideration when determining if a rights violation has occurred is the set of principles that guides such decisions. This might take the form of explicit guidance concerning the law or treaty in question, precedents set by previous similar cases, and other considerations such as various international standards. This can be illustrated with regard to the ECHR, which, unlike some other conventions (including the CRC), takes on legal cases and has therefore developed explicit guidance. Kilkelly (1999) identifies several principles that have developed in the process of applying the convention. One involves taking into account the particular morality and culture of the country concerned. Thus the ECtHR has been reluctant to interfere with national decisions about alternative care for children or the custody of children following divorce. Another principle is that the ECHR must be interpreted in the light of contemporary standards. Circumstances that might not have been conceived of when the document was written, or that have not previously been dealt with in a rights context, might therefore be deemed to constitute infringements. This has been particularly evident with regard to methods of punishment, the treatment of 'illegitimate' infants and the consultation of children.

Stage 2: Codifying rights violations

Having decided that a rights violation has occurred, the fact needs to be codified or marked. How does this happen? First there is case law, in other words law made by courts interpreting cases and laws as opposed to law made by legislatures. This is the obvious place to start because it contains the considered judgments of impartial referees on specific situations in which a rights violation is alleged to have occurred. These judgments serve as precedents, indicating how an international treaty or national law is, and to some extent will continue to be, interpreted. This is because courts must take the outcomes of previous cases into account when assessing new cases that have some similar characteristics. For example, the judgments handed down by the ECtHR have contributed both to international human rights law and also to national jurisprudence (Kilkelly, 1999), while the UK 1998 Human Rights Act 1998 requires courts to look at case law relating to the ECHR and even other jurisdictions (Drew, 2000). Previous judgments therefore help to clarify what does and what does not constitute a breached right. For example, the outcomes of two cases taken to the ECtHR suggest that a child's rights are infringed by corporal punishment but that they are unaffected by sex education in school (Dale-Risk, 2001). One of the strengths of using case law to identify rights infringements is that matters are clear-cut; either a person's rights have been violated or they have not. Deliberations also require hard evidence and so decisions are likely to be consistent, and the principles on which they are based transparent. The main drawback with case law is the small number of cases that reach the courts; are they the tip of an iceberg or anomalies?

Formal complaints lodged by individuals are a second indicator that a rights violation has occurred. Allegations concerning the violation of children's rights can be directed at various bodies, from confidential telephone helplines to independent quasi-judicial adjudicators. In Norway, for instance, the child ombudsman produces an annual report that counts and categorises complaints by topic – family circumstances, school problems, treatment in institutions and so on. Some complaints are unfounded, however, and it is difficult to gauge the wider prevalence of the kinds of situations that generate complaints.

Treaty Articles that states decline to sign might be taken as a third indicator of who in that country has had their rights infringed. For example, the UK government registered reservations against provisions in the CRC concerning economic exploitation, detaining children with adults, and immigration and citizenship (Bisset-Johnson, 1994): it reserved the right to apply Article 32 'Protection from Economic Exploitation' subject to national employment legislation; it pushed for children to be detained with adults where appropriate facilities are lacking or in instances where mixing is deemed mutually beneficial (Article 3(c) 'Torture and Deprivation of Liberty'); and it required national legislation to be preserved in relation to immigration and citizenship (Article 10 'Family Reunification'). This suggests that children in the UK who at the time were working, locked up or seeking asylum were disproportionately likely to experience rights violations. However, a drawback with using reservations as a marker is that violations invariably occur in relation to Articles that countries *have* signed.

A fourth measure of rights violations is provided by the independent bodies that monitor some international rights laws. By identifying groups of people whose needs are treated inadequately, or policy areas in which states have failed to implement appropriate services or procedures, these bodies effectively highlight rights violations. Signatory states to the CRC, for instance, must report regularly to a panel of experts known as the Committee on the Rights of the Child (see Kilkelly, 2006). Against headings such as 'basic health and welfare' and 'special protection measures' they are required to provide evidence both of the number of children in particularly disadvantaged groups, and also of the existence of an infrastructure conducive to upholding CRC standards.

The response of the Committee to such reports conveys a sense of the extent to which children's rights are breached. For example, its first report on the UK raised concerns about efforts to alleviate poverty, discrimination against Travellers, schools making unilateral decisions about a child's education, and the treatment of 12-year-olds in custody (Price Cohen and Wolthius, 1995). One step on from this is an official declaration that national legislation is incompatible with human rights. The implication is that anyone affected by such law has had their rights violated. In the same report, the emergency measures in Northern Ireland allowing children as young as 10 to be detained by the police without charge were deemed incompatible with the convention.

Based on the conceptual discussion earlier in this chapter it is clearly appropriate to use judgements about infrastructure as a measure of whether rights are being upheld or violated by the state. However, a drawback of the approach is that it does not look at the circumstances of individual children before adding together those whose rights have been infringed (a necessary step since how children are *actually* treated will vary).

Stage 3: Aggregating the number of people with violated rights

A search of the literature suggests that nowhere has the number of people affected by rights violations at any one time been calculated. The nearest kind of evidence derives from human rights indices applied to countries, for example the UN Human Freedom Index. This includes a range of indicators, including rights to peaceful assembly and independent courts, and the freedom from unlawful detention or child labour; each country receives a score, ranging from 0 (poor human rights record) to 40 (good human rights record) (UNDP, 1991). However, such measures provide an indexed figure rather than a proportion of the population. Certainly there is nothing on which to draw at a community level and in a survey format. Consequently, the approach adopted in the study described here could only draw on rather than replicate what exists. Fortunately there are several useful pointers.

Social indicators are sometimes used as proxies for rights violations. Lansdown and Newell (1994) employed this approach in their extensive assessment of the UK's compliance with the CRC. One premise of this approach is that an individual's right is violated when their well-being falls beneath a designated standard. For example, children who are malnourished – according to a scientific measure of calorific intake – are deemed to have had their nutritional rights infringed (based on CRC Articles 6, 24(2c), (2e), and 27(3)). (The same approach is adopted in relation to standards of housing, income, educational opportunities, environmental quality and so forth.) Also implicit in the approach is the idea that certain situations represent an infringement, for instance having a parent in prison raises concerns against Article 9 on children not being separated from parents unwillingly. Other indicators in the report concern provision for children. For instance, a family's ability to afford basic necessities is used to measure respect for the right to adequate living standards (CRC Articles 24, 26, 27 and 31). The results are presented as proportions of the national child population who are, by definition, deemed to be victims of a rights violation.

States at the 'World Summit for Children' in 1990 adopted a similar method. They endorsed targets corresponding to CRC Articles, including a reduction in infant mortality, and universal access to clean water and sanitation, and made commitments to monitor progress on these indicators (the relevant CRC Articles are 6 and 24(2a), and 24(2c), (2c), respectively; Ledogar, 1993). There is also the official CRC monitoring process, which incorporates a series of indicators for each cluster of Articles (Ennew and Miljeteig, 1996; UNICEF, 1998). For example, among the indicators for 'Family Environment and Alternative Care' are the proportion of girls under 16 years who have given birth and the existence of a legal mechanism for the unscheduled inspection of care establishments (Harwin and Forrester, 1999).

The main benefit of using social indicators as proxies for rights violations is that they provide a wider perspective than the somewhat restricted number of formally recognised infringements outlined in the previous section. They also include indicators of treatment or infrastructure, which is appropriate given that the focus should be on outputs and not outcomes. That said, it can still be difficult to judge if a right has been breached, mainly because a hardship or circumstance is not the same thing as a violated right; they might be a *product* of a breached right, but this will depend on several factors, including whether or not the individual or public body responsible for guaranteeing that right has defaulted. There are also complications in adding together the children scoring against social indicators because some are likely to have violated rights in several areas. Further, well-being indicators tend not to cover all aspects of the CRC or extend to evaluating in a qualitative way how children are treated and the extent to which they enjoy all of their rights (Kilkelly, 2006).

Conclusion (2)

The measurement of rights and their violation is clearly underdeveloped. Some approaches are in danger of ignoring the concept of rights altogether, others offer little data to back their polemic, and many indicators are borrowed or unsuitable. In addition, systematic links between deciding, codifying and aggregating violations (the stages 1–3 described in this chapter) are drawn infrequently: judgements are made but not aggregated; markers that refer to outputs or infrastructures tend not get linked to individual cases; and aggregated statistics portray people's circumstances and level of disadvantage without permitting a judgement as to whether or not they represent rights violations. The study reported here sought to tackle some of these problems by taking each element in the measurement process in turn and linking them together explicitly. In doing so it draws on some of the strengths of the approaches reviewed earlier.

The CRC was used as the organising framework for five reasons. First, it relates specifically to children. Second, it incorporates various aspects of children's lives – living standards, treatment by others, opportunities for self-expression and so on. The various Articles can be neatly summarised in terms of *provision* for children's basic needs, *protection* from discrimination and all forms of neglect and exploitation, and facilitating children's *participation* in decisions that affect them (the 'three Ps') (Van Bueren, 1995).

Third, signatory states are obliged to transform the moral rights enshrined in the CRC into legal rights that are to be realised in practice. (This is because the convention is *hard* law, comprising binding norms; it arose out of the *soft* law of previous declarations on children's and human rights, which express aspirations, principles and international custom and tend not to be binding.)

Fourth, it describes obligations in terms of conduct rather than result (Hammarberg, 1995), with Article 4 mandating states to take appropriate legislative and administrative steps to implement rights. Both the monitors and the signatory states therefore tend to focus on the following:

- facilities for groups with special needs, for instance children with learning difficulties;
- eligibility criteria for state assistance, such as free school meals;
- mechanisms for eliciting children's views, notably youth councils;
- independent inspectors of standards, for example ombudsmen;
- legislation relating to children;
- specific initiatives, such as anti-bullying measures;
- structures designed to assist children, including planning mechanisms; and
- the numbers of children receiving specified services, for instance the ratio of numbers in foster care compared with residential care (Ledogar, 1993; Price Cohen and Wolthius, 1995; Kent, 1997).

This resonates with the idea that rights are about outputs, not outcomes.

Fifth, the convention has been central to most attempts to measure children's rights. Although it continues to be abused and has had a limited impact on domestic legislation (Archard, 2004), it has high legal and moral standing and is comprehensive in scope (Kilkelly, 2006).

For each child in the sample the study was able to use data on the following: the child's current circumstances, or events in the recent past; how (if at all) individuals and public bodies have caused or responded to these circumstances; and what else caused or perpetuated the circumstances in question. This information was used to decide for each child if CRC rights had been infringed (Stage 1). The test that was applied is based on three principles. First, there must be a problem with at least one of the 'three Ps'. Second, this problem should be the result of, or have been made worse by, the action (commission) or inaction (omission) of the state, an individual or another third party. The primary reason for the problem should not be genetic inheritance, the individual's own self-harming action (or inaction) or accidents or misfortune. Third, the violation must be current; if the person or body that trespassed or failed to provide has made amends, or has been prevented from reoffending, or if the circumstance that followed as a result of the incident in question no longer pertains, the violation is considered void. Cases where a rights violation has occurred were marked (Stage 2) and then added together (Stage 3).

FOUR

Poverty

Nobody seriously defends poverty, and few doubt the intrinsic value of strategies aimed at its eradication, but there is less agreement on exactly what 'poverty' is. It conjures up images of starving children in Africa, homeless beggars outside the theatre or downtrodden parents struggling to make ends meet. Numerous factors contribute to the confusion. Political values are influential, the right–wing perspective generally more at ease with harsher, subsistence thresholds. Then there are different languages and cultures; Persian alone has over 30 words for poverty (Rahnema, 1999), and Spicker's (1999) typology reveals the many-shaded western understanding. Lister (2004) makes a similar point when she identifies different discourses of poverty, and there is a proliferation of associated terms – 'underclass', 'deprivation', 'social exclusion' and so forth (Roll, 1992).

Consequently, there have tended to be wildly contrasting views about the extent of poverty and the profile of the poor. Like the pantomime villain, some people see it clearly, others deny its existence; interpretation depends on definition, which in turn reflects one's values. Yet as social policy interest in the subject has increased, the need for precise definition and good-quality research has become a priority (Gordon, 2006). For those working in children's services, a better understanding of poverty is crucial for making decisions about the fair distribution of resources and for understanding how other aspects of child well-being can be improved.

Concept

Science or value judgement?

It has been suggested by some commentators that 'poverty, like beauty, lies in the eye of the beholder' (Orshansky, 1969, p 37). The implication is that identifying someone as poor is value-laden – a subjective rather than an objective statement – and is, as such, of little substance. This is misleading. Poverty *is* defined in relation to the standards of society, but this is not the same as making a moral assessment of what such conventions should be or asking individuals what they feel about them. The standards are matters of fact. As Sen (1981, p 17; emphasis in original) put it, 'There is a difference between saying that the exercise [of poverty measurement] is *itself* a prescriptive one and saying that the exercise must *take note* of the prescriptions made by members of the community. To describe a prevailing prescription is an act of description, not prescription.' So, defining and measuring poverty is primarily a descriptive rather than an ethical exercise, and different value judgements and perspectives do not prevent this being done using a robust scientific process (Pinker, 1999).

Resources and living standards

Definitions of poverty are dominated by two dimensions: resources and living standards. Combining them produces thresholds of income beneath which the capacity to meet one's material and social needs in a manner commonly enjoyed in wider society diminishes rapidly. The idea that poverty is the inability to participate fully in society owing to deficient resources is adopted by some of the most respected studies. Rowntree's (1901) study of York defined the primary poverty threshold in terms of the earnings required to obtain the minimum necessities for maintaining physical efficiency, while Townsend's (1979) seminal research on poverty in the UK focused on the level of income below which deprivation multiplies disproportionately fast.

This approach to conceptualising poverty raises three questions, the first of which concerns how resources and participation are defined. In a classic definition, Townsend (1993) suggests that 'resources' include income, assets and goods in kind, and that 'participation' means 'the conditions of life, that is the diets, amenities, standards and services which allow [people] to play the roles, participate in the relationships and follow the customary behaviour which is expected of them by virtue of their membership of society' (p 36).

Of course, this approach involves the potentially difficult task of defining the style of living that is generally approved or shared in society. Townsend (1979) argues that, notwithstanding the absence of a unitary, clear-cut national style of living, common *types* of consumption and customs do exist. So, 'Christmas may be celebrated by an exchange of gifts from Woolworth's, a few glasses of beer and a chicken from a broiler factory; or by an exchange of gifts in the best tradition of Harrods or Heal's, together with all the luxurious trappings of a country-house weekend party' (p 249). The message is clear: government, travel, media and education produce diffuse cultural norms that supersede ethnic, class, regional and familial variations. Put another way, social groups remain somewhat distinct but essentially they adopt and accept as appropriate society's modes of behaviour; activities are shared, they just differ in substance.

Indirect and direct definitions

The second question raised by the approach to defining poverty outlined above is why the link between resources and living standards? It is not self-evident, indeed for Kangas and Ritakallio (1995) the issue that most divides researchers is whether poverty should be defined and measured *indirectly*, that is through income and other resources, or *directly* in terms of consumption and living conditions (p 1).

Ringen (1988) contends that studies often operationalise deprivation (a direct definition) using income (an indirect measure), a step that for him is illogical and invalidates the results. Low income does not necessarily mean poor living standards or impaired participation in society. It may be a temporary blip or be offset by savings or informal support. Equally, living standards do not always reflect resources; material hardship may be the product of a simple style of living, or wastefulness, or involuntary expenditure – such as debt repayments or medical bills – rather than of low income. Accordingly, somebody who has a low income but decent living standards (for example because of accumulated wealth), or a reasonable income but poor living standards (perhaps they have heavy debts) is not poor (Gordon, 2000b). Similarly, if a person is prevented from participating in various customary activities by ill-health, poor education or discrimination they are *deprived* but not poor (unless of course resource deficiency contributes to their disadvantage) (Whelan and Whelan, 1995). The logical conclusion is that poverty should be defined as poor living standards connected with a lack of resources. Indeed, Ringen (1987) advocates this connection. It is about establishing that an individual lives as if he is poor *because he lacks the means to avoid (or get out of) it.*

Absolute and relative poverty

The third question raised by the dual approach to defining poverty is what constitutes *poor* living standards? According to *absolute* definitions it means living at beneath the level of subsistence. For example, Rowntree's (1901) 'primary poverty' threshold was concerned with the minimum necessities for maintaining physical functioning, notably food, clothing, shelter and fuel. This conception dominated in Europe during the first half of the 20th century. For some, absoluteness also suggests constancy over time and invariance between societies (eg OECD, 1976). *Relative* definitions focus on a person's inability to participate fully in the society to which they belong, as reflected in Townsend's (1993) definition cited earlier. This perspective informed the development of a wider range of poverty thresholds during the second half of the 20th century.

The strength of absolute definitions is their moral authority; that everyone needs basic physical items is beyond dispute. Relative measures are more vulnerable because the 'basic' living standard and its calculation are open to question. This will become more apparent later in the chapter in the section on measuring poverty. However, absolute definitions have been challenged on the grounds that by concentrating on physiological efficiency they overlook social needs, notably recreation and the ability to fulfil obligations as workers, parents, friends and citizens (Gordon and Pantazis, 1997; Gordon and Spicker, 1999). For example, anyone living on Rowntree's (1901) poverty threshold would have been unable to afford newspapers, concerts or bus travel; they would be denied the essence of humanity, namely the capacity to make choices and participate in society. Moreover, minimum nutrition requirements cannot be translated seamlessly into minimum food requirements, and anyway such diets tend to be unrealistic as people's consumption habits are rarely based on cost minimisation (Sen, 1981). It is also impossible, arguably, to define a universal minimum because basic needs – or at least the satisfiers that meet them – depend on climate, taste, occupational hazards, individual constitution, the availability of goods and expectations generally (Alcock, 1997). Goods that were once deemed luxuries are now considered necessities (Roll, 1992); for example, refrigerators are needed for storing food in western developed nations today because most houses have central heating and groceries are packaged to be chilled. Thus, the absolute minimum for staying healthy and participating in modern Britain is higher than 100 years ago (Blackburn, 1991). 'Absolute' is as problematic as 'relative'.

In reality, then, absolute conceptions of poverty necessarily involve relative judgements in order for them to be applied to any particular society. But for some commentators, they are still less relative than relative definitions of poverty, which are thought merely to be measures of *inequality*. Roach and Roach (1972, p 23), for example, define relative poverty as 'the bottom segment of the income distribution', suggesting that the threshold is drawn simply by comparing the worst off with the better off. Theoretically this *pure* relative position can result in the same number of people being deemed to be in poverty in times of national prosperity as during a recession; indeed, if everyone were starving – total equality – nobody, perversely, would be poor (Piachaud, 1981). Sen (1981) makes the point that since all people need nutrition, shelter, clothing and freedom from disease, poverty has an irreducible absolutist core. Starvation and hunger constitute poverty whatever the relative conditions (Sen, 1983). Relative definitions of poverty therefore require some absolute core in order to distinguish them from broader inequalities.

What are the implications of this discussion? Four are of particular relevance here. First, the distinction between absolute and relative standards, outlined above, remains. One means not having the basic necessities of life to keep body and soul together, the other not being able to do the things that most people take for granted (Gordon, 2000a).

Second, some of the semantic confusion has hopefully been addressed. 'Relative' should be interpreted as relative to a minimum standard rather than in pure terms, which would be vis-à-vis the living standards enjoyed by others in society. The 'absolute' minimum must be understood relative to society (Townsend, 1985), in other words it is not defined by physiological efficiency or invariance between places and constancy over time (Sen, 1985a). Core needs include travel, education and living without shame in addition to shelter, clothing and escape from avoidable disease (Sen, 1983). Their concrete form varies, for example with medical technology, climate and fashion.

Third, absolute and relative definitions are virtually indistinguishable *in operational terms*, that is they can be measured using the same methods and criteria (Gordon, 2000a). With both it is necessary to take into account prevailing living standards and the minimum acceptable level. Townsend (1979, 1993) and others since (eg Gordon et al, 2000; Pantazis et al, 2006) have done this.

Fourth, poverty and inequality are related but different. Inequality can increase but leave the poverty rate untouched, notably when income is transferred from the poor to the non-poor, or from the very poor to the less poor (Osberg, 2002). Equally, inequality can remain static while poverty increases: 'a general decline in income that keeps the chosen measure of inequality unchanged may, in fact, lead to a sharp increase in starvation, malnutrition and obvious hardship; it will then be fantastic to claim that poverty is unchanged' (Sen, 1981, p 15).

Duration and depth

The discussion thus far implies that a straightforward dichotomy exists between the poor and the non-poor. Reality, inevitably, is more complicated. For example, in the US Ashworth and his colleagues (1994) traced the poverty history of 21,000 children over 20 years, identifying six categories of poverty based on the spacing and duration of episodes. These included the *transient* – one short spell (10%), the *recurrent* – multiple intermittent poverty spells (16%), and the *permanent* – one continuous spell (2%) (see also Leisering and Walker, 1998; Hill and Jenkins, 1999). The depth of poverty, by contrast, is the extent to which the incomes of the poor fall short of the poverty line (Osberg, 2002); there are gradations of deprivation even below the poverty line, from those whose income is marginally short to those with barely two pennies to rub together. These observations prompt the question of whether researchers should treat all poverty equally.

Conclusion (1)

Poverty is defined here as poor living standards owing to deficient resources. Children are poor if, because their family's income is inadequate, they cannot enjoy the goods, services and activities that most children in the society concerned take for granted. Poverty has the following characteristics.

First, whereas need is about agency, and rights are about status and treatment, poverty is about resource-related ability to participate in customary living patterns in a given society.

Second, poverty is an outcome/output hybrid in that it captures the standard of living that is potentially attainable given a certain level of income. It can be defined solely in terms of outputs, for instance receipt of basic social assistance or free school meals (in the UK), but usually it is defined in terms of resources – in particular money – and the goods, activities and services to which these afford access. It does not capture health or development directly, focusing on a lack of need–satisfiers rather than unmet need per se.

Third, the concept of poverty is fairly limited in scope. It concerns material hardship owing to a lack of resources and is generally described in terms of income and living standards. The narrowness of this perspective becomes evident if it is linked to the four other main concepts considered in this book. It is an unmet need for economic security (Doyal and Gough, 1991) and hints at the infringement of the right to adequate living standards (Article 27 of the UN Convention on the Rights of the Child; CRC). It represents a low score on the socioeconomic component of quality of life (QoL) (Smith, 1977; Commins, 1995) and might be taken to indicate exclusion from the economic sphere (Lister, 1997).

Fourth, poverty research usually concerns the wherewithal to live a minimally adequate life. To be poor is to lack sufficient resources to secure *basic* necessities. A subsistence approach suggests that people are only poor if they lack bare essentials like food, safe drinking water, sanitation facilities and shelter (UN, 1995). Even higher poverty thresholds often allow only for a modest living standard – the absolute minimum level of participation in a given society.

Fifth, poverty concerns material and objective phenomena (Abrahamson, 1995). Although normative judgements shape estimates of sufficiency, it can be defined objectively. Generally, a person whose income and living standards fall beneath a certain level is poor irrespective of their feelings on the matter. Several definitions heed public opinion regarding adequate living standards, but purely subjective approaches are rare.

Sixth, poverty lines demarcate clearly between the poor and the non-poor. The choice of threshold affects the poverty rate and the composition of the poor, but on any one measure the calculation is reasonably straightforward; an individual's income is either greater or less than the specified minimum, and they either do or do not enjoy certain possessions and activities. The only caveat concerns the duration and depth of low-income spells, nuances that invariably get glossed over.

Seventh, poor living standards must be linked with resource deficiency, but otherwise the antecedents of a situation have no bearing on the existence of poverty. Most mainstream commentators agree that poverty has structural roots, for example unemployment or low pay (Abrahamson, 1995). Some, however, attribute it (controversially) more to personal disposition and criminal, immoral lifestyles (eg Murray, 1990). Alternatively, misfortune or natural disaster may result in extra expenditure or loss of income.

Measurement

Two ideas cut across all of the poverty measures described in this section. The first is the distinction between the poverty *rate* – the number of people who are poor against a specified standard – and the poverty *gap* – the aggregate shortfall of income of all the poor from the selected poverty line (Sen, 1981). The former approach is the most common, and is used in the present study. It is resolutely quantitative, as compared with the numerous rich *qualitative* accounts of poverty that exist, both in academic studies (eg Townsend, 1979) and in more popular ethnographies (eg Abrams, 2002; Toynbee, 2003).

The second important idea is *equivalisation*. Meaningful comparisons of household income must take family size and composition into account, since what is adequate for one person may not stretch for a larger family. The common method involves converting families into standardised units using equivalence scales. Individuals in a household are weighted according to how much they are thought to need, incorporating the economies of scale that exist for many items and the different consumption needs of adults and children. This information is used to gauge whether specified resource bundles are adequate for certain groups of people. Throughout the rest of the chapter, 'income' means equivalised income. Because each equivalence scale uses a different weighting system, the choice of one over another can affect the results, with the *composition* of the poor apparently more sensitive than the poverty *rate* (eg Buhmann et al, 1988). Furthermore, equivalisation does not address the problematic assumption that children share the same living standards as fellow household members (eg Huston, 1991; Daniel and Ivatts, 1998). Relatively little is known about the intra-household distribution of resources but there is evidence that some non-poor households contain poor children and vice versa (Middleton et al, 1997). Ideally, then, children would be the primary unit of analysis with any of the following thresholds.

Percentage of average income

It is common for households below an agreed point of the income distribution to be deemed to be poor. National governments and international bodies such as Eurostat – the European Union statistics agency – conventionally use 40%, 50% or 60% of the mean or median. The volume of poverty is affected by the percentage threshold that is selected, although comparative data suggest that countries maintain their relative position irrespective of which one is used. The poverty rate is also consistently lower for median (as opposed to mean) income, although the extent of this disparity varies between countries; those with more equal income distributions are more likely to have medians that are close to the mean (Bradshaw, 1999). Whether average income is calculated before or after housing costs are subtracted affects the poverty rate as well. The rationale behind the 'after housing costs' option is that whereas a significant chunk of most individuals' earnings goes towards a mortgage, many people on the lowest incomes have their rent – or a large proportion of it – covered by the government (the function of Housing Benefit in the UK) (Roll, 1992).

The main advantages of the percentage measure are that it is standardised and adapts to changing demographics and living standards. It does not require detailed information on living standards, thereby avoiding some of the complications associated with need-based measures (see later), and it lends itself to crude cross-national and longitudinal comparisons. However, it also has its drawbacks, two of which are salient in the context of the study described in this book. One is that it applies arbitrary cut-off points that bear little relation to scientific or social criteria of need (Townsend, 1979). Often these are fairly conservative, overlooking the fact that individuals with higher proportions of average earnings may also struggle. The other disadvantage is that if average income falls, people who become worse off in real terms may be seen to move out of poverty (Blackburn, 1991).

Benefit levels

Several measures compare household or individual income with the minimum entitlement guaranteed by the state, namely basic social assistance (eg Abel-Smith and Townsend, 1965). (Every industrial country has some scheme of social assistance, a floor below the social insurance system, providing relief in cash for those with limited resources [Atkinson, 1995]; the level is usually based on a test of the claimant's income and assets, and, in some cases, their behaviour [for instance their availability for employment] [Bradshaw, 2001].) Those with incomes below that amount are in poverty. This will include the very low paid, people who have delayed applying for benefits, the wilful unemployed and those whose benefit claims were under-assessed or who are eligible for but not claiming assistance – reasons include a lack of awareness, resistance to the stigma of 'charity' and a belief that navigating the bureaucracy involved will outweigh any financial gain (Townsend, 1979).

The advantages of benefit-level measures are that they take need into account, they represent some kind of socially approved minimum and they do not require detailed information on living standards. However, they have weaknesses. First, unless social assistance rates are regularly updated with prices or earnings, or based formally on a standard budget (eg Sweden), any original scientific notion of adequacy is lost; this is certainly the case in the UK (Veit-Wilson, 1998), where successive studies suggest that 150% to 160% of basic social assistance is a more realistic approximation of the amount of money required for participation in society (Desai, 1986; Oldfield and Yu, 1993; Parker, 1999). This occurs easily because other criteria besides need, including fiscal prudence and a desire to engender conformity with social norms, affect the rate at which benefits are set. For example, rates may be set low to act as an incentive for recipients to seek paid employment. Second, receipt of basic social assistance is not inevitably associated with poverty (Bradshaw, 2000). In countries with realistic rates, even those with incomes *lower* than the state minimum may not be poor against other conventional standards. This is because the package of state help, in the form of cash and in-kind benefits (services), can boost recipients' incomes and living standards significantly (Townsend and Gordon, 2000). Third, the *actual* income of benefit recipients is likely to deviate from the rate of basic social assistance (Townsend, 1979). Some claimants receive more, perhaps through one-off payments for exceptional needs or money from savings or casual work. Fourth, as benefit levels increase, so, paradoxically, does the poverty rate (Alcock, 1997); this is because there are more people with incomes beneath that threshold.

Deprivation indicators

This measure takes the point on the income distribution below which a significantly large number of people reduce disproportionately their participation in the community's style of living. It was pioneered by Townsend (1979) in a nationally representative survey of over 2,000 households in the UK. That study explored different spheres of life and identified elements common to or approved by the majority of the population. The resulting 60 indicators covered diet, clothing, fuel and light, home amenities, housing, the quality of the immediate environment, work conditions, family support, recreation, education, health and social relationships. The majority of these correlated highly significantly with income and were therefore used to develop a summary index comprising 12 indicators (this included lack of a refrigerator, no holiday away from home in the last year, and lack of a cooked breakfast most days of the week). The mean score per household was 3.5 (out of 12), with 6.0 or more regarded as highly suggestive of deprivation (20% of households). By plotting income against this index, Townsend found evidence of a 'break of line' – a threshold of resources below which there was a marked increase in the proportion of people who might be regarded as deprived (or a significant increase in the mean deprivation score). This became the poverty line. In the light of critiques of the previous measure it is worth noting that, depending on the family type, Townsend's threshold varied between 102% and 133% of the prevailing rate of basic social assistance (then Supplementary Benefit).

The advantages of this approach are that it takes a range of needs into account and makes an explicit link between income and living standards. However, critics consider it unrealistic because experts rather than the public determine what constitutes an unacceptable standard of living (eg Piachaud, 1981). It also overlooks taste – the possibility that people lack items because they do not *want* them rather than because they cannot *afford* them; even the economically secure forgo holidays or cooked breakfasts, and members of religious orders often opt for austere living standards. Townsend (1979) acknowledges this weakness, noting that deprivation is difficult to detect at the margins because of individual idiosyncrasies and that in itself the lack of any single item is not symptomatic of deprivation.

Consensual indicators

This approach identifies people who lack a number of socially perceived necessities because they cannot afford them. Initially, respondents in a survey are asked to select from a list the items and activities that they think are needed for a reasonable standard of living in a given society. Next, the respondents are identified who, owing to insufficient resources, lack necessities (classified as such by at least 50% of the sample). Finally, the income level is ascertained of respondents at the greatest risk of being forced to go without (those lacking a specified number of items). This is the poverty threshold. The method is exemplified by the *Breadline Britain* studies (Mack and Lansley, 1985; Gordon and Pantazis, 1997; Gordon et al, 2000; Pantazis et al, 2006). In addition, Middleton and her colleagues (1997) constructed an index for children comprising 32 items, 21 of which parents regarded as essential for living in modern Britain. These included two substantial meals a day, parties on special occasions and a garden to play in. The study measured 10,500 children, classifying those lacking three or more necessities as 'poor' and those without five or more as 'severely poor'.

On the positive side, this approach addresses the main criticisms of deprivation indicators. It asks the public to define necessities and requires individuals in the study sample to say whether or not their lack of something is linked to inadequate resources. Another strength is the inclusion of items that reflect the place in customary living patterns of participation in activities and access to services; in other words, it moves beyond a focus on material goods. However, the approach also has weaknesses. First, 'necessities' are probably revealed more by people's *behaviour* than by their *opinions*; it is easy to deny that something is a necessity when one already has it (Roll, 1992). Second, it is debatable whether the approach is truly consensual. Experts compile the original list and may omit items that individuals regard as necessities, while respondents have no opportunity to reflect on their views, either independently or collectively (Walker, 1987). If anything, the approach might be considered to be more *majoritarian* than consensual, requiring as it does 50% agreement for an item to be deemed a necessity. Third, with this emphasis on majority views, it has been argued that the technique risks disregarding important cultural differences (Veit-Wilson, 1987).

Budget standards

Another method for measuring poverty involves costing the items, activities and services that experts deem necessary for a basic lifestyle. This 'basket of goods' is based on normative judgements, supported by scientific and behavioural evidence (Roll, 1992). Careful attention is paid to the commodities included, in particular their quantity, quality and estimated lifetimes and prices (Bradshaw, 1993). The sum is converted into a weekly budget, with anyone whose income (or expenditure) falls beneath it considered to be in poverty. For example, Rowntree and Lavers (1951) spelt out in their budget detailed amounts and prices of foods like rice, swedes and tea. Budgets for families with children have included nutritional needs, clothing, an annual seaside holiday, heating and lighting (Piachaud, 1979; Oldfield and Yu, 1993; Parker, 1999; see also Deeming, 2005).

The main strengths of the method are its transparency and adaptability; it can be adjusted to suit different family types, to represent different living standards, to use prices from national or local outlets, and to reflect inflation (Bradshaw, 2001). A persistent criticism, however, is that commodity baskets are unrealistically frugal. Families with a standard of living acceptable to Rowntree (1901) would have been forced to forgo all luxuries and buy the cheapest version of any item. More recent studies underestimate how much people spend on 'non-necessities' such as alcohol, pet food or videos (Alcock, 1997), and few allow for emergencies like an exploded boiler. Budget standards can account for unexpected items of capital expenditure, but only to a point. The problem lies in the hypothetical, expert-defined nature of such budgets. They capture what people *ought* to spend, not what they *do* spend, and they are based on average expenditure, when actual spending patterns vary with people's environment, needs and culture. For example, a person might live far from a reasonably priced supermarket, or have to pay extra for transport because of a disability, or be expected to wear special clothes – school uniform maybe (Roll, 1992). Budget standards also tend to be weighted towards market commodities at the expense of services or social activities and, as such, encompass only some of the elements that contribute to living standards. Ironically, Rowntree's budget standard was *deliberately* inadequate so that opponents of reform could not dismiss it as 'extravagant'; it was an heuristic device rather than a realistic prescription (Veit–Wilson, 1986).

In response to these criticisms, some studies have taken *actual* expenditure patterns as their starting point. For example, Bradshaw and his colleagues (1987) identify the point on the income distribution below which households, following ordinary expenditure, spend more than a given proportion on basic needs. Even this approach poses difficulties, although largely because defining 'luxuries' is tricky (Bradshaw, 2001). Other studies have become more sophisticated at taking into account social expectations. For instance, in recognition that a coat might be warm but unfashionable, and that food may be nutritious but unpalatable, Parker's (1999) 'low cost but acceptable' budget only includes goods that most people would find acceptable. Nothing, however, can prevent the method from being labour intensive and quick to become dated.

Component and multiplier method

Orshansky (1965) developed the 'component and multiplier' threshold, still widely used by US authorities. It involves calculating the costs of a minimal food budget for different-sized families and multiplying the amount by three (at the time this was the inverse of the proportion of income spent on food by an average American family). Bradbury and Jantti (1999) use the measure with Luxembourg Income Study data. Its scientific origins are a strength but it also has several disadvantages, not least that the multiplier – three times the food budget – is anachronistic because the cost of food has fallen (Citro and Michael, 1995).

Subjective approach

This approach obtains estimates from the population of the minimum income level at which it is possible to live decently in a given society. The average response can be used as the poverty line (eg Gordon et al, 2000). However, because people's estimates tend to rise systematically with their actual income (eg Citro and Michael, 1995), using the income standard derived from households that are only just able to balance their budget is sometimes preferred; it is considered that people in this position are best placed to know what amount is needed to participate in normal living standards. One way to identify these households is via a follow-up question enquiring how difficult it is to get by (Deleeck et al, 1988).

Another avenue is to select those households with an actual income equivalent to their estimate of the minimum required (van Praag et al, 1980).

The main strength of subjective measures is that they are socially realistic; the poverty threshold is defined by society itself (Gordon, 2000a). Another advantage is that the results are often corroborated by more objective measures; for example one study in Britain found that four fifths (80%) of those saying that their income was 'a lot below' the amount needed to avoid overall poverty were poor by a more objective measure (Gordon et al, 2000). So 'false consciousness' is fairly contained. Critics, on the other hand, argue that subjective thresholds are too high; many households below them encounter *some* difficulty in participating in normal living standards but few are actually *excluded* (Deleeck et al, 1992). Subjective measures also make international and longitudinal comparison difficult because they vary with the socioeconomic circumstances of countries and reference groups (Gordon, 2000a).

Selecting a measure

Thus far the section on measurement has described various methods of drawing a scientifically robust threshold between the poor and the non-poor. The discussion has effectively assessed the options against six criteria:

- First, does the measure incorporate income and living standards, looking at income (an indirect indicator) to establish how people can afford to live (a direct indicator)?
- Second, does it capture negative relative deviation from the absolute minimum needed to participate in the society's customary living patterns?
- Third, is the standard based on an objective, socially approved notion of adequacy (normally this means taking account of goods and activities, normal patterns of expenditure, fashion and taste, and individuals' needs)?
- Fourth, according to the definition in question, does the poverty rate fall as real incomes increase (so indicating that it is not measuring inequality)?
- Fifth, does the threshold account for the duration and depth of poverty episodes, that is, not treating short-shallow spells and long-deep spells equally?
- Sixth, how far is the measure transparent and easy to apply?

Having made these judgements, which measure should be used? The choice that is made has far-reaching ramifications, with different measures producing contrasting poverty rates. For example, in 1999/2000 one third (34%) of children in Britain were poor on the percentage of income measure (Bradshaw, 2002), compared with a fifth (20%) using the subjective threshold (Gordon et al, 2000). The selection of one measure over another also affects the composition of the population segment that is defined as poor. When Bradshaw and Finch (2001) explored the relationship between three poverty measures using nationally representative data from Britain, they found that the child poverty rate according to each measure was about the same (between 17% and 20%) but that the children designated as poor varied considerably. Indeed, the measures were almost completely uncorrelated, with only 6% of children in poverty according to all three.

Each of the measures reviewed here is better in some respects than others; none are perfect. Given this, researchers have three options. One is to use a single measure. This is the most common but least satisfactory option. An alternative is to identify 'core' poverty, that is, those people who are poor against several standards. Work to date on this topic suggests that 'the more dimensions that people are poor on, the more unlike the non-poor and poor on only one dimension they are – in their characteristics, in their attitudes and in their social exclusion' (Bradshaw, 2001, p 10; see also Bradshaw and Finch, 2003). This approach is probably the best, but thus far it has been little used. A compromise is to apply several measures and compare results. This is the approach taken in the study reported here. Recent years have witnessed a growing awareness of the value of using several poverty standards simultaneously in empirical studies (eg Oyen, 1999; Layte et al, 2000).

Conclusion (2)

For the purposes of this study, a child was deemed to be in poverty if they lived in a low-income household *and* had poor living standards. Several variations of this approach were applied using the data available, the results from which are compared in Chapter Eight. However, for the purposes of the analysis one measure was selected. (The data imposed restrictions, but every effort was made to incorporate the strengths of the measures described earlier.) *Low income* was measured in terms of receipt of basic social assistance, being in the lowest income band, or belonging to a sociodemographic category known to be strongly associated with low income. *Poor living standards* were captured in terms of substandard housing, limited leisure opportunities, lack of basic items, and financial problems such as debts and utility disconnections. Any intra-household variations in living standards were identified since children were the unit of analysis. Moreover, the dual approach – requiring evidence of low income *and* poor living standards – reduced the likelihood that temporary or shallow low-income spells are recorded as poverty. Finally, researcher and parental analyses were combined, thereby providing objective and subjective perspectives on whether the family's participation in society reached minimum accepted standards and how far it was limited by resource deficiency.

FIVE

Quality of life

Philosophers going back to Aristotle have struggled to articulate the meaning of 'the good life', and since the Garden of Eden scholars have conjured up visions of 'utopia'. The popular media seems obsessed with how the human existence can be enhanced, be it humorous depictions of assorted attempts to cheer up residents in Britain's officially most miserable town (the BBC television series *Making Slough Happy*) or earnest magazine columns on the 'science of happiness'. The term 'quality of life' (QoL) is often at the heart of such discussions and appears in common parlance and in technical settings, bridging the worlds of popular magazines, political rhetoric and academic journals. It represents a global assessment of the human life experience (Smith, 1977) and reflects the natural inclination of human beings to evaluate the quality of their existence (Hopkins, 1992); in one study, for example, fewer than 1% of respondents said that they had never assessed their overall QoL (Andrews, 1974).

The actual term 'QoL' was popularised in the 1960s by US Presidents seeking to trumpet their administration's success and show an interest in the electorate. It was Lyndon Johnson, for example, who proclaimed in 1964 that 'the Great Society is not concerned with how much, but with how good – *not with the quantity of the goods, but with the quality of their lives*' (cited in Day and Jankey, 1996, p 40, emphasis added). Since then, the profile of QoL concerns has been elevated by sociocultural trends such as environmentalism and a dawning recognition of the limits of wealth. This has stimulated a focus on measuring positive well-being and strengths or quality in people's lives and reorientating policy and practice to that end (eg Pollard and Rosenberg, 2003; Marks and Shah, 2005; Seligman, 2005; Jordan, 2006a, 2006b).

Concept

QoL has diverse conceptual and operational representations, particularly in the fields of philosophy, development economics, medicine and ecology (Nussbaum and Sen, 1993; Renwick and Brown, 1996). It is a somewhat elastic term (Roche, 2001), covering topics such as relationships, health, material and financial circumstances, and leisure activities (Bowling, 1995; Farquhar, 1995). Together with the potential conflict between personal taste and universal values, these factors make QoL a complex concept to define and measure.

Defining the 'good life'

Underpinning definitions of QoL are responses to the question 'what is the good life?'. These may be categorised in terms of three broad perspectives, the first of which focuses on *utility* – maximising happiness and satisfying people's preferences (Cohen, 1993). It sees well-being as a person's state of mind, which is in turn dependent on how far their desires are fulfilled and whether or not they are able to enjoy chosen activities and relationships (Dasgupta, 1993). QoL should therefore be evaluated subjectively. The perspective could be seen as *bottom-up* because it draws conclusions about the components of QoL from concrete experience.

There are various criticisms of this position. One is that it legitimises the pleasure a person derives from hurting others, counting it as equal to other satisfactions in the calculus of what is good (Rawls, 1971). It also risks overlooking actual deficits if the victim has a positive disposition. Thus, someone whose affliction is countered by a phlegmatic outlook or limited aspirations would not be found wanting by the utilitarian; critics of this position object, arguing – to paraphrase Cohen (1993) – that 'the disabled but sunny-spirited child *should* get a wheelchair'. A further criticism is that fulfilled preferences do not necessarily enhance a person's well-being; someone's QoL is unaffected by whether or not their preference for, say, the number of Saturn moons is fulfilled (Scanlon, 1993). Lastly, utility is hard to quantify, partly because it can be distorted by the experience of and adaptation to oppression or deprivation (Sen, 1993).

The second approach to defining 'the good life' therefore involves identifying the major *ingredients* of utility – the substantive goods that always make life better (Scanlon, 1993). Rawls (1971), for example, argued that well-being should be defined in terms of an individual's bundle of primary goods. These are the things that every rational person is presumed to want, including liberties, opportunities, income, and other factors that contribute to self-respect. Similarly, the *basic needs* approach to eliminating destitution defines QoL in terms of commodities like food, shelter, clothing and healthcare (Sen, 1993). For Dasgupta (1993), this approach stresses the human capacity for deliberation and doing and can be judged externally or objectively. It is *top-down* in that it involves identifying at a level of philosophical generality the rules that generate the good life.

Critiques of this perspective target what Sen (1982, p 366) calls 'commodity fetishism' – interpreting goods as the embodiment of advantage. Rigid lists of items overlook the fact that different people derive different benefit from the same good. For example, food intake and nutritional achievement vary with culture, climatic conditions and a person's metabolism and body size (Drèze and Sen, 1989). People also have different tastes; what one person likes leaves another cold. The focus should therefore be less on *ownership* of primary goods than on what they *do* to people. This emphasis is captured well by Sen (1985b, p 28) when he writes that 'a person's well-being is not really a matter of how *rich* he or she is ... commodity command is a *means* to the end of well-being, but can scarcely be called an end in itself'.

In the third interpretation of 'the good life', Sen (1982, p 30) christens the missing link between goods and utility 'capabilities'. He conceives life as a combination of beings and doings ('functionings'), ranging from the elementary – being well nourished, sheltered, clothed and disease-free – to the more complex – such as having self-respect and participating in community life. A person's *capability* refers to the various alternative combinations of functionings from which they can choose (Nussbaum and Sen, 1993). The stress is on what people are free to do and be – the ability to lead a life of one's choosing (Sen, 1999). *Utility* is evidence of that capability, while *goods* are the source of the capability. The following example, drawn from Sen (1982, p 30), illustrates these connections:

Goods (bike) → Characteristics (transport) → Functioning (moving) → Utility (pleasure)

Some commentators have attempted to put meat on these bones, for instance Nussbaum (1995) identifies a number of basic capabilities, such as avoiding unnecessary and non-beneficial pain, being able to laugh and play, being able to have attachments to things and persons, and reflecting critically on life. (The theory of need advanced by Doyal and Gough, 1991, and elaborated in Chapter Two also fits here.) Greater specificity is problematic because one gets into disputes over the merits of, say, particular pastimes or foods.

Although difficult to operationalise, Sen's contribution is important because it demonstrates that neither the substantive good nor the utility approaches in isolation capture QoL: 'a comparison of – say – malnutrition of different people is *neither* a comparison of foods they had consumed (they could consume the same amount of food and still have different levels of malnourishment), *nor* a comparison of utility (they could be equally malnourished but their levels of satisfaction or desire-fulfilment could still be quite different)' (Sen, 1982, p 30). Instead, QoL includes both: it entails being happy *and* the ability to fashion and pursue goals (the two are not exclusive, but nor are they intrinsically linked). In other words, QoL has two aspects: *inputs* or commodity determinants, notably goods and services, and *outputs* or the constituents of well-being, in particular utility and freedoms (Dasgupta, 1993). Rogerson (1995) describes the relationship in terms of an *internal* psychological-physiological mechanism that produces a sense of happiness and satisfaction, and those *external* conditions, for example health or the environment, which trigger this mechanism. In the same vein, Lane (1996) uses the formula QoL $= f$ (QC, QP) where QC is quality of objective conditions and QP is a sense of subjective well-being combined with personal development, learning and growth.

Common QoL themes

There are at least five recurring themes in the myriad definitions of QoL. First, QoL is an *holistic* concept in which people are seen as 'biopsychosocial beings' whose well-being hinges on efficiency of body, mind and spirit (Bowling, 1997).

The World Health Organization QoL Group (WHOQOL Group, 1993, p 30) considered it 'a broad ranging concept affected in a complex way by the person's physical health, psychological state, level of independence, social relationships, and their relationships to salient features in their environment'. Accordingly, most QoL definitions break life into several domains and incorporate similar components (Table 5.1; the items listed are drawn from the studies referenced in this chapter). Approaches range from the simple (for example two categories) to the elaborate (for example 15 categories grouped under five headings), and some are fairly philosophical. Renwick and Brown (1996), for instance, identify three areas of life in which all people strive for quality: *being* – the basic aspects of individuals; *belonging* – the fit between individuals and their environment; and *becoming* – purposeful activities to realise one's goals.

Table 5.1: Standard components of QoL definitions

Dimension	Examples of common items
Physical	Pain, mobility, sleep, appetite, nausea, ability to perform household duties, healthy eating, appearance, hygiene
Material	Income, consumer goods, inequality, general living standards, ability to do work
Psychological	Adjustment to illness, life satisfaction, morale, stress, happiness, self-esteem
Social	Family, friends, cultural and recreational activities, belonging to people, sexual relationships, prejudice, inclusion/normalisation, non-violence
Environmental	Housing (size and quality), access to green spaces/beauty spots, transport, neighbourliness, pollution, security/crime, architecture, belonging to a place
Spiritual	Personal development and fulfilment, growth and mastery, striving for and attaining goals, achieving aspirations and hopes, choice, respect, independence, balance

The dimensions outlined above broadly apply to children, although Bullock and his colleagues (1994) argue that it is harder to define QoL for children than it is for adults. They suggest that the importance of items changes as children develop, for instance competence matters more at 17 years than at six years, and that the relevance of items for QoL varies over time: a century ago moral fervour was focused on basic nutrition and school attendance, whereas today there is greater emphasis on self-expression. Further, sociodemographic shifts mean that criteria date rapidly, with divorce and unemployment arguably less harmful for children now than in the past.

A second theme in the QoL literature concerns the importance of looking beyond material goods (Burchardt, 2006). Put another way, a minimal quantity of certain goods is necessary but not sufficient for a meaningful QoL. Indeed, as inputs increase, their impact on the level of living is less than proportional – a law of diminishing returns (Drewnowski, 1974). In the US, for example, further increments above an annual income threshold of about $20,000 have a negligible effect on subjective well-being when viewed from an aggregate perspective (Ahuvia, 2000; see also Layard, 2005). (This is not to deny that people in rich countries tend to be happier than those in poor countries, and there is a small blip at the top of the income distribution where the most wealthy appear to experience greater subjective well-being – perhaps because they can avoid what they most dislike.) Moreover, beyond a certain point, there is evidence that additional quantity can actually bring about deterioration in QoL (ICPQOL, 1996); for instance, people with the most valuable possessions tend to worry most about their security. Offer (2006) marshals such evidence to argue that restraint and more emphasis on relationships contribute more to QoL than the immediate gratification of appetites for food, sexual experiences, drugs, television and so on.

These so-called 'disutilities of overabundance' are associated with the search for *non-material* sources of satisfaction. In Britain and the US after the Second World War, the term 'QoL' referred predominantly to material goods – a house, a car, consumer gadgets and so on. As these societies became more affluent, the emphasis switched to personal freedom and leisure (Farquhar, 1995). The same pattern occurs with individuals. People on higher incomes are not especially happier than their poorer counterparts (Fuentes and Rojas, 2000; Cummins and Lau, 2006), which confirms that other factors besides the economic affect QoL. Indeed, the emphasis with QoL is on grades of goodness (Bowling, 1997), or how excellent one's life is (Brown et al, 1996). In relation to children, QoL shifts attention away from their basic needs, such as protection, to wider, more eclectic concerns such as cultural activities and emotional health (Roche, 2001). The watchword is *quality*. A related point is that the absence of disease or pathology is not the same as flourishing; for example, Keyes (2005) argues that mental health and mental illness are different, albeit correlated, dimensions.

A third theme running through research on QoL is the possibility of trade-offs between different items; that is, because QoL has many ingredients, more of one item may compensate for less of another. At an individual level, for example, a person may choose to invest time in fulfilling work or study at the expense of interpersonal relations (Lane, 1996). It follows that individuals can have broadly the same level of QoL even though it is composed of a different *balance* of items. That said, the potential for trade-offs is limited. Someone who is starving would be hard-pressed to enjoy life, and Nussbaum (1993) is surely right to argue that each person should have minimal functioning in the key areas. So although in practice it is the rounded picture that counts, a particularly low score in one area of life will have a significant ripple effect.

The fourth common theme in debates about QoL is the value of self-determination – a person's capacity to exercise choice in forming and pursuing a coherent life plan. The importance of self-determination is crystallised in discussions about critically ill newborn infants. This is a highly sensitive and controversial area, but medical ethicists and moral theologians tend to argue that life should be preserved when it has the potential to be meaningful. In other words, there should be the possibility of positive conscious experience and sufficient longevity that the life moves from being biological to being *biographical* (eg McCormack and Richard, 1974; Rhoden, 1985). The implication of such a stance is that a good QoL requires the formulation of desires, hopes and plans for the future; it is life lived from the inside.

The fifth emphasis in the literature on QoL concerns the need for objective and subjective perspectives. Since QoL comprises inputs and outputs, judgements about it are necessarily composed of *observable facts* – for example regarding a person's functional capabilities, environment and state of mind – which can be apprehended by an external social group, and the *person's valuation* of those facts. The two aspects are captured in Renwick and Brown's (1996, p 80) definition of QoL as 'the degree to which a person enjoys the important possibilities in his or her life'. It is how objective circumstances are perceived relative to one's outlook and time of life that determines how much pleasure one enjoys.

Combining objective circumstances and subjective appraisal in this way is important because they can be at odds (Cummins and Lau, 2006). At the aggregate level, living standards and happiness do not correlate strongly. For example, in the US the steady increase in material wealth since 1957 has been accompanied by declining levels of happiness (Lane, 2000). A similar disjunction is evident with individuals. For instance, an important study of seriously debilitated people found that, surprisingly, fewer than half were dissatisfied with their health, indeed a handful (6%) were 'completely satisfied' (Campbell et al, 1976). Other medical research reveals similar patterns. So, a clinical measure of airways obstruction may not reveal a problem, despite the patient's experience (for example breathlessness when walking up stairs) (Hopkins, 1992). Similarly, patients detect significant changes in their health that clinical measures miss (Fitzpatrick, 1996). Greenspoon and Saklofske (2001), meanwhile, showed that children can have high levels of externalising psychopathology but also high self-reported subjective well-being.

There are various reasons for the objective–subjective disjunction. One is that objective measures may focus on factors that are important to the researcher or professional but are of little consequence to the subject (Raphael, 1996a). Another reason is that vulnerable populations can exhibit a 'false awareness' borne of a lack of hope about attaining goals and a consequent lowering of expectations (Raphael, 1996a). Thus, many report a good subjective QoL despite their objectively inferior conditions. Prior experience also mediates the relationship between objective circumstances and subjective appraisal. Offer (1996), for instance, remarks that the labour camp inmate described by the Soviet dissident Solzhenitsyn would consider it a good day on which nothing worse than the usual privations occurred. In a similar way, slight gains to health may seem very significant to someone with a history of illness; for example one study showed that three years after a cancer operation patients were happier than a control group of non-patients (Fitzpatrick, 1996). And if suffering can lose its bite, so comforts can lose their appeal – hence the desire of the better off for new things and experiences.

Personal resources and traits are also important in this regard, in particular motivation, cognitive ability, patience, an optimistic outlook, sociability, a meaningful view of the world and a sense of control (Day and Jankey, 1996). These enable people to overcome disadvantage and maintain a cheerful disposition; for example some patients with crippling injuries adjust their aspirations and find happiness despite their newly limited functional capacities (Fitzpatrick, 1996). Others, meanwhile, struggle to exploit favourable circumstances and remain miserable. As Lane (1996, p 273) put it, 'Opportunities in the environment contribute to quality of life only if there are matching receptive properties in the person involved'. The ability to enjoy fulfilling work requires some degree of cognitive understanding and motivation, while the benefits of friendship come only to those with at least a modicum of self-esteem and ease of interpersonal relations.

Taken together, these points suggest that either the objective or the subjective approach to capturing QoL is inadequate in isolation (Brock, 1993). Some commentators have therefore attempted to bring the objective and subjective together by focusing on the perceived gap between the 'actual self' – what an individual can do – and the 'ideal self' – what that person would like to be able to do (Calman, 1984). Taking this a step further, Michalos' (1986) 'multiple discrepancies theory' holds that QoL is the product of comparing one's current life to various standards – other people, the past, expectations, an ideal and so forth.

Conclusion (1)

Based on the foregoing discussion, QoL is defined here as 'subjective well-being and personal growth in a healthy and prosperous environment' (Lane, 1996, p 258). As in previous chapters on need, rights and poverty, aspects of this definition can be summarised in terms of cross-cutting themes.

First, QoL is a multidimensional concept that embraces all aspects of life. It is strongly influenced by the well-known World Health Organization (WHO, 1948) definition of health as a state of complete physical, mental and social well-being and not merely the absence of disease or infirmity.

Second, QoL is distinguished primarily by its concern with outcomes such as health, self-realisation, happiness and fulfilment. Outputs or service-related indicators are relevant insofar as income, relationships, a pleasant environment and so on affect how people feel. But it is how they are *used* that affects a person's QoL.

Third, as an holistic concept QoL encompasses more than a person's material well-being. The level of contentment that people feel is only partially captured by the way they deploy resources and the goods they consume.

Fourth, the notions of enrichment and the satisfaction of desires are central to the definition of QoL, and certainly given greater emphasis here than the other four concepts explored in this book. In other words, QoL concerns a higher level of existence or well-being than, say, need or poverty. Having enough to be able to function adequately or enjoin customary living patterns in society is a necessary but insufficient condition for a good QoL.

Fifth, a person's subjective conception of what is good – what they want – is central to their QoL. QoL depends on how a person evaluates their objective, material situation – for example, whether it makes them happy or depressed. It therefore depends considerably on a person's likes and dislikes as well as on their expectations and past experiences.

Sixth, assessing an individual's QoL is not as simple as scoring them against a set threshold (the approach most common in the measurement of poverty). All aspects of a person's life must be taken into account, and some appreciation is required of how an individual evaluates their circumstances.

Seventh, the antecedents of a situation are irrelevant when assessing QoL; outcome is far more important than process, notwithstanding the bearing on that outcome of past experiences. A person's QoL is a product of structural *and* individual factors.

Measurement

Economic indicators

From the 1940s onwards Gross National Product (GNP) per capita has been a widely used indicator of QoL: GNP (national income) divided by a country's population. This measures well-being in terms of access to market goods and services. It has been used extensively by international organisations such as the World Bank to measure the progress of so-called 'underdeveloped' countries. Income and consumption measures have also tended to be treated as proxy indicators for the QoL of individuals.

Unfortunately, and as already indicated, economic indicators are generally poor measures of well-being, and, in most cases, were not designed to capture QoL anyway. In particular, GNP was used as a proxy indicator on the grounds that it signifies relative QoL and economic growth would spread other benefits widely and speedily (Streeten et al, 1981). It was never intended as an end in itself. Indeed, in cross-national comparisons income explains just over half the variations in life expectancy and infant mortality (Doraid, 1997), and many countries with different GNP per capita have similar levels of subjective well-being (Stewart, 1996). In the US the material well-being of children increased between 1975 and 1997 but levels of intimacy fell (Land et al, 2000).

There are several reasons for these disjunctions. First, economic measures tend to overlook key determinants of QoL such as environmental and labour conditions, community cohesion, receiving affirmation and gifts from other people, aesthetic values and psychological satisfaction (Townsend, 1979; Lane, 1996; Stewart, 1996). Second, they include items that may not enhance well-being (Offer, 1996). Economic growth, generated by high levels of consumption, has negative side-effects like inequality and environmental degradation (Stewart, 1996), indeed, wars and oil spillages both – perversely – *increase* national wealth by generating economic activity. Third, not all consumption is equally valuable; few would argue seriously, for example, that pornographic videos are as life-enhancing as water or Mozart, yet such nuances are overlooked in measures of consumption. Fourth, people make choices that do not necessarily maximise their utility, and some people – including very young children – rarely make their own consumer choices. To sum up, there are many good reasons for not using an economic measure as a proxy for QoL.

Social indicators

In response to these criticisms, a plethora of social indicators emerged in the 1960s. Using or adapting a selection of these, then, could offer an alternative approach. Mostly dealing with objective external conditions – health, housing, education, transport, recreation facilities, civil liberties and so forth – these indicators have been mapped at different geographic levels, especially in the US and western Europe (eg Knox, 1975; Smith, 1977; Gordon and Forrest, 1995; SEU, 1998a; Dorling and Thomas, 2004). Many have been collated in statistical series produced by national statistics agencies (for example *Social Trends* in the UK) and international organisations (for example the United Nations Development Programme [UNDP] *Human Development Reports*), and the approach is reflected in the UK's official national QoL indicators (DETR, 1999a, 1999b; Audit Commission, 2005; National Statistics/DEFRA, 2006).

In relation to children, data have been compiled under the auspices of bodies such as the United Nations Children's Fund (UNICEF), whose annual *State of the World's Children* reports review basic indicators on children's development (for example, infant mortality, school enrolment, nutrition and percentage immunisations). In a similar vein, Micklewright and Stewart (1999) compiled Eurobarometer data for 15- to 19-year-olds in European Union (EU) countries against indicators such as health, education, material well-being, social inclusion and life satisfaction. A more recent publication charts trends in the physical, cognitive, behavioural and emotional well-being of children in the UK – significantly in response to the lack of any such regular official analysis (Bradshaw and Mayhew, 2005) – while Bradshaw and his colleagues (2007a) developed and applied an index of child well-being to the 25 EU states. These and similar developments are significant given that children have traditionally been invisible in statistical returns (Saporiti, 1999).

Of course, some social indicators are more useful than others. Work on children has seen a move away from measures of survival and deficiency towards positive indicators such as satisfaction, neighbourhood facilities and participation in activities (Ben-Arieh, 1997; Ben-Arieh et al, 2001; Ben-Arieh and Goerge, 2006). This is important, since the most widely used indicators – calories per head, literacy, access to sanitation facilities and so forth – are better at capturing levels of basic need-satisfaction than QoL (Gordon and Spicker, 1999). However, indicators continue often to be little more than collections of readily available figures, especially where children are concerned; they are not informed by theory (Casas, 1997).

A further major drawback with many social indicators is that without translating them into a common denominator it is difficult to compare QoL between areas and individuals. Attempts to rectify this include the *Human Development Index* (HDI), which includes life expectancy at birth, educational attainment and living standards (Doraid, 1997) and has been used in successive UNDP *Human Development Reports*. Similarly, the *Indicator of Sustainable Economic Development* (ISEW) attempts to 'green' GNP by adding value for goods such as unpaid domestic work and public services, and subtracting for inequality, pollution and money spent clearing up human-made problems, for example smoking-related illness (Jackson et al, 1997).

Such indices have both substantive and methodological strengths and weaknesses. On the positive side, they incorporate factors beyond the economic, are relatively straightforward to apply and, up to a point, lend themselves to cross-national and longitudinal comparison. However, indices like the HDI tend to be better at measuring the *length* rather than the *quality* of life, focusing on basic needs and overlooking much that contributes to the higher levels of well-being that QoL seeks to capture (Streeten et al, 1981; Doraid, 1997). The composition of the ISEW is also controversial; for instance, consumer durables are counted as a *minus* benefit for welfare, yet appliances such as washing machines have arguably made life better for people by radically cutting the time and effort spent on more menial tasks (ICPQOL, 1996).

Taken together, these points suggest that a robust measure of QoL should ideally be broad in scope, have a theoretical underpinning, embrace more positive indicators (extending beyond basic needs), focus on quality or enrichment and capture an individual's situation. To what extent does research on health-related QoL meet these standards?

Health-related indicators

Origins and development

QoL research in medicine expanded rapidly from the 1970s onwards, particularly in the fields of nursing, gerontology, health promotion and rehabilitation (eg Renwick et al, 1996). Until fairly recently the study of the QoL of infants and children was a neglected area (Skevington and Gillison, 2006) and adolescent health had not been examined in a QoL framework (Raphael, 1996b). However, a number of generic and disease-specific QoL measures have been developed recently in paediatrics and childhood studies more widely (Eiser et al, 2000a; Skevington and Gillison, 2006).

Most of the research in health has tended to concern post-treatment outcomes. New measures emerged in part because standard indicators such as increased longevity were inadequate for assessing the value of modern medical interventions, the majority of which are dedicated to relieving symptoms, improving mental health and restoring functioning (Najman and Levine, 1981). Standard health status indices typically include survival, morbidity or service use, but such measures generate little information about the 80% to 90% of the population who are healthy by such definitions (Bowling, 1997, p 4). In addition, the capacity afforded by technological advances to manage life-threatening conditions needed to be weighed against often painful and distressing treatments, not to mention the diminished quality of the extra years. For example, while 80% of children with acute lymphoblastic leukaemia – the most common form of childhood cancer – can expect five years of disease-free functioning following treatment, many suffer fatigue or cardiac damage together with social and psychological maladjustment (Vance et al, 2001).

This observation led to the development of Quality Adjusted Life Years (QALYs), which are based on individuals' assessment of the disability and distress associated with a series of health states (Rosser and Watts, 1972; Bowling, 1997) and used to identify interventions with the maximum cost-benefit ratio (Mulkay et al, 1987). There are drawbacks with this approach, however. The results from different valuation techniques are not concordant (Buxton, 1992) and the results often have an unreliable relationship with measures of health-related QoL or subjective well-being, suggesting that QALYs have poor criterion validity (Cummins and Lau, 2006). Hunt and McKenna (1992) question the implicit mechanistic conception of humans in terms of their ability to function. The valuation of health states also depends on *who* is asked (Williams and Kind, 1992).

Is there an approach that manages to maintain the link established in the QALY approach between objective circumstances and subjective appraisal of the associated degree of happiness or suffering, while also holding onto the relative simplicity that lends itself to research with children?

Standardised QoL instruments

As it happens, most QoL research uses psychometric instruments and questionnaires, of which there are a profusion (Raphael, 1996a). These offer more promise in the present context. Bowling (1997) describes 58 scales for capturing functional ability, broader health status, psychological well-being, social relations and support, and life satisfaction and morale. There are also numerous standardised instruments for assessing aspects of children's QoL, including self-esteem, feelings of hopelessness, ability to function normally, perceived support from friends and exposure to violence (eg Rosenberg, 1965; Currie, 1995; Brooks, 1996; CDC, 1998; Bru et al, 2001; Bolland, 2003) as well as more generic or multidimensional scales (eg Cummins, 1997; Cummins and Lau, 2005; Ravens-Sieberer et al, 2005; Funk et al, 2006).

Most health-related instruments cover one or more of three dimensions (Fitzpatrick, 1996): *functions* of a biological, mental, physical and social nature – all of which are necessary for the pursuit of relatively full and complete life plans (these include rest, eating, work, recreation and home management); *self-determination*, as defined earlier in this chapter; and *conscious experience* – subjective reflections ranging from abject misery to happiness. Instruments generally list items against life domains and elicit responses to each on set scales. Some are self-administered, while others are completed by a third person such as a carer or professional; the vast majority of measures for the under-eights are completed by carers or doctors on children's behalf (Eiser et al, 2000a). Results are calculated in different ways but commonly result in an *index* in which item scores are summed to form a composite score. The robustness of a measure is assessed in terms of validity – whether it captures the underlying attribute – and reliability – whether it consistently produces the same results if applied to the same subjects at different times when no change is evident.

Standardised QoL instruments are subjected to at least four general criticisms. First, the choice of indicators can appear to be arbitrary and, beyond their immediate context, occasionally bizarre. Najman and Levine (1981), for example, identified studies that used height, weight or desire to work, none of which, arguably, are essential attributes or determinants of a good QoL. Meanwhile, important items are often excluded; many instruments use only objective indicators, ignoring any distress experienced by the patient (see the fourth point below), and health-related measures pay insufficient attention to socioeconomic determinants of QoL such as income and housing (Day and Jankey, 1996). Certainly it may be contended that children's QoL is best ascertained by eliciting from them the *indicators* as well as the responses (MacGillivray and Zadek, 1995), in other words by involving them in the process of designing a meaningful instrument that addresses inherent developmental problems regarding communication (Skevington and Gillison, 2006).

Second, while health-related QoL research emphasises the function of the *whole* person (that is, beyond individual body parts), instruments tend to emphasise particular aspects of QoL. This holds especially in relation to children, although more comprehensive measures are emerging. In part the focus on discrete elements is practical, as overarching instruments can be unwieldy and time-consuming to complete (Bowling, 1997). Further, many QoL measures are disease-specific rather than generic, tailored to capture the known effects of specific conditions – for example the *Paediatric Cancer Quality of Life-32* scale (Vance et al, 2001).

Third, there are doubts about the validity of some health-related QoL measures. For example, self-reported physical functioning should concur with objective mobility tests (criterion validity), and scores for psychological well-being should correlate with self-report data from recognised depression tests (convergent validity). These indicators should not correlate with factors unrelated to general health, such as height (discriminant validity). Many indices fall short of these standards (Muldoon et al, 1998).

Fourth, instruments often struggle to capture an individual's subjective experience. Sometimes only objective indicators are included. Then there is the fact that many instruments use third parties as their source. This issue deserves greater attention, holding in mind the main lessons from this section, namely that measures should ideally be: multidimensional rather than focusing on one aspect of a person's life; generic rather than condition-specific; informed by theory rather than focusing on objective circumstances or subjective appraisal in isolation; and made up of as few items as possible (so that it is not unwieldy) but more than one (so that it is meaningful).

Subject or third-party response?

For some commentators it is vital that *subjects* express their views when measuring their QoL (Muldoon et al, 1998). This is because of the widely acknowledged discrepancies between judgements made by two individuals (Cummins and Lau, 2006). Patient and doctor ratings of post-treatment QoL are frequently at odds (eg Slevin et al, 1988) and adults often struggle to reflect children's views accurately; for instance, Eiser and her colleagues (2000b) identified significant differences between parent and child accounts using the *Childhood Asthma Questionnaire*. Various factors account for such divergence. One is knowledge: chronically ill children tend to evaluate their QoL more positively than their parents do, perhaps because the latter are more aware of likely future effects such as missed schooling and reduced fertility (Vance et al, 2001). This can work the other way too, of course; Skevington and Gillison (2006) argue that disjunctions may arise more in the psychological domain since it is less susceptible to parental observation. Underlying values and preferences also play a role, with children known to have different thought patterns and priorities than adults – a product of their earlier stage of cognitive development and generally more limited life experience (Hill and Tisdall, 1997). And different individuals also have different baselines. In particular, third parties base their judgements on intuition concerning the transition into ill-health, forgetting that to some extent patients get accustomed to being ill and adjust their expectations accordingly (Fitzpatrick, 1996). Lastly, extraneous factors impinge on third-party valuations, for example parents' stress levels have some bearing on how far their views tally with their child's (Vance et al, 2001).

Lane (1996) advances a counterview, namely that while there can be no QoL except as that quality as perceived and appraised by living persons, the judgement need not be made by the person living that life. There are various reasons for adopting this position. It may not be appropriate to seek the subject's views, perhaps because neurological or psychological dysfunction limits their ability to report accurately (Muldoon et al, 1998). Self-report may also be misleading, particularly given the tendency for some subjects to give socially desirable responses – to please their care-giver, for example – or to be reluctant to express dissatisfaction for fear of losing a service (Raphael, 1996a). There are also individual idiosyncrasies to take into account in the sense of different people meaning different things by 'very satisfied' or the same individual responding differently depending on mood or time of day (Day and Jankey, 1996).

Methodologically it may prove difficult to elicit the subject's view. Administering QoL instruments to children, for instance, may encounter challenges such as short attention span, less-developed language and reading skills and limited understanding of conventional scaling techniques (eg Spieth and Harris, 1996). Of course, such obstacles are not insurmountable; even young children can process fairly complex tasks competently and compare their own experience with that of others (Eiser et al, 2000a), particularly where concrete examples, pictures and other props are used (Skevington and Gillison, 2006). Moreover, numerous qualitative studies have successfully incorporated children's reflections on their QoL, for example in relation to the boarding-school experience (Lambert and Millham, 1968), receipt of various children's services interventions (Little and Kelly, 1995) and ordinary family life (Moore et al, 1996). Even so, it may be argued that by drawing on a combination of personal experience, lay definitions of QoL, and how the public evaluates a particular condition, so the argument goes, an outsider can make an educated assessment of an individual's state of mind (Brock, 1993).

Conclusion (2)

It is usually easier to measure quantity than quality, and it should be apparent from the preceding discussion that this applies to QoL. Applying the concept to children presents particular difficulties since there is uncertainty about its components and establishing subjective perspectives can be awkward. Nevertheless, it is possible. Drawing on the main points in the second part of this chapter, then, the study described in this book used an holistic measure of QoL that takes into account the main components identified by the studies discussed here. It is multidimensional, and goes further than financial and material items to include recreation, enrichment and happiness. Although it was beyond the scope of this study to ask children directly about their QoL, attention is focused on factors known to contribute to subjective well-being, as well as on evidence of emotional state visible to parents or carers, for instance distress or depression. A child's QoL was be deemed to be poor if this was so both objectively and subjectively, so forging this critical link. Finally, the measure needed to be succinct and generic.

SIX

Social exclusion

Exclusion and inclusion are universal features of human interaction, from global migration patterns to playground cliques. Divides are often given concrete form, for example the security gates that bar non-residents from elite housing developments, or the membership criteria that preserve the integrity of social clubs. These divisions are imposed formally, but often they arise from more subtle judgements about appearance and creed. The experience of being excluded can also be positive, although usually it entails a sense of losing out; this depends largely on whether it is volitional or coerced. Whichever way, one group's inclusion implies de facto another's exclusion (Silver, 1994; Jordan, 1996).

The concept of *social exclusion* is now widely used by policy-makers and social policy analysts in the UK, European Union (EU) and beyond to describe all manner of phenomena (Percy-Smith, 2000b; Hills et al, 2006; Levitas, 2006; Sheppard, 2006). It has been associated with the 'highly visible disorders of youth' (Roche and Tucker, 2003, p 440) that the majority finds hard to accept (Hill et al, 2004); indeed some have argued that all children are socially excluded because they are not part of the adult-dominated processes by which inclusion is defined (Ridge and Millar, 2000). But is this perspective useful or does it add little value to the understanding of child well-being, as some have suggested (eg Micklewright, 2002)? The first half of this chapter examines the origins of the concept of social exclusion and its defining features to see whether Sen's (2000) claim that the term is often used to recast traditionally recognised problems in a new light without offering any fresh insight is true, or if, used carefully, it can provide significant analytic advantage.

Concept

Origins of the concept

The concept of social exclusion originates in France. When the then government minister René Lenoir (1974) estimated that 10% of the French population were excluded from society he was referring to groups unprotected by social insurance – mentally and physically disabled people, the elderly and infirm, drug addicts, delinquents and so on. Subsequently the term 'social exclusion' came to be used widely to describe the product of a clutch of empirical trends, notably increasing and persistent unemployment, the failure of the state to protect those so affected, and the concentration of deprivation and ensuing social unrest in suburban social housing estates (Yépez del Castillo, 1994; Evans et al, 1995). Similar problems were experienced across Europe during the last two decades of the 20th century

(Room, 1995; Mingione, 1997; Byrne, 1999), with young people particularly affected (MacDonald, 1997a).

Arguably these developments might have been explained using existing concepts. For example, Wilson (1987) showed how the collapse in demand for unskilled and semi-skilled men in US cities had produced an *underclass* – spatial concentrations of the long-term poor and unemployed. The concept of *poverty* also captures a lack of resources and associated deprivations (Chapter Four) and may be closer to social exclusion than some commentators suggest (see Chapter Seven), notwithstanding important differences (see Levitas, 2006). So why did social exclusion become such a popular descriptor and explanatory concept for phenomena of the kind just described? At least six reasons may be given, all of which help with drawing out the essence of this approach to conceptualising ill-being.

First, French Republican thought provided it with a fertile environment, and it also translates well into various contexts. In France the state is considered to embody the general will of the nation, thereby engendering a sense of collective responsibility for any citizen suffering from its failures (Silver, 1994). Exclusion is viewed as a threat to society as a whole – a deficiency of solidarity, a violation of the social contract.

A second reason why social exclusion became ubiquitous as a descriptor of disadvantage concerns cultural and economic trends, notably consumerism and globalisation. Young (1999) argues that market forces and the increased emphasis on the individual caused advanced industrial society to move away from being inclusive, stable and homogenous to instead become exclusive and characterised by social change and division. People have grown increasingly aware of the diversity of the global village and the risks of daily life, including the fact that jobs, homes and relationships are rarely guaranteed for life (Paugam, 1995). Such insecurities cultivate a climate in which projection and moralising prosper, bringing into starker focus the divisions between 'us' and 'them', between the included and the excluded. Young (1999, p vii) puts it more colourfully:

> Social blame and recrimination ricochets through the social structure: single mothers, the underclass, blacks, new age travellers, junkies, crackheads – the needle spins and points to some vulnerable section of the community to whom we can apportion blame, and who can be demonised.

A third factor driving the rise of the concept 'social exclusion' involved broader social shifts in society, in particular perceived changes in social differentiation. Abrahamson (1997, p 147) argues that poverty is

> an early modern condition for the majority of people (the working class) brought onto them because of the exploitation by the rich (the bourgeoisie). Social exclusion is a postmodern condition for the

minority of people who are marginalised from mainstream middle mass society.

Linked to this is the idea that the class system is eroding:

> We are currently living in a time of transition from a *vertical* society, which we have come to know as a class society with people at the top and people at the bottom, to a horizontal society where the important thing is to know whether we are in the centre or on the periphery ... today, it is no longer a case of being 'up or down' but 'in or out'. (Touraine, 1991, cited in Abrahamson, 1997, p 4)

Thus, traditional ways of viewing the world became, in the eyes of some, anachronistic.

Fourth, 'social exclusion' found a niche because the idea of an underclass had largely been discredited. Theoretically it is weak; class distinctions are traditionally based on *economic* theories of social division, yet the underclass took on moral and behavioural overtones (Procacci, 1996) – the notion that beyond society and standard social classes there is a group characterised by work-shy attitudes, involvement in drugs and crime, and a rejection of monogamy and the nuclear family structure (eg Murray, 1990; Dennis and Erdos, 2000). Moreover, empirically the underclass appears not to exist; data suggest that its protagonists see only a mirage or phantasm – that it refers to a heterogeneous and transient group lacking a distinctive culture. An ethnographic study of deprived neighbourhoods in Britain, for example, failed to find an underclass of socially excluded, welfare-dependent young people (MacDonald and Marsh, 2005); instead, it painted a picture of young people subscribing to the same working-class culture as previous generations but left behind by the macroeconomic processes of globalisation, deindustrialisation and the 'casualisation' of labour.

Fifth, social exclusion as a concept won admirers because it draws attention to non-material deprivation and the longitudinal dimension, factors that are commonly acknowledged in poverty research but often overlooked in practice (Burchardt, 2000). For example, by focusing attention on relational factors it helps with analysing some of the effects of unemployment: the weakening of family harmony, the loss of self-confidence that makes forging new relationships difficult, the cynicism about social arrangements that reduces the willingness of the aggrieved to be self-reliant or act lawfully and so on (Sen, 2000). Social exclusion therefore represents a shift of emphasis rather than a change of direction (Atkinson, 1998); it offers what Sen (2000, p 9) calls 'investigative advantage', not 'conceptual novelty'.

Sixth, and more cynically, it might be argued that 'social exclusion' provided centre-right politicians with a convenient euphemism for poverty. Exclusion is something that can be ignored because it focuses attention – supposedly – on a small minority (Procacci, 1996) and because it can be portrayed as something that is *normal*, thereby diverting attention from its *cause* (Messu, 1993). Poverty is more threatening as it highlights the desire of the excluded for inclusion and political transformation (Balibar, 1992).

To sum up, social exclusion became popular partly because it offered some analytic advantage, partly for reasons of expedience and partly for its grassroots appeal. The fact that disadvantage was being created and experienced in new and different ways demanded a new mode of analysis, just as a shift in imagination saw the genesis of concepts like poverty in the 18th century (Silver, 1994). At the same time, social exclusion suited politicians and provided social welfare commentators with a versatile concept: 'the success of the notion of exclusion is due precisely to its social neutrality and pseudo-scientific garb' (Procacci, 1996, p 14). For campaigners, it put a human face on the plight of the worst off at a time when economists were in danger of reducing all differentials to monetary ones (Messu, 1994).

Defining features

The term 'social exclusion' is used lazily in popular speech to refer to social and economic disadvantage generally. In the academic literature authors have sought to outline its contours more precisely. This section discusses two definitions that include the most widely agreed components. Burchardt and her colleagues (1999, p 229) suggest that

> an individual is socially excluded if (a) he or she is geographically resident in society but (b) for reasons beyond his or her control he or she cannot participate in the normal activities of citizens in that society, and (c) he or she would like so to participate.

Room (1999, p 171), meanwhile, identifies as excluded people who are

> suffering such a degree of multi-dimensional disadvantage, of such duration, and reinforced by such material and cultural degradation of the neighbourhoods in which they live, that their relational links with the wider society are ruptured to a degree which is in some considerable degree irreversible.

Here it is argued that five criteria – drawn from these definitions – must be met for a person to be described as excluded (1-5). A further three factors (6-8) are commonly associated with – but not defining of – social exclusion.

First, an individual must be resident in a society in order to be excluded from it. Some writers have described exclusion as loss of citizenship (eg Lister, 1990). Yet a young person living in, say, India who is barred from settling in the UK by immigration restrictions is more likely to be part of their own society than a person of Indian extraction experiencing racial discrimination in Britain. *Internal* rather than *external* exclusion is what is as stake (Burchardt et al, 1999).

Second, an individual's participation in that society must be diminished if they are to be deemed to be 'socially excluded'. 'Society' here means normal activities, the kind of exchange systems through which one derives autonomy and status. Thus, if inclusion involves membership of a range of human collectivities – state, family, labour market and various social or cultural clubs – then exclusion implies the breakdown of the systems of mutual obligation and interdependence that these entail (Berghman, 1995). (Different commentators identify different spheres of participation, but all classifications cover broadly the same ground; for example, Euvrard and Prelis, 1994, p 115, define exclusion as 'the failure of one or more systems [of belonging] regarded as fundamental for the functioning of society ... the democratic and legal systems, the job market, social protection, the family and the community'.) This approach contrasts with what Sen (2000, p 28) calls 'unfavourable inclusion'; for example, exploitative labour conditions might be described in terms of 'exclusion from equitable arrangements', when arguably *anyone* who is employed is more accurately described as *included* in the labour market. Thus, it is better, and clearer, to reserve the descriptor 'excluded' for those who are outside the labour market – or whichever collectivity is under consideration – for reasons *other than* their own volition.

So an individual must be *excluded* in some sense, but at what point is this threshold crossed? Put another way, when does inclusion become exclusion? Castel (1991) sought to address this by distinguishing between four degrees of exclusion, from 'integration' (long-term employment and social support), through being 'at risk' and then 'in need of help' to 'disaffiliation' (a lack of work and social isolation). For some commentators the rupture of the social link must be pretty severe – a catastrophic discontinuity in relationships with the rest of society (Room, 1999). Others contend that this definition is unduly narrow and takes in only the extremes of exclusion – people effectively outside society altogether, for instance because of chronic drug or alcohol problems or because they live on extremely run-down housing estates (eg Hills, 1999). Whichever way, social exclusion is purely relative; it refers to reduced participation in a particular society at a particular time (Tsakloglou and Papadopoulos, 2002). In other words, 'diminished' means compared to others: 'We cannot judge whether or not a person is socially excluded by looking at his or her circumstances in isolation.... People become excluded because of events elsewhere in society' (Atkinson, 1998, p 7).

Third, relational factors must be central to the cause of predicaments that merit the individual concerned being described as socially excluded. Thus, if a child is starving because of crop failure it is unhelpful to say that they are 'excluded from access to food'; such a claim *is* appropriate, however, if food subsidies were removed thereby reducing their family's purchasing power (Sen, 2000). Intellectual clarity demands going beyond linguistic similarity to discriminate between concepts, and the insights that social exclusion offers stem from its emphasis on the relational factors that shape the genesis and experience of deprivation.

Fourth, the excluded person must not only *want* to participate in certain activities but be *prevented* from doing so by some excluding agency: 'an individual who *voluntarily* withdraws themselves from society – a hermit, a recluse, a Scrooge – is not socially excluded' (Burchardt et al, 1999, p 229). Thus, the condition of exclusion must lie beyond the narrow responsibility of the individual; a third party or outside force must have propelled them there. Sometimes this might be wilful but it might arise from circumstances where there is no intent, for instance industrial restructuring may inadvertently prevent young people from securing employment. Sen (2000) refers to these as *active* and *passive* exclusion respectively. It is not possible, however, for someone to be excluded by virtue of their handicapping characteristics – what Veit–Wilson (1998) calls *weak* exclusion (as opposed to the *strong* type just described). The difficulties of distinguishing between voluntary and involuntary behaviour are discussed later in the chapter.

Fifth, social exclusion implies a state of ill-being and disablement. This is largely implicit in the previous four conditions, but it is worth stating since some 'exclusion' is a positive experience. For example, many of the children in the UK who were evacuated during the Second World War were removed from their family and community but placed in secure substitute environments (eg Jackson, 1985). Some children removed from their families and cared for by foster carers or in residential homes have a similarly positive experience (eg Bullock et al, 1994).

Sixth, diminished participation is invariably brought about by multidimensional and accumulating disadvantage. The different systems from which people can become detached were outlined earlier in this chapter. For each one there are different types of disadvantage, for example unemployment (the labour market) or low warmth/high criticism (family). In relation to the process, Room (2000) advances a model in which an individual's *initial endowment* (for example income) influences their living conditions, a process interrupted by *shocks* (for example redundancy) or *opportunities* (for example a job offer). The effect of shocks is mediated by the individual's *buffers* (for example strong social networks), while the ability to take advantage of opportunities depends on having *passports* (for example access to childcare). The detail of this analysis is unimportant; what it illustrates is the dynamics of exclusion and the way that structural and personal factors conspire to weaken the position in society of certain unfortunate individuals.

Seventh, the disadvantage that creates social exclusion is invariably of substantial duration. The evidence from various longitudinal studies suggests that only a very small proportion of children remain highly disadvantaged for a prolonged period (eg Rutter et al, 1970; Wedge and Essen, 1982). Atkinson (1998) goes further, arguing that *forward-looking* indicators are needed to capture the sense of having little hope for the future: 'social exclusion is not merely a matter of ex post trajectories but also of ex ante expectations' (p 8). This is the catastrophic or largely irreversible rupture of social bonds described by Room (see earlier in this chapter).

Eighth, area features such as location and the housing market often exert an influence on patterns of exclusion that is above and beyond that of macro factors (Glennerster et al, 1999; Lupton and Powers, 2002). Because communities are differentially affected by social and economic change, disadvantage often becomes concentrated geographically (Byrne, 1999). For example, the rapidly deindustrialised northern UK regions have suffered most from the labour market shifts described earlier (Berghman, 1995; SEU, 1998a). It is difficult for people who live in environments of concentrated disadvantage to integrate into society (Garbarino and Kostelny, 1992; Jack and Jordan, 1999; Jack, 2002) since neighbourhood characteristics determine access to social goods such as education and leisure facilities.

Conclusion (1)

Social exclusion is defined here as an individual's involuntary and somewhat catastrophic detachment from mainstream society owing to an accumulation of relational disadvantages. This definition is informed by the following points, which are drawn from the preceding discussion.

First, exclusion concerns the extent to which a person is participating in mainstream society. It involves having connections to integrating systems such as the market, family and friends, voluntary organisations and the state (Berghman, 1995).

Second, although exclusion is not a good thing, either for the individual or for wider society, it does not necessarily entail actual or likely harm (unlike the concept of need). Technically, at least, a person may be excluded without having poor outcomes against health and development; it is their limited participation that is of primary concern.

Third, social exclusion is a multidimensional concept. It concerns degrees of participation in several spheres of life. It extends beyond income and material resources and living standards – the focus with poverty – to incorporate other factors that can exert an exclusionary effect. It also takes into account forces operating at the individual and area levels.

Fourth, social exclusion reflects the non-existence or damaged nature of social ties rather than their quality. For example, the fact that someone has paid employment is more important than whether or not they have safe and pleasant work conditions, interesting tasks and secure employment status. This contrasts markedly with quality of life (QoL), where the quality of an individual's experience is everything.

Fifth, exclusion does not reflect a person's evaluation of their external circumstances. There is a view that an individual's perception of themselves in relation to society and the future affects whether or not they are excluded (Abrahamson, 1995). Certainly there are symbolic and psychological phenomena associated with a loss of status (eg de Gaulejac and Taboada Leonetti, 1994), and those who *feel* excluded may become objectively so if they live out a self-fulfilling prophecy (Lessof and Jowell, 1999). But in terms of identifying exclusion the subjective perspective is important only insofar as the predicament must be involuntary.

Sixth, social exclusion is reasonably straightforward to identify as it requires a high threshold to be applied. It refers to catastrophic and to some extent irreversible detachment from society.

Seventh, the antecedents of a person's situation are crucial in determining whether or not it constitutes social exclusion. In particular, the predicament must have relational roots, arise from an external influence and be involuntary. The associated disadvantage must also be of long-term duration. Attention is thereby focused less on personal disposition or failure and more on relationships of power and control (Abrahamson, 1995; Williams, 1998).

Measurement

Specific problems

One approach to the measurement of social exclusion involves the study of specific, often extreme, problems. The first method under this heading entails selecting populations deemed to be at risk of exclusion by virtue of their social characteristic (for example disability) or service/administrative category (for example the incarcerated). In the UK, government studies using the rubric of social exclusion have looked at truancy and school exclusion, rough sleeping, teenage pregnancy, 16- to 18-year-olds not in education or training, and young runaways (SEU, 1998b, 1998c, 1999a, 1999b, 2002). Unemployment is commonly used in EU studies concerned with social exclusion, largely because returns are satisfactorily available at the macro level (eg Mayes, 2002). Further afield, case studies of social exclusion in Tanzania, Yemen and Russia have focused respectively on beggars, the long-term unemployed and migrants (Gore and Figueiredo, 1997).

The second method of studying specific problems focuses on poor neighbourhoods, the characteristics of which are widely acknowledged: high unemployment and crime rates, weak local economies, expensive food and transport and so forth. For example, one study mapped for England the 44 local districts with the highest concentrations of deprivation on an orthodox index (*Index of Local Deprivation*) (SEU, 1998a). Similarly, Glennerster and colleagues (1999) identified the 284 wards in England and Wales that are in the top 5% of rankings for both another well-known deprivation index (*Breadline Britain*) and being 'work poor'. The assumption is that people living in these areas are socially excluded (or at least extremely vulnerable to exclusion).

The third method involves aggregating yearly income data or rates of social assistance receipt – effectively measures of poverty (Saraceno, 1997). For example, data from the UK *Households Below Average Income* series have been used to identify the proportion of the population (12%) in the bottom three income deciles for five continuous years (Oppenheim, 1998). Using a narrow definition, namely persistent material hardship, this group might be considered socially excluded.

These approaches do not really meet the criteria set out earlier in this chapter for what constitutes social exclusion. Indeed, it seems fair to suggest that many empirical studies in this vein do not so much measure social exclusion as borrow the term to 'sex-up' otherwise familiar topics. It is possible, however, within these various approaches to see elements of the three policy discourses of social exclusion identified by Levitas (1998), and in that sense they do reflect how social exclusion is interpreted by policy-makers. According to this typology, the cultural explanation of social exclusion is based on a self-excluding moral underclass discourse (MUD), a residuum of the long-term unemployed, criminally inclined and sexually irresponsible – or what Bagguley and Mann (1992) satirise as 'idle, thieving bastards'. The social integrationist discourse (SID), meanwhile, defines inclusion as attachment to the labour market in the form of paid work, and the redistributionist discourse (RED) interpretation equates exclusion with poverty.

A lack of participation

The other main approach to measuring social exclusion focuses on a lack of participation in important aspects of society. This tends to involve collating social indicators. Usually these capture disadvantage in different areas of people's lives, including economic circumstances, employment, health and education (SPC, 2001; Ferrera et al, 2002). Sometimes these are arranged into stages of the life cycle, for instance in the UK the New Policy Institute (NPI) uses the categories of children, young adults, 25 years to retirement and older people (eg Howarth et al, 1998; Palmer et al, 2002, 2006). For each indicator there is a specific measure, thus the Department of Social Security (DSS, 1999) operationalises 'low birth-weight babies' as live births under 2,500 grams. The approach draws primarily on data collected routinely for official government purposes or for large longitudinal studies such as the *National Child Development Study* (NCDS) (eg Hobcraft and Kiernan, 2001). Atkinson and his colleagues (2002) refer to other indicators at the EU level.

Measuring social exclusion as a lack of participation can be further developed by exploring how different indicators overlap. Four studies illustrate what can be done. Paugam (1995, 1996a) examines the risks of exclusion among the working population (18- to 64-year-olds) in several European countries. His indicators of social and economic precariousness are based on being linked to the *labour market* (poverty and flexible employment), to the *interpersonal sphere* (marital instability, inadequate social and family life, and inadequate support networks), and to the *community* (low levels of participation in social activities). In France, for example, he shows that 'relational poverty' was particularly high (49%) for those with high 'occupational precarity' (unemployed for two or more years) (Paugam, 1995, p 65).

Next, Gordon and his colleagues' (2000) major national survey of Britain distinguishes four dimensions of social exclusion:

(1) exclusion from adequate income and resources;
(2) exclusion from the labour market;
(3) lack of access to basic services, whether in the home or outside it; and
(4) exclusion from social relations.

As part of the same study, Bradshaw and his colleagues (2000) explore the overlap in the data, showing, for example, that 55% of adults were excluded on one dimension but only 2% on three (p 8) (the analysis was based on dimensions (2)-(4) only). This study is referred to throughout the remainder of this chapter as the 'MPSE' (after its title, the *Millennium Poverty and Social Exclusion Survey*).

Then, in a Europe-wide study, Tsakloglou and Papadopoulos (2002) define exclusion as chronic cumulative disadvantage and measure it using data from the first three waves (1994-96) of the *European Community Household Panel* survey (ECHP). Exclusion is operationalised using four deprivation indicators: income, living conditions, necessities of life and social relations. A person is considered at high risk of exclusion if they are excluded on two or more dimensions at least twice in the three-year period.

Lastly, Burchardt and her colleagues (1999) adopt a similar approach, examining levels of exclusion in Britain on five dimensions selected to represent the 'normal activities' in which it is most important that individuals participate. For example, *consumption* is selected because it enables people to achieve a reasonable standard of living, and *social activity* because of the importance of being able to draw support from informal networks. The study uses 1991-95 data from the *British Household Panel Survey* (BHPS), a nationally representative survey of 10,000 adults reinterviewed annually. In any one year about a quarter (27%-28%) were excluded on one dimension, decreasing to around 5% for three dimensions and 0.1%-0.2% for all five (p 236). In the following discussion the study is sometimes referred to as the 'CASE' study (after the research team at the *Centre for the Analysis of Social Exclusion*).

Evaluation of the measures

The strengths and weaknesses of these measures inform the measure of social exclusion used in the study described in this book. The first strength is the way that some studies consider explicitly what it means to participate in society and then operationalise exclusion in terms of impaired participation on those dimensions. For example, Burchardt and her colleagues (1999) identify five activities that constitute inclusion on the basis that they have value to individuals and wider society: having a reasonable living standard (consumption); possessing a degree of security (savings); engaging in activity valued by others (production); having some decision-making power (political); and being able to draw support from family, friends and the community (social). This list is not definitive, but it resonates with work by others.

Some studies, however, are prone to include indicators of *outcome*, even though exclusion is properly identified using indicators of *inability to participate*. Palmer and his colleagues (2002), for instance, include indicators of subjective well-being (dissatisfaction with area and feeling unsafe at night) and health (longstanding illness or disability). Similarly, Hobcraft and Kiernan (2001) use responses to a general health question and measure symptoms such as anxiety and depressed mood. A corresponding error is to confuse *risk factors* for *indicators*. For example, one of the indicators used by the UK government concerns the proportion of young people aged 19 with at least a level 2 qualification (DSS, 1999; DWP, 2005); while not reaching this level could *lead to* impaired participation in society through low employability it does not indicate social exclusion per se (Levitas, 2000).

A second strength of most studies is their multidimensional perspective. In some cases this is very systematic and rooted in theory about the nature of participation (for example, CASE, MPSE). Moreover, it often means going beyond economic hardship to examine social ties such as job security, the strength of social relationships, the level of participation in social activities, access to services and so forth (Paugam, MPSE). This is important, since, as has been seen, social exclusion cannot be captured using deprivation indicators alone (Bradshaw et al, 1998). For example, services fulfil various functions that enhance participation in society, from ensuring basic health (water) to facilitating access to other goods (transport).

Of course, some measures are less 'multidimensional' than they purport to be; work- and income-related variables continue to loom large in studies of exclusion (eg Oppenheim, 1998; Mejer, 2000; Gordon et al, 2000). Also apparent is an unfortunate by-product of the multidimensional perspective, namely what Sen (2000, p 2) calls the 'bulging list' of the excluded. Such heterogeneity undermines the coherence and analytical advantage of the concept.

The third feature of robust measures of social exclusion is the combining of components to capture the way that disadvantage overlaps and accumulates (for example, Paugam, CASE, MPSE). Too often, however, measures relate to *components* of social exclusion rather than the phenomenon per se. For example, none of the indicator studies referenced earlier includes a composite index. Yet while being in trouble with the police, or lacking basic skills or becoming pregnant as a teenager might indicate impaired participation in one area of a person's life, they do not provide prima facie evidence of social exclusion (Bynner, 1998; Pullinger and Matheson, 1999).

Fourth in terms of commendable approaches to measuring social exclusion are attempts to incorporate the temporal perspective. Some studies do this by following respondents over time. For example, Burchardt and her colleagues (1999, p 239) track household circumstances over a five-year period and identify the proportion of respondents excluded on multiple dimensions over several years (see earlier in the chapter). Similarly, Tsakloglou and Papadopoulos (2002) take a three-year perspective to capture what they call 'chronic cumulative disadvantage'. They found that 7% of respondents were excluded on two or more dimensions during all three waves of data collection. Others track the progress of an indicator over time, for example the NPI includes data on the five-year trend as well as the current situation.

Significantly, however, none of the studies described uses forward-looking indicators, indeed the majority only examine an individual's circumstances at a specified point in time. Sometimes these incorporate indicators that have a time dimension, for instance *long-term* unemployment (SPC, 2001; Paugam), *persistently* low income (DSS, 1999), and no involvement in civic activities *in the last three years* (MPSE). But the vast majority of indicators in snapshot studies are static.

A fifth feature of many studies is the way that they grapple with the thorny issue of threshold. Martin (1996, p 387) writes that the process of exclusion is 'almost as if the person in question left the track on which they were running and went off at a tangent, down a slope'. As noted earlier, theorists differ about where on this trajectory the line between integration and exclusion is crossed, and most empirical studies tend to skirt around the question. Some explore different degrees of exclusion, for example the CASE study shows that whereas many people are excluded in one dimension in any one year, only a tiny proportion are excluded on all dimensions several years running. Tsakloglou and Papadopoulos (2002) appear to be unique in specifying a cut-off point using the axes of multidimensionality and chronicity.

A sixth strength of some measures is that they try to capture the involuntary nature of social exclusion. The CASE study adopted the strategy of 'setting the threshold of "exclusion" so low that it can be assumed that anyone who wanted to, and was able to, participate more fully would do so' (Burchardt, 2000, p 392). On the social interaction dimension, for example, few would wish to be without anyone to turn to in a time of need. Gordon and his colleagues (2000) establish whether not enjoying certain activities or amenities is enforced or from choice by asking respondents to indicate if a lack of resources is responsible.

Few studies go to these lengths, however, which is unfortunate since exclusion, by definition, must be forced. It is also understandable, however, as measuring freewill is difficult. Non-participation can be less voluntary than it appears. It may be a product of stunted preferences or limited expectations of life. As Burchardt (2000, p 389) put it, 'The simple fact of not wanting to go to university may not be enough to establish that I am not excluded from going to university'. Non-participation may also reflect the quality of choices available (Barry, 2002). For example, ethnic groups may withdraw from society in the face of hostility, just as the apparent self-exclusion from school of disruptive pupils may indicate an *inability* to take advantage of educational provision more than an unwillingness to participate (Littlewood, 1999). A counter-argument is that constrained options in the present may be the consequence of previous decisions, and are in that sense volitional; being excluded from a graduate job, for instance, may be a consequence of deciding to leave school at 16 (Burchardt, 2000). One way round the dilemma is to distinguish between *total* and *problematic* social exclusion, where the former refers to all exclusion and the latter concerns only people excluded against their will. Most studies measure *total* exclusion.

A seventh advantage of some measures of social exclusion is the spatial aspect. For example, Levitas et al (2000) include access to services such as shops, transport, libraries and banks, as well as fear of walking alone after dark. Others go further and identify entire areas that are 'no-go zones' for outsiders and places of no escape for residents (eg SEU, 1998a). However, not everyone living in places with high levels of exclusion is excluded, just as people living in apparently well-off areas may be excluded. As Burchardt (2000) argues, living on a run-down estate does not constitute exclusion per se, but rather contributes to the risk of becoming excluded.

An eighth benefit of many of the studies of social exclusion referred to earlier is the reliability of the data. This is a product of using government survey data and various long-running cohort studies, and reflects the fact that studies have largely been driven by pragmatic concerns. For example, central criteria for selecting one set of indicators were that they should be capable of being clearly defined, measured and tracked (Robinson and Oppenheim, 1998). The flipside is that the resulting indicators can be atheoretical, based more on what data exist than on a coherent definition of social exclusion. Certainly this accusation is levelled at the NPI indicators (see Lessof and Jowell, 1999). Reliability effectively takes precedence over validity, so that 'rather than moving, as research ideally should, from definition to operationalisation to data collection, the process is largely reversed; we move from available data to an implicit definition embedded in the flawed data sets which already exist' (Levitas, 2000, p 366). Other drawbacks of official statistics are well known (eg Dorling and Simpson, 1998), not least the omission of residents of prisons, hospitals, children's homes and mental illness institutions, some of whom are potentially very vulnerable to exclusion.

Childhood exclusion

Empirical studies of childhood social exclusion mostly involve the first approach described in the previous section, namely identifying specific sociodemographic groups or administrative categories. Particular attention has been paid to young people who are disabled, in public care, homeless, or aged 16-17 years but not in education or work (MacDonald, 1997b), while Ridge (2002) has studied children from families receiving basic social assistance. Kenway and Rahman (2000) identify what they call 'hot spots' of youth disadvantage in England and Wales using an index comprising items for 12- to 25-year-olds such as school absenteeism and residence in public care.

There is comparatively little research under the second heading of impaired participation. The DSS (1999) uses 13 indicators that specifically concern children, while the NPI employs nine for children and a handful for young adults that include 15- to 17-year-olds. When it comes to children, the MPSE study focuses on exclusion from activities owing to the inability of parents to afford them, 'service exclusion' (for example utility disconnection) and exclusion from school but without indicating overlap between them (Lloyd, 2006). Indeed, studies that measure the volume of exclusion by showing how disadvantage overlaps mainly focus on adults. This is usually because the indicators are unsuitable for children or because of the age range or unit of analysis in the datasets.

Many of the strengths outlined in the previous section are evident in work on the social exclusion of children. For example, there are indicators that capture the idea of impaired participation in different spheres, in particular a lack of purposeful activity (truancy, school exclusion, unemployment), restricted consumption (living in a workless household) and withdrawal from civic and community life (incarceration, problem drug use) (DSS, 1999; NPI). There is also some analysis of overlapping disadvantage. Wedge and Essen (1982), working before the concept of social exclusion really existed, identify chronic multiple disadvantage – children who at the ages of 11 *and* 16 were from lone-parent or large families, *and* badly housed *and* on low incomes.

Other work on children is also instructive. It is certainly arguable that many young people entering residential care are socially excluded, and that residential care often compounds that exclusion (Kendrick, 2005). Often children enter residential care with multiple problems relating to the breakdown of relationships with family, difficulties at school and socioeconomic deprivation, and once in care it is common for them to experience feelings of displacement, loss, a lack of control, stigma and isolation from family and friends (eg Bebbington and Miles, 1989; Berridge and Brodie, 1998; Sinclair and Gibbs, 1998; Little et al, 2005). In addition, Ridge's (2002) in-depth interviews with 40 children paint a picture of exclusion from children's perspective. She shows, for example, how the lack of pocket money makes it hard to afford fashionable clothes, how limited transport curtails social activities with peers, and how living in a poor neighbourhood results in worries about stigma and security.

The flaws identified in relation to work on adults also appear in research on childhood exclusion. Some children in selected groups are not excluded, for instance young people with disabilities do not necessarily experience unemployment (Baldwin et al, 1997), just as not all of those outside education or work have less secure relationships (Williamson, 1997). Another tendency is to use the exclusion terminology rather loosely, with children variously deemed to be excluded from a normal childhood (war victims), the adult world (unemployed youth) or decision-making (a lack of say in their upbringing) (eg Brannen, 1999; White, 1999). Lastly, some of the indicators used in relation to children reflect *risks* or *outcomes* of social exclusion, whether in relation to health (for example low birth-weight babies) (NPI) or academic attainment (for example literacy and numeracy test scores) (DSS, 1999). They are not indicators of social exclusion per se.

Longitudinal studies in developmental psychopathology offer an alternative perspective by tracking the aetiology of multidimensional disadvantage (eg West and Farrington, 1973; Kolvin et al, 1990). They use the concept of risk factors to describe how unfavourable attributes and circumstances in children's lives can interact in causal chains to produce negative social and psychological outcomes (Rutter, 1989, 1999). The language of risk is evident in some discussions of social exclusion (eg Bynner, 2001; Hobcraft and Kiernan, 2001), and its use in relation to children suggests that it has potential in the present context. The potential of such research in relation to measuring social exclusion is perhaps more apparent than real, however. First, only a constellation of several risks in any one child's life could constitute exclusion; individual risk factors are more suitable as indicators of vulnerability to exclusion rather than exclusion per se. Second, *attributes* such as low birth-weight or temperamental difficulties are not indicators of exclusion, only *circumstances* are (as in the aforementioned examples). Third, researchers working in psychology or psychiatry, such as Michael Rutter, are primarily interested in children's developmental trajectories; they are less concerned with degrees of participation in mainstream activities, or the relational antecedents of particular circumstances, or the role of agency – all central aspects of social exclusion. Indeed, Bynner (2001, p 287; emphasis in original) notes that social exclusion 'puts alongside risk and protective factors the social and economic context of development and the various kinds of policy-driven *obstacles* to development that children (and adults) have to surmount'. In other words, it is *structural* factors that make the *individual* trajectory one of exclusion.

Conclusion (2)

In order to operationalise the definition of social exclusion given earlier in this chapter it is necessary to combine indicators of impaired participation from several dimensions of the child's life to capture cumulative, chronic disadvantage. The measure used in the study reported in this book therefore used indicators for:

- the labour market/education (economy);
- families (domestic sphere);
- various leisure and cultural groups (civil society); and
- the nation state (citizenship) (Jordan, 1996).

Adjustments were made for children (following Ridge, 2002, among others) and a high threshold was selected – the rupture or attenuation of social ties on all four of these dimensions – to identify diminished participation that is both involuntary and likely to be of substantial duration. The spatial dimension was captured in two ways: first, the children in the study all lived on the same inner-city housing estate, and second, their parents/carers offered perspectives on local factors such as facilities, environmental quality and fear of crime. Brief social histories and prognoses provide some insight into how entrenched each child's difficulties are.

SEVEN

Relationships between the concepts

The five concepts

Chapters Two to Six have looked in turn at how each of the five concepts of well-being is defined and measured. This chapter explores how far each one makes a unique contribution to the understanding of child well-being. It starts by aiming to get to the heart or essence of each concept (see Table 7.1). The exercise might be likened to distinguishing between personality types using techniques such as *Myers-Briggs*, which are based on the premise that pure types do not exist but the key traits of different personalities may be identified. So it is with the five concepts discussed here, and the task of separating them out offers analytic advantage.

Thus, a child is 'in need' if their health or development is actually impaired or likely to become so without some remedial intervention. This reflects an understanding of *need* as being concerned with 'agency' – the capacity to act in society and avoid harm. Needs are thus related to outcomes and in that sense should be defined and measured in terms of aspects of health (physical and psychological) and development (physical, behavioural, emotional, social and intellectual). People have needs in all areas of their lives, all connected with the ability to lead a minimally adequate life, and all objective, universal and timeless. However, the satisfiers that meet needs are relative, varying for example with climate, age and the standards prevailing in society. Subjective taste also has a role to play. Determining whether or not a person has unmet need requires a rounded appraisal of their situation, in other words some knowledge of the context. That said, the antecedents of a person's circumstances have no bearing on whether that person may be considered to be in need. Nor is the type of antecedent relevant: unmet need can reflect personal deficiency or structural injustice.

Rights are defined here as the resources, liberties and opportunities to which children are entitled. Violated rights are therefore identified by contrasting what a child is owed with how they have actually been treated by the person or body with the corresponding duty to assist or forbear. In that respect, rights are legal or moral claims that derive from and reinforce a person's status; they allow right-holders to claim their due (assistance or forbearance from another) with dignity rather than having to grovel. Consequently, the extent to which rights are upheld is evident from *outputs* (infrastructure, regulations and action) rather than from outcomes – or from how the individual is treated rather than from the effect of that treatment on their health and development. Claims can be attached to a range of goods, from housing and health provision to freedom of speech, and are a mixture of aspiration and ideal on the one hand, and minimum standards and

Table 7.1: Distinguishing features of the five concepts

	Need	Rights	Poverty	QoL	Social exclusion
(1) The aspect of well-being that the concept draws attention to	Agency – the ability to act in society – and the avoidance of harm	Status – the entitlement to be treated appropriately and fairly by others	Living standards – the standard of living (with a focus on the material) that one can afford	Enrichment – the extent to which one's life is a life worth living	Participation – how far one is included in society by virtue of participating in common spheres of activity
(2) Whether the concept concerns an individual's health and development	Yes – explicit concern with actual or likely impairment to health and development	No – focus is rather on ensuring that child is treated appropriately, whether by individuals or by organisations	No – focus is on resources and the standard of living that this enables	Yes, but viewed in particular from a positive perspective (a concern with flourishing as opposed to the absence of ill-being) and taking into account how the individual feels about their life	No – more concerned with whether individual is participating in society, for example through work, family, social networks, civic engagement

continued

Table 7.1: (continued)

	Need	Rights	Poverty	QoL	Social exclusion
(3) Extent to which concept embraces a multidimensional perspective	High – needs relate to all areas of an individual's life and can be categorised in various ways	High – often categorised in terms of rights to provision, protection and participation (the three Ps)	Limited – living standards takes in a range of things, including quality of neighbourhood and participation in social activities, but the orientation is towards material goods	High – encompasses the many varied inputs at different levels (eg personal health, relationships, quality of neighbourhood) that contribute to an individual's appraisal of their well-being	Varies but can be high – some approaches focus on a narrow area only (eg the labour market) but participation in (or exclusion from) society can cover several spheres of activity
(4) Whether the concept is orientated towards notions of adequacy/minimising ill-being or quality and maximising well-being	Adequacy – essentially concerned with preventing or alleviating harm, although quality may be a consideration in relation to need-satisfiers	Mixed – essentially concerned with protecting basic standards of treatment and preventing or tackling abuses, although some would argue that those standards are often ambitious aspirations	Adequacy – by definition the concern is with people's ability to afford a fairly basic standard of living and with lifting those who are below the poverty line above it (but not necessarily any further)	Quality – extends beyond whether the basic requirements of health and development are in place to whether an individual's life is enriched and appraised favourably by the person whose life it is	Adequacy – issue is whether people are participating in different spheres of activity, even if only at a fairly minimal level

continued

Table 7.1: (continued)

	Need	Rights	Poverty	QoL	Social exclusion
(5) Whether the concept encourages attention to objective or subjective indicators (the extent to which the individual's view matters)	Objective (when considering normative need) – although the relevance of choice as regards need-satisfiers is acknowledged	Objective – although the importance of the right to participation is acknowledged	Objective – although poverty can be measured subjectively	Objective and subjective – concerns the individual's appraisal of their circumstances, so the fulfilment of wants and preferences is relevant	Objective – although some attention is given to whether individuals 'feel' excluded
(6) The extent to which measuring the concept is clear-cut or more convoluted	Extent of actual or likely impairment to an individual's health or development can be fairly clear-cut, but decisions about 'need for support' – which take into account availability of resources – involve greater discretion	Fairly clear-cut once entitlements have been operationalised, notwithstanding the issues of gathering and interpreting evidence, but moral rights tend to be vague and therefore hard to pin down	Fairly clear-cut once measure and threshold have been agreed, as extent of poverty and profile of the poor can vary considerably depending on the indicator used	Standardised instruments give the appearance of measurement being clear-cut, but generally more convoluted than other concepts owing to emphasis on relating situation to experience, desires, expectations and goals	Fairly clear-cut once measure and threshold have been agreed, as extent of social exclusion and profile of the excluded can vary considerably depending on the indicator used

continued

Table 7.1: *(continued)*

	Need	Rights	Poverty	QoL	Social exclusion
(7) The extent to which antecedents to the presenting situation are relevant when measuring the concept	Not really relevant, insofar as need can arise from structural injustice and individual deficiency, although 'need for support' may be affected by considerations of desert and personal wherewithal	Relevant in that violations can only arise from a third party's failure to act or forbear in order to uphold an entitlement; they cannot arise from accidents, personal fault or biological/genetic mechanisms	Relevant insofar as the poor living standards must be a product of deficiency of resources, but not relevant insofar as the deficiency of resources could have structural or individual origins	Not really relevant, although the subjective appraisal of one's circumstances is shaped by past experiences	Relevant because one is excluded involuntarily by something or someone; it is not possible to exclude oneself

procedures aimed at protecting against improbable disaster or gross negligence on the other. An individual's subjective opinion need not be considered when judging if their rights have been infringed. Indeed, such assessments should be straightforward given sufficient information about a person's entitlements, the nature of attendant duties and events leading up to the pertaining situation. Ascertaining the antecedents of the situation is crucial as a violation can only arise from an act of omission or commission by a third party; for example, organic deficiencies, misfortune/accidents or self-infliction cannot be responsible.

Poverty is defined in the study described here as poor living standards owing to deficient resources. Children are therefore poor if, because their or their family's income is inadequate, they cannot enjoy the goods, services and activities that most children in the UK take for granted. This is based on the view that poverty concerns the resource-related ability to participate in customary living patterns. Insofar as it captures the level of well-being that is potentially attainable given a certain level of income it is an outcome/output hybrid, but the focus is more on the ownership of material goods and the enjoyment of certain activities than on health and development. Poverty is a multidimensional concept but within the limited bounds of living standards (for example, food, clothes and housing); for example, relational factors are often acknowledged in definitions but they tend to be overlooked in empirical studies of poverty. Poverty is also defined primarily in relation to the wherewithal to live a *minimally* adequate life, although what this means can range from the bare essentials of survival to modest but acceptable standards in a given society. In light of this, several definitions of poverty heed subjective views regarding adequate living standards, but most require objective judgements. On any particular threshold these decisions are clear-cut, and the antecedents of the situation are only relevant insofar as low income (or deficient resources) must be a contributing factor to the poor living standards (underlying reasons can be structural and personal).

Quality of life (QoL) is defined here as a child's subjective well-being and personal growth in a healthy and prosperous environment. It is concerned both with outcomes, such as health and happiness, and also with outputs in the form of material goods, relationships, a pleasant living situation and so forth. It is also an holistic concept that embraces every aspect of a person's life. In particular, many definitions of QoL go beyond material well-being to include less tangible goods such as trust and aesthetic values, and most take into account enrichment and the satisfaction of desires as well as basic functioning. Since there are many versions of 'the good life', an individual's QoL is affected significantly by how they appraise their circumstances and the extent to which they can exercise choice. Ascertaining a person's QoL therefore requires a rounded evaluation of their situation and, preferably, a first-hand perspective. The antecedents of a person's circumstances should have no bearing on the assessment of their QoL (whether or not it came about by choice is included de facto).

The study described in this book defines *social exclusion* as a child's involuntary and somewhat catastrophic detachment from mainstream society owing to an accumulation of disadvantages. Exclusion is primarily concerned with degrees of integration and in that sense, exclusion is not an outcome; its existence is not established by assessing an individual's health or development but rather by examining the degree of their participation in society. It is, however, a multidimensional concept, taking into account participation in various systems that 'include' people into society – work/education, families, communities and so on. Broadly speaking, the existence of a social tie is more important in the equation than its quality, and taste and choice are irrelevant; for example, a hazardous, poorly paid and dull job at least represents a connection with the labour market. In that respect, and put crudely, an individual's subjective views hold little weight. If exclusion is defined as the somewhat irreversible rupture of social ties – a high threshold – it is relatively straightforward to identify. However, it is vital to uncover the antecedents of a situation as exclusion must be involuntary and have relational roots, and prognoses are also instructive since the person's predicament must to some degree be irreversible. Moreover, the study sides with commentators who emphasise structural or third-party causes as opposed to personal deficiency or a failure to perform one's duties; someone who excludes themselves is not socially excluded.

Similarities and differences between the concepts

The main similarities and differences between the concepts can be summarised in relation to seven dividing lines. First is the aspect of well-being on which attention is focused: agency (need), the status that demands and is afforded by proper treatment (rights), resource-related living standards (poverty), enrichment and enjoyment (QoL) and participation or integration (social exclusion). Clearly there is some overlap in terms of content. For example, to achieve agency people generally need economic security (that is, to be non-poor), and most definitions of poverty take need into account (for example, equivalence scales, or the lack of socially perceived necessities). Living standards are often defined in terms of participation in the customary living patterns in a given society (also the main basis for measuring exclusion), and the primary goods to which rights can be attached are derived from theories about the essential components of QoL. There are also important differences, however. Several are discussed in the points that follow, but it is particularly important to note that whereas rights refer to the *normative form* in which a claim is couched, need – and for that matter decent living standards and so on – refer to the *content* of the claim (Waldron, 1993, p 576). Thus, when children are said to have a right to adequate living standards it means that they are entitled to certain provision from their carers and wider society to ensure that they do not experience deprivation. The content of such claims is fiercely disputed, with some arguing that rights should be attached to needs (eg Wringe, 1981).

A second dividing line concerns the extent to which impairment to health or development is an indicator of the concept in question. This is essentially about whether outcomes or the things that contribute to outcomes are at stake. Need is concerned with the former, in other words the individual's actual well-being rather than the services they receive or the policies and procedures that affect them. QoL deals with a mixture of the two – on the one hand outcomes like health and self-realisation, and on the other outputs like shops, parks and entertainment venues. By contrast, respect for rights tends to be measured in terms of outputs, namely third parties' acts of omission or commission; it may be true that when entitlements are forthcoming they often increase utility (Dasgupta, 1993), but this is not the acid test of whether rights are upheld or infringed.

The third heading against which to contrast the concepts is multidimensionality (including the relative importance of economic and material conditions). All take an holistic perspective but in slightly different ways. Needs are spread across different areas of people's lives, from adequate shelter and significant primary relationships to physical health and autonomy. Technically speaking, rights can be attached to almost anything, but in relation to children they are often categorised under the headings of provision, protection and participation. Poverty is arguably the narrowest in scope out of the five concepts, focusing as it does on economic and material well-being, but even then this takes into account involvement in various activities as well as having the bare necessities. QoL encompasses all aspects of life – it is very much a global judgement – and social exclusion is defined as a product of dissociation from several milieux. At the same time, some concepts give more weight to particular dimensions than others. For example, geographic features and the nature of relationships are particularly prominent in measures of QoL and social exclusion, whereas poverty is defined more in relation to material resources. QoL pays the most attention to indicators of utility such as happiness and distress.

The fourth point of comparison is whether the concept deals primarily with standards of adequacy or rather goes further to assess quality and enrichment. Four of the concepts are essentially conservative in scope; they are concerned with the protection of basic standards and the ability to act or participate. Only QoL captures aesthetics and desire-satisfaction, for example whether or not people are happy with how their needs are satisfied, or if their participation in certain relationships and activities affords them intimacy and security.

The fifth dividing line is the relative contribution of objective circumstances and subjective appraisal to how the concepts are measured. Again, it is only really with QoL that the latter has a strong influence. For instance, measures of rights and poverty are only concerned with one aspect of personhood, namely goals or substantive goods, and do not capture utility.

A sixth perspective suggests that whereas with some of the concepts it is very clear when a person's situation constitutes a problem, with others considerable deliberation is required. For example, poverty can be measured with relative ease once a threshold based on income and living standards has been agreed. Similarly, there are varying degrees of social inclusion, but if a high threshold is selected using the axes of multidimensionality and chronicity, it is relatively straightforward to delineate the excluded population. Need is more difficult to identify because it requires taking context and likely long-term effects into account. Compared to, say, a rights perspective, where entitlements are spelt out clearly, need can also be quite pliable and therefore subject to varying interpretations – a frequent complaint of recipients of needs-led as opposed to rights-based interventions (eg Oliver and Barnes, 1998). QoL is arguably the most difficult to gauge because technically the same objective circumstances can leave one person deliriously happy and another miserable, just as different goods can produce the same level of utility.

The seventh and final dividing line concerns the relevance of the antecedents of a given situation. These are of greatest significance when measuring rights violations and social exclusion. An individual's predicament cannot constitute a violation of their rights if it is attributable to genetic inheritance, misfortune or personal fault; rather, it must stem from the negligence or trespass of a third party (individual or collective). Similarly, social exclusion must be involuntary and derive from attenuated or ruptured social ties; an individual who withdraws by choice from society, or who is isolated by virtue of a personal deficiency is not socially excluded. Calculations like these are not really required when measuring the other concepts. For example, poverty and unmet need can have structural or individual roots, and although QoL is in part a product of past experiences – and how these shape future expectations – this is accounted for in the individual's perspective.

It is clear from this discussion that these concepts act as different lenses through which to view child well-being, with each one bringing a uniquely valuable perspective. This analysis relates to the first aim of the study described in this book, and supports the hypothesis that the concepts are related but not as closely as is often assumed. The next question is whether the concepts concern the same people seen in different hues or rather draw attention to different groups of people. This is now explored.

Connections between the concepts

A systematic comparison of relationships between the five concepts requires that the 10 two-way combinations are examined, focusing on overlap and disjunctions. The analysis that follows draws on a mixture of theory, observation and reliable empirical studies. Since relatively few studies operationalise the concepts for children before comparing them empirically, it is often necessary to use evidence relating to adults rather than children and to *aspects* of the concepts rather than data on the concepts per se.

Need and rights

It was noted earlier in this chapter that rights may be regarded as an entitlement to have one's needs met. Consequently, assuming that an individual does have such a claim, and if that claim has been breached by the action or negligence of a third party, unmet need can be an indicator of a violated right. Equally, the violation of a need-based right will, generally, result in unmet need. Moreover, respect for rights is broadly conducive to need-satisfaction (Plant, 1991), just as meeting need is to some extent a prerequisite for the exercise of various rights. For example, it is difficult for a person to exercise freedom of speech if they are living in squalor or debilitated by illness (Plant, 1990).

That said, there are several ways in which a person can be in need without their rights being violated. First, the content of their entitlements may be very limited or even non-existent; it has been argued, for instance, that welfare entitlements are insufficient to guarantee adequate housing, health, economic security and so forth (Campbell, 1983). Second, the untrammeled enjoyment of rights to liberty may expose individuals to harm; for example, allowing children the freedom to play outdoors unsupervised increases the risk of them getting hurt and so sacrifices their need for health and a non-hazardous environment (Phillips, 1996). Third, in a litigious climate, efforts to respond to rights claims often give rise to reactive responses that overlook or perpetuate need, for instance social workers may place children in care unnecessarily for fear of being sued if the child is subsequently abused at home (Hirst, 1999). Fourth, need arises for reasons besides the action or negligence of third parties, including illness and accidents.

From the opposite angle it is apparent that the violation of rights does not automatically render an individual 'in need'. Sometimes drastic action is regarded as a means to an end, for instance the decision to forcefeed a person who is on hungerstrike. In the case *T & V v United Kingdom* [1999, European Court of Human Rights] two boys convicted of murder in an adult court were deemed to have had their rights to a fair trial (Article 6) breached, yet having been placed in secure accommodation with a reasonable standard of education there is reason to think that their needs were met (Little, 2002). Needs may also be met in a manner that, in the minds of some, leaves structural discrimination intact, for example providing disabled children with special facilities that segregate them from the wider community rather than making mainstream transport or education more accessible (Pinney, 2005; Rabiee et al, 2005). Contextual factors, for example the family environment and wider community, are also important because they may moderate the developmental effects of child maltreatment, thereby accounting for some of the heterogeneity in the outcomes associated with abuse and neglect (Zielinski and Bradshaw, 2006; Berry, 2007); thus, the extent to which children who get hit experience impaired health or development depends on its frequency and if it occurs in a low-warmth/high-criticism environment (DH, 1995). One-off actions or incidents in which the duty-holder defaults can therefore constitute rights violations without causing unmet need.

Need and poverty

Most measures of poverty take need into account, indeed some are based purely on, unmet need – the direct approach of Ringen (1988). This would suggest that the majority of poor people have unmet needs. There are caveats to this rule but certainly there is strong evidence that poverty is associated with impaired health and development, for example disability, conduct disorder and illness (eg Blackburn, 1991; Pantazis and Gordon, 1997; Gordon, 2000b; ONS, 2000; Pantazis et al, 2006). This is partly because a lack of resources makes it harder to afford decent housing, a nutritious diet, adequate winter clothing and so forth; it means that intermediate needs go unmet. It is also because individuals with an illness or disability often struggle to avoid poorly paid work or dependence on basic social assistance and, in addition, are likely to incur extra costs for equipment, treatment, special transport and so on (MacGregor, 1981). Parents with a disabled child often encounter similar difficulties (Sharma, 2002).

Of course, some people have unmet needs despite not being poor because they use adequate resources inappropriately (Spicker, 1999). But there are other reasons for such a disjunction. Health needs may require additional resources that even the non-poor struggle to afford. They may also arise for reasons that are unconnected to a lack of resources, for example organic developmental disorders relate to genetic make-up, and some respiratory conditions have environmental roots. Meanwhile, some needs are arguably a product of affluence, for example stress and isolation are prevalent in some of the world's richer countries (Seabrook, 1999; Layard, 2005; James, 2007). Technicalities of measurement also distort the picture: when poverty indicators underestimate human needs they give the impression that some people are *not* poor even though their needs are not met (Gordon and Spicker, 1999).

At the same time, not everyone who falls beneath a specified poverty line is automatically 'in need'. Children in poor households, as defined by level of income, often have their needs for food, clothes, recreation and so forth met (Adelman et al, 2000; Lloyd, 2006). This is partly because the families make sacrifices, stretching scarce resources to make ends meet, and maybe because they also secure income and goods in other ways. If a person's needs are minimal, or if their immediate financial history is healthy, they can also often manage – at least for a short period – on a low income (Walker, 1995). Again, the way that poverty is calculated is a factor: measures that define poverty in terms of items that people do not need, or that overestimate what people need, can produce results in which people whose needs are met are counted as poor (Spicker, 1999).

Need and QoL

The close overlap between unmet need and poor QoL is reflected in the fact that physical health and autonomy (basic needs) are central components of many medical or health-related QoL instruments (eg Skevington and Gillison, 2006;

see also Chapter Five), while aggregate social need is frequently estimated using area QoL indices (Long, 1994; Porteous, 1996). Clearly, the failure to meet basic needs such as sanitation and nutrition can result in diseases like gastroenteritis that cause their victims extreme physical suffering (Nkrumah, 1992; Stewart, 1996). Even beyond such extremes, unmet need can contribute to a poor QoL. For example, children whose developmental needs for play or new experiences are not addressed adequately often lack a sense of excitement and self-esteem (Kellmer-Pringle, 1974; Waldfogel, 2006). Turning the equation around, living in a poor-quality environment – defined in terms of buildings, leisure facilities and the strength of social bonds between neighbours – is known to exert a negative effect on children's health and behaviour (Furstenberg and Hughes, 1997; Chaskin, 2006).

However, a decent QoL can accompany unmet need. People often choose to fulfil desires in ways that jeopardise their health, for example by participating in dangerous sports, or consuming particular drugs and substances, or fasting to attain a spiritual experience; effectively they put pleasure above meeting their needs (eg Godfrey and Powell, 1990; Ponton, 1997). Making altruistic sacrifices may have a similar effect (Hamlin, 1993); the carers of disabled children often report that the responsibilities involved, while stressful and time-consuming, bring particular kinds of satisfaction (Baldwin and Gerard, 1990). A person's expectations, temperament and previous experiences are also important factors and help to explain why chronically ill children can be surprisingly content (Graham et al, 1997; Skevington and Gillison, 2006). Gilbert (2006), for example, argues that humans have developed a psychological immune system that helps them make the best of very bad circumstances – a blind spot metaphorically embedded in human perception, which creates the realities or 'silver linings' we might unconsciously prefer, such that 96% of cancer patients consider themselves to be in better shape than the average cancer patient. Lastly, there are circumstances, such as following a bereavement, when good subjective well-being may indicate cause for concern – a sign of unmet need (Abrams, 1973).

The varied quality and desirability of need-satisfiers means that meeting a person's needs does not guarantee that that individual has a good QoL. Some satisfiers are intrinsically unpleasant, for example chemotherapy may address health needs but it tends to make patients nauseous and miserable (Miller, 1999) – a point illustrated graphically in the autobiography of record-breaking cyclist Lance Armstrong (2001). Others have unfortunate side-effects, for instance paid work enables people to meet their needs but for many whose employment involves laborious tasks, long hours or unpleasant conditions it is soul-destroying and requires sacrificing time with loved ones (Parker, 1990; Schluter and Lee, 1993, 2002; Leach, 1994). A need-satisfier is also unlikely to enhance a person's QoL if it is not of their choosing or taste. But it is not just about need-satisfiers. Often what is sufficient to facilitate agency is insufficient to help people attain the sublime, be that a personal ambition – say, a safari, or playing a musical instrument well, or a trip to the moon – or a sense of meaning (Doyal and Gough, 1991; Soper, 1993;

Miller, 1999). Put another way, the absence of illness or psychopathology is not the same as the presence of health or flourishing (eg Greenspoon and Saklofske, 2001; Seligman, 2005; Keyes, 2005). Thus, most people in post-war Soviet societies had the bare essentials but at a cost to individual freedom, the environment, relationships and spirituality (Feher et al, 1983). Moreover, some people lack the necessary personal qualities to convert good objective circumstances into subjective well-being (Lane, 1996); challenging work, for example, cannot be exploited by people who are incapable of rational reasoning.

Need and social exclusion

Meeting children's needs equips them to participate in various spheres of activity, which in turn contributes to need-satisfaction (eg Rubin, 1980). Disruption of this virtuous circle has significant ramifications. For example, children who witness domestic violence may learn hostile, rejecting behaviour that ultimately leads to school exclusion, while those who lack stability often struggle to form strong attachments (Ridge, 1998; Cullingford, 1999). And if unmet needs contribute to fractured social ties, so exclusion from some settings results in impaired health and development. In India, for instance, excluding people from land on the basis of caste deprives them of adequate nutrition and water (Appasamy et al, 1995), while children who are not locked into supportive networks are disproportionately susceptible to maltreatment (Garbarino and Kostelny, 1992; Jack and Jordan, 1999).

That is not to say that unmet need always implies exclusion. If needs are relatively minor, likely to be temporary, unrelated to relational factors, or the product of the characteristics or actions of the individual concerned then they cannot constitute exclusion, which must, by definition, have certain antecedents (described earlier in this chapter). Moreover, individuals sometimes sacrifice their basic needs in order to feel included, for instance by buying status goods (Bugra and Irzik, 1999), while formal measures aimed at 'including' the marginalised – young offenders, minority ethnic groups, pupils with learning difficulties and so forth – do not always address the target group's needs (Barry, 1998; Daly, 1999). It is also true that being linked into relationships can create need if those relationships are dysfunctional; for example the tradition in some South Pacific islands for sharing childcare with extended families has proved physically and emotionally damaging for many children because of their relatives' systematic favouritism towards *biological* offspring (Mills and Davies, 1999).

Depending on the definitions used, exclusion does not necessarily entail unmet needs. For example, an unemployed young person (in the social integrationist discourse [SID] of exclusion) may have alternative sources of material and emotional support, while a modicum of physical health and autonomy are required to engage in crime and sexually inappropriate behaviour (moral underclass discourse [MUD]). From another perspective the means of meeting need can attenuate the social ties of the individuals concerned; for example children with learning difficulties may be taught in specialist remedial units (Cullingford, 1999), and it can be stigmatising to depend on state assistance (Ignatieff, 1984). In addition, the retreat from society of, say, mystics or reclusive artists, is often with a view to meeting their needs. (The degree to which such actions are volitional is a moot point since choices are based on the quality of what is available.) However, it is unlikely that someone could be excluded in the sense of catastrophic detachment from society and simultaneously not have unmet needs.

Rights and poverty

On face value the entitlement to adequate living standards enshrined in international law (for example Article 27 of the UN Convention on the Rights of the Child) means that the poor have de facto had their rights violated (eg Rosenfeld, 1989, cited in Corden and Duffy, 1998, p 110; Wresinski, 1994). This is contentious but certainly poverty restricts people's ability to enjoy their rights to protection and participation; for example, it has long been known that women and children seeking to escape domestic violence are often forced to remain with the perpetrator because they cannot afford alternative accommodation (Kempson et al, 1994; Kaufman Kantor and Jasinski, 1998). Equally, in some situations poverty is brought about by the infringement of rights. Sen's (1981) compelling analysis shows that the world's worst famines have arisen not through lack of food but because individuals' command over – or entitlement to – that food has broken down, and in the UK it is known that race discrimination in the employment market has contributed to some minority ethnic groups being overrepresented in low-paid jobs (Alcock, 1997). Further, people who are denied the opportunity to affect political decisions are vulnerable to economic changes that leave them in poverty (Freire, 1970).

Notwithstanding these observations, the link between violated rights (to protection and participation) and poverty is not axiomatic: not every abused child is from a low-income family, and in oppressive societies even the non-poor may struggle to make their voices heard. Some commentators go further, however, and argue that to alleviate poverty it may be necessary to trade in some civil and political rights in return for economic development (eg Friedmann, 1996; Donnelly, 1999). Supporting this view is the sustained growth achieved by repressive regimes such as South Korea in the 1970s and 1980s.

However, even if a person's rights are protected it does not follow that they are necessarily safe from poverty. First, the content of their legal entitlements may be meagre, with successive studies in the UK finding that basic social assistance is insufficient to afford what experts define as acceptable living standards (eg Piachaud, 1979; Oldfield and Yu, 1993; Parker, 1999). Second, the hardship might be caused by something besides rights violations, for example natural disaster. Third, restrictive understandings of rights also alter the picture. For instance, some theorists contend that rights are only valid if they concern liberty (thus erasing positive rights) (Nozick, 1974) or if the resources required to enact them exist (thus relegating many 'rights' to aspirations) (Cranston, 1967); such limited entitlements might remain intact even for a right-holder who is destitute.

Rights and QoL

The violation of rights often impairs the QoL of those concerned. This applies particularly to rights of *participation* since the freedom to make choices about living situation, relationships, use of time and so on is a major contributor to life satisfaction. But QoL is also diminished by the violation of rights both to *provision* – for example the failure to provide accessible leisure facilities for disabled children (Widdows, 1997; Lansdown, 1998; Morrow, 2000) – and also to *protection* – for instance the failure of relevant authorities to prosecute factories in residential areas that exceed legal toxic emission levels. The objective and subjective well-being of the individuals concerned is likely to suffer in such circumstances.

As with need, the extent to which the violation of an individual's rights affects their QoL will depend partly on context; for instance a child who is prevented from expressing an opinion in court may enjoy an otherwise enriching life. Similarly, a person's expectations and previous experiences play a role; life in prison, even with the associated constraints and abuses, might be safer and more stimulating for some young people than being at home (Bullock et al, 1994). Temperament and constitution are also important: people may derive significant benefit from goods that fall short of their full entitlement, and history shows that some people remain remarkably positive despite appalling treatment – as memoires of many Holocaust survivors testify. One might also think here of the pleasure associated with exposure to risks that, morally and/or legally, individuals are entitled to be protected against. Children may get a thrill, for example, from climbing through a fence that should have been mended by the responsible authority and then playing on a railway line.

The violation of rights is not necessarily implicated in poor QoL. Some of the reasons outlined in relation to rights and need are pertinent here, but four additional points can be made. First, some measures to protect children make their lives less healthy and enriching; for example tight security at schools aimed at guarding against lone gunmen or paedophiles may curtail outdoor play and make the atmosphere less relaxed (Guldberg, 2000; Jeffs 2002). Second, the right to participate in decisions about one's life does not necessarily lead to preferences being fulfilled, and the process of expressing choices can be distressing, especially if it concerns sensitive matters or involves alien settings (courtroom interrogations are cases in point) (eg Kemshall and Littlechild, 2000). Third, rights–orientated services risk being sterile and perfunctory rather than warm and nurturing (Cooper, 1998). Smith (1997) contends that in some UK residential and foster care settings, for instance, adherence to checklists of standards and procedures – the product in part of the children's rights agenda – has undermined the quality of the care experience. Similarly, Jordan (2006a) argues that the provision of packages of services by professional assessors and risk monitors, often with little choice for clients, can lead to the relational and emotional elements of service provision being overlooked or underestimated. Fourth, respect for rights arguably only provides the *foundations* for QoL; attaining higher levels of well-being is dependent on numerous other factors (see the section on need and QoL).

Rights and social exclusion

Social exclusion has been defined as the denial or non-realisation of social rights (Duffy, 1998). The EU Observatory on Social Exclusion, for example, has suggested that 'social exclusion can be analysed in terms of the denial – or non-realisation – of social rights [ie the rights] each citizen has … to a certain basic standard of living and to participate in the major social and occupational institutions in society' (Room et al, 1992, pp 14-15). Whatever the merits of this formulation, the infringement of rights often contributes to exclusion. For instance, in undermining the 'non-optional altruism' that welfare states embody (Campbell, 1983; Lister, 1997) it can prompt individuals to feel 'hard done by' and to opt out of mutually beneficial relationships by refusing to contribute to the collective good (for example tax evasion), or by breaking the law, or by using alternative (often private) services. Similarly, the exclusion of ethnic groups from their communities follows when oppressive regimes ignore legitimate claims to land and basic civil liberties (Twine, 1994). Exclusion can also further the denial of rights. This is partly because some legal entitlements are conditional on participation. For example, in a social insurance welfare state, where cash benefits, healthcare and other basic services are earned through paid work, the long-term unemployed are vulnerable to having their moral rights infringed (Figueroa et al, 1995). There is also some evidence that children who become detached from their families or excluded from school are particularly susceptible to maltreatment – a violation of their right to protection (Blyth and Milner, 1996; SEU, 2002) – and that differential access to 'cultural capital', which includes the personal networks that facilitate active civic engagement, impedes the effective exercise of political citizenship by disadvantaged young people (Fahmy, 2006).

Of course, some violations occur in contexts that signify inclusion, from corporal punishment at school and hazardous conditions at work to the abuse of women and children in the family home (Hyams-Parish, 1996; Hester and Pearson, 1997; Pettitt, 1998). Indeed, a recurring theme in the social exclusion literature is that measures aimed at integrating people into mainstream society often do so at the expense of individuals' rights. 'Workfare' policies, for instance, tend to be coercive and are accused of paying little attention to safety in the workplace (Jordan with Jordan, 2000), while attempts to assimilate minority ethnic groups in society generally run the risk of violating communities' cultural rights (Barry, 1998). Tokenistic efforts to include people in decision-making processes ('co-option') violate the right to participate (Levitas, 1998). Drawing these themes together, Corden and Duffy (1998) note that unequal access to rights and institutions (what they call *relative exclusion*) does not automatically lead to *absolute exclusion* – the complete biographical 'break-off' from social relations.

On the other hand, upholding an individual's rights may entail, or at least contribute to, the attenuation of social ties. In the UK, for example, the acknowledgement in the 1972 Education Act of severely disabled children's right to education resulted in a form of de facto segregation with many such children being educated in special schools outside their communities (Jones and Basser-Marks, 1997; Mittler, 2000). It has also been noted already that the process of cashing in some entitlements, notably to basic social assistance, can be stigmatising. It is further argued in some circles that, as egoistic claims against the community, rights make citizens more combative and society less cohesive (eg Waldron, 1984; Glendon, 1991; Etzioni, 1997). Some commentators (eg Cooper et al, 1995) think that this concern with the individual explains, in part, the relatively sanguine attitude among the UK population towards separating children from their families to protect them from abuse (the practice is less common in France where the state, families and children are regarded as inseparable members of a contract). However, in some instances the link between upheld rights and exclusion is more apparent than real. For example, it is true that strong rights enable people to disaffiliate from certain spheres of activity without losing out: in countries with generous unemployment benefit, individuals have the realistic option of severing their ties with the labour market (Esping-Andersen, 1990). But the social tie is cut by choice, so the individual has not been excluded. Similarly, it may appear that exclusion does not entail the violation of any rights, particularly in the case of individuals with minimal legal entitlements (for example immigrants without full citizenship) (Roche, 1995; Stewart, 1995; Lister, 1997). In many such cases, however, the person's *moral* rights might be judged to have been infringed.

Poverty and QoL

Below a certain level, material resources are the primary determinant of a person's QoL (Cummins and Lau, 2006), but even above that threshold poverty affects QoL in at least five ways. First, poor people often live in poor environments, in some cases because in desperation they exploit resources to destruction – as in the Brazilian rainforests (Church, 2000) – and in others because the housing market concentrates deprivation spatially (Glennerster et al, 1999). This produces a correlation between low income on the one hand and poor services, a lack of community spirit and feeling unsafe in the neighbourhood on the other (Bradshaw and Williams, 2000; ONS, 2000). Second, poverty restricts access to the goods and activities enjoined by society, from food to theatre trips. Third, poverty contributes to poor health, for instance inadequate diet and heating are important factors in malnutrition and asthma respectively, while the constant need to juggle resources is one reason why poverty is associated with undue stress, anxiety and depression (Pantazis and Gordon, 1997; Payne, 2006). Fourth, because poverty constrains a person's choices, the poor must put disproportionate effort into survival, leaving less time for recreation; this, and a lack of resources generally, arguably helps to explain why poverty has a negative impact on the use of leisure facilities such as the theatre/cinema (Bramley, 1997; Fisher and Bramley, 2006). Fifth, economic hardship sometimes prompts those affected to engage in unpleasant and harmful pursuits such as sex work or street vending in order to secure resources (eg Vafea et al, 2000). It is a vicious circle too: all of these 'effects' of poverty number among its causes.

However, there are important disjunctions too. These are partly artefacts of the fact that many QoL measures overlook socioeconomic status (Farquhar, 1995). But substantive disjunctions also arise. It is possible, if difficult, for an individual to be counted as poor but to have a decent QoL: the low income episode might be brief, shallow or offset by alternative resources such as savings (Ringen, 1987); the intra-household distribution of goods may be weighted in the individual's favour (Bradbury and Jantti, 1999); and community facilities may compensate for the lack of individual resources (Furstenberg and Hughes, 1997). In addition, outlook, character and constitution affect how much utility people derive from particular goods or circumstances (Sen, 1982; Cohen, 1993; Roker, 1998). For example, people may be satisfied with very little if they have an ascetic outlook or are ignorant of their *relative* socioeconomic status (Runciman, 1966). A person may also *choose* to go without, indeed a small minority in the West adopt simpler, less stressful and more environmentally friendly lifestyles; they 'drop out' (Bliss, 1996). Certainly there is evidence, partly from poor countries, that happiness is largely a product of things that money cannot buy – health, fulfilling relationships, natural beauty and so on (eg Norberg-Hodge, 1996) – and that hardship can foster solidarity. The phrase 'slums of hope' has even been conjured up to describe parts of some third world cities (Gordon and Spicker, 1999). Further, most parents have marveled at the joy that young children derive from playing with spoons and saucepans (as opposed to expensive toys), and most of the world's major religions stress the benefits of poverty; one need only think of Christ's teachings in the Gospels – 'What does it profit a man if he gains the whole world but loses his soul? ... Blessed are the poor, for they shall inherit the earth ... I tell you, it is easier for a camel to pass through the eye of a needle than it is for a rich man to enter the kingdom of heaven.'

It is becoming increasingly apparent that relative affluence has some drawbacks. First, securing adequate resources often entails sacrifice and struggle – one reason why many western developed countries have high rates of dislocated relationships and alcoholism (Argyle, 2000). Second, the means of generating wealth can have destructive side-effects – for example, the virtual elimination of poverty in Maoist China should be viewed against the backdrop of what Friedmann (1996) described as a shabby, grey and regimented society. Third, the happiness that people derive from improved living standards fades as they become accustomed to their new situation, or as they feel heightened security concerns, and also because they compare themselves against a new adjacent social group (to 'keep up with the Joneses') (Layard, 2003, 2005). For example, although East Germans' living standards soared following reunification, their reported happiness declined because they started comparing themselves more with West Germans rather than with Soviet bloc countries. Similarly, a study of 5,000 British employees found that reported satisfaction was more strongly related to *relative* income – how workers thought their income compared with that of similar colleagues – than to absolute *income* (Clark and Oswald, 1995). Fourth, as indicated earlier in this section, many important determinants of QoL are priceless, meaning that the economically secure can be afflicted by, say, chronic illness or family discord, and it is also to their detriment if public services and infrastructure are dilapidated. Nor is cost an accurate indicator of value: water is usually free or at least very cheap compared with, say, diamonds (Offer, 1996). Fifth, 'income' may not translate into 'ability to afford'; this applies particularly to people whose resource base is depleted following a prolonged period of poverty, those who receive less than their share of household resources, and people repaying debts. Taken together these points help to explain why there appears to be an income threshold above which extra income has little effect on happiness (Ahuvia, 2000; Fuentes and Rojas, 2000; Layard, 2005).

Poverty and social exclusion

Social exclusion is sometimes equated with poverty – the redistributionist discourse (RED) of exclusion in Levitas' (1998) typology – and some commentators have identified particular *kinds* of poverty with exclusion – Paugam's (1996b) 'disabling poverty'. Certainly poverty is associated with attenuated or severed social ties, largely because it is often hard for people with deficient resources to participate fully in mainstream society. The inability to afford gifts or to invite friends to parties, for example, can frustrate attempts to sustain relationships (Kempson et al, 1994), and restricted choice in the housing market means that the poor gravitate towards so-called 'sink estates' (Lee and Murie, 1997; Murie, 2000). Further, children in poor households are at elevated risk of being unable to participate in activities such as going to the swimming pool or having friends round for tea or a snack (Lloyd, 2006). Poverty also weakens individuals' attachments to integrative systems such as the labour market and local communities. For instance, it is a risk factor in children and young people for lower educational attainment – which increases the likelihood of unemployment (Hobcraft, 1998) – and for antisocial behaviour – which may incur custodial penalties (Cullingford, 1999). The relationship works the other way too: for example, people are often poor because they cannot obtain paid work (Alcock, 1997).

For some theorists the poor are not excluded unless they are practically destitute (eg Paugam's [1996b] 'integrated poverty'). Low pay means that people can be poor without being detached from the labour market (SID exclusion) (Duffy, 1998), and few – if any – families with low income and poor living standards inhabit the 'underclass' (in the sense of a culture distinct from the rest of society) (MUD exclusion) (Gordon and Pantazis, 1997). In addition, most poor people live outside so-called 'excluded neighbourhoods' (Gordon, 2000b), and many are locked into supportive families and communities (eg Cainkar and Abunimah, 1998). Indeed, some informal networks form as a rational response to poverty (Jack and Jordan, 1999). Lastly, in a society where everyone was poor, no one would be socially excluded; this is because social exclusion is relative in the pure sense, whereas poverty is relative to an absolute standard.

The evidence shows that not everyone who is considered excluded is poor (eg Muffels et al, 1992; Bradshaw et al, 2000). There appear to be two main reasons for this. First, a range of factors besides resource deficiency prevent people from participating in different spheres, including illness, fractured relationships, discrimination, a lack of time, fear/anxiety and inadequate transport (eg Golding, 1986). ('Gated communities' might also be offered as an example, but they represent a choice taken by the rich to exclude themselves from society [Scott, 1994; Gordon, 2000b] and so do not count.) Second, even where exclusion does entail some loss of resources it may be adequately compensated, whether by the shadow economy (Paugam, 1996a) or, in some social-democratic welfare regimes, by reasonably generous unemployment benefit (Papadopoulos, 2000).

QoL and social exclusion

Sometimes poor QoL and social exclusion are treated as if they are the same – the 'miserable excluded' versus the 'happy included'. Writing in the early 1990s, for example, de Foucauld claimed that

> There are already two Europes. *One relatively happy*, which has work (with two salaries), takes holidays, is well-covered by the social welfare system. And there is *the unhappy Europe*, the one which takes precarious work – lonely, put-down, hidden; it can hardly express itself, has no clear representation, and lives 'on the margin'. These two Europes are afraid of each other, do not want to see each other, do not meet, and perhaps do not even realise it. (cited in EC, 1994, p 12; emphasis added)

Clearly there are connections between poor QoL and social exclusion. Becoming detached from the labour market, for example, often causes feelings of rejection and a loss of control (Parsons, 1999), and young children who become separated from a parent or friends usually experience distress (Downes, 1990; Ridge, 2002). Being denied access to recreational or cultural facilities, perhaps by discrimination of some kind, may prevent the excluded from enjoying an enriching/fun experience (Hillman, 1993). Equally, a poor QoL often impedes participation in various activities. Debilitating illness can make it very hard for the sufferer to participate in various activities, and feelings of anxiety and low self-esteem are known to cause some adolescents to withdraw from social contact or to behave antisocially (eg Rutter et al, 1998).

This is not to say that inclusion in certain settings, activities or relationships necessarily entails a good QoL. It is possible to be neither extremely poor (RED exclusion) nor criminally inclined (MUD) but still to be confined to bed in extreme pain – an existence that many would consider to be 'worse than death' (see Chapter Five). In addition, some forms of participation can be dangerous or uninspiring (for example work in coalmines or call centres), and any parent knows that children are generally less likely to enjoy activities into which they are coerced. Indeed, it is arguable that forcing individuals such as seasoned rough sleepers to conform to mainstream modes of living is unlikely to enhance their sense of well-being (Cheetham and Fuller, 1998). Then there is the way that outlook and experience can produce negative subjective responses to good objective circumstances (see earlier section on need and QoL). A connected point is that because individuals with good personal resources and lifestyles do not rely on community facilities, they can live in a poor environment without being excluded from society as a result (Room, 1999).

Of course, forced exclusion can be beneficial: a child removed from very abusive parents is likely to gain from the attention and activities provided in a good children's home (Bullock et al, 1994). However, some *apparent* exclusion is really a product of an individual's efforts to improve their QoL. For instance, the fear of conformity attracts some young people to subcultures that share distinctive – and to outsiders often bizarre – clothes, language and music tastes (Krooshof et al, 2000). For similar reasons to those given earlier (see previous section), this does not count as social exclusion. Moreover, it might be argued that people who claim to be content despite being objectively excluded are exhibiting false consciousness (Burchardt et al, 1999). Generally speaking, forced exclusion and a good QoL are unlikely to go together.

Conclusion

The research drawn on in this chapter lends support to the second general hypothesis explored by the study described in this book. There is overlap between groups of people affected by different conditions, and, without exception, it appears that individuals with condition X are disproportionately likely to exhibit condition Y. However, there are also disjunctions; different concepts *do* draw attention to different groups of people. For example, there is evidence that individuals may not be in need despite having had their rights violated, and that it is possible to be in poverty while enjoying a reasonable QoL and participating in various spheres of activity. Based on this analysis, and also on the discussion earlier in this chapter and in Chapters Two to Six, it is now possible to explore the study's second hypothesis properly, namely that the prevalence of the conditions varies considerably, and that although there is greater overlap between some conditions than others, none subsumes another. Part Two of this book reports how this was tested empirically for a population of children in an inner-London community.

Part Two
Measuring child well-being

EIGHT

Child well-being through different lenses

Data and measures

This chapter presents findings about child well-being measured in terms of need, rights, poverty, quality of life (QoL) and social exclusion. They are drawn from a reanalysis of data from phase one of an exploratory study in the UK funded by the Department of Health and aimed at providing evidence on the nature of need among children in the community, the extent to which they and their families use children's services and how these agencies, together with coping strategies, affect children's development (Axford et al, 2003). The dataset contained information on 689 children and their families living on a moderately deprived and ethnically diverse inner-city housing estate in London. This represents 62% of the 1,116 children estimated to have lived on the estate at the time. Tests indicate that although the sample was not representative of children in England and Wales, it was representative of all children on the estate (measured in terms of age, first language and number of children resident). Data were collected in the period April-July 1998 and covered the child's situation at the time as well as providing a retrospective view of the previous year. In most cases (528 children) the main source was the child's principal carer, from whom information was gathered by way of one-hour semi-structured interviews. The sample was boosted by 161 other children from the estate using data that were collected from social services and education welfare files using a separate schedule. The two data collection instruments covered the same topics: risk and protective factors in different areas of the child's life; coping strategies used by the child and their family to address difficulties; and interactions with a number of children's services agencies.

Just over a third of the children (*N*=234) were judged against the five concepts using this decision-making instrument and the summary forms. A sample of this size was deemed to be sufficiently large for the statistical procedures used in analysis, and, since the decision-making process itself required exhaustive analysis of each case, it would not have been feasible with the given time and resources to apply the measures to all children in the dataset. The subsample is broadly representative of the 689 children in terms of demographic characteristics and data sources. The analysis that follows is based on five dichotomous measures that were applied to the data (Table 8.1). There is statistical support for the choice of *all* of the measures, which correlate highly (>0.7) or moderately (0.4-0.7) with at least one other measure of the same concept. The choice of measures was theory-driven for poverty, QoL and social exclusion but other concerns (mainly scientific and political) meant that the preferred measures for need and rights were discarded in favour of alternatives. The method is described more fully in Appendix A.

Table 8.1: The five measures

Concept	Measure
Need	The child has actual impairment to their health or development (which includes behaviour and education)
Rights	The child is victim of a serious violation of any of their rights to provision, protection or participation; for example, rape, assault, abuse, war/oppression, victim of official negligence or poor practice
Poverty	The child lives in a low-income household and has poor living standards (including substandard accommodation, a lack of basic items, few/no leisure opportunities, and money problems)
QoL	The child has poor objective circumstances (including poor living standards, ill-health, fractious relationships and little enrichment) and displays a negative subjective outlook (signs of being anxious, unhappy or distressed)
Social exclusion	The child's ties to all four of the following spheres are attenuated or ruptured: economic, domestic/interpersonal, social/civil and political/civic

Prevalence and distinguishing features

As expected, the conditions have different prevalence rates, and therefore to some extent they affect different groups of children (Table 8.2). A more fine-grained picture of the children affected by each concept can be gained by exploring the extent to which each condition is distinguished by a different set of factors in children's lives. Taking each condition in turn it compares the children who were affected by the condition with those who were not. It does this using 60 variables that cover sociodemographics, risk factors and service use. These were selected from the 330 in the dataset on the grounds that they relate to at least one of the

Table 8.2: Prevalence of the five conditions

Condition	Number (N)	%
In need	87	39
Rights violated	97	42
In poverty	138	61
Poor QoL	54	23
Socially excluded	14	6

concepts being studied. Thus, a distinction is made between those factors that were presumed in advance to apply to particular conditions, and those that emerged as significant from the data and their analysis. But first the $N=234$ dataset is described to provide a point of comparison; unless stated otherwise, the profile of children affected by each condition resembles that of the overall sample.

All children in the *N*=234 sample

The sample splits approximately equally between males (47%) and females (53%), and there is a spread of ages, from the very young (26% aged 0-4 years) to older adolescents (11% aged 16-17 years) (Table 8.3). About half (52%) of the children lived with a lone parent, with slightly fewer (42%) in two-parent families and the remainder (6%) with relatives or substitute carers or living independently. Most children (73%) lived in a household with three to six people resident, but about a fifth (17%) lived either by themselves or with one other person (usually a parent), and one in 10 (10%) lived in households where seven or more people were resident. Nearly two thirds (63%) of the children came from families where English was the second language, and in a quarter (25%) of cases the family had

Table 8.3: Sociodemographic profile of the *N*=234 sample

Factor	% of children (*N*=234)
Gender	
Male	47
Female	53
Age (years)	
0–4	26
5–9	29
10–15	34
16–17	11
Who child lives with	
Lone parent	52
Both parents	42
Other (step-parent, substitute care, independently)	6
Number of residents	
1–2	17
3–4	43
5–6	30
7+	10
English as a second language	63
Forced by war/oppression to leave home country	25
Child in house <6 months	11
Frequent movement	12

been forced by war or oppression to escape their home country. A significant proportion of children (11%) had been living in their house for less than six months, and there was also evidence of frequent movement (12%) – defined as two or more house moves in the last year.

In relation to living situation, two fifths (39%) of children lived in overcrowded dwellings (effectively more than one person per room), and a fifth (22%) lived in accommodation defined as substandard – for example, damp or with fixtures and fittings in need of attention (Table 8.4). Respondents identified safety problems such as broken windows in about one in seven (16%) cases, and half (50%) said that they feared or had experienced crime or antisocial behaviour in the neighbourhood. A substantial number of children lived in households where the family were reported to feel unhappy in the house (48%) or in the area (49%).

Table 8.4: Living situation of children in the *N*=234 sample

Factor	% of children (*N*=234)
Overcrowded accommodation	39
Substandard accommodation	22
Safety problems	16
Fear or experience of antisocial behaviour	50
Family unhappy in the home	48
Family unhappy in the area	49

Family and social relationships were also explored (Table 8.5). Although about two fifths (38%) of children had either a poor relationship or no contact with their father, the comparable figure for the mother was much lower (6%). There was positive evidence of loving family relationships in nearly two thirds (62%)

Table 8.5: Family and social relationships of children in the *N*=234 sample

Factor	% of children (*N*=234)
Poor relations/no contact with mother	6
Poor relations/no contact with father	38
Poor relations/no contact with relatives/siblings	15
Loving relationships	62
No significant adult	3
Abuse	8
Low-warmth/high-criticism environment	8
Poor relations/no contact with peers	10
Isolated	7
Lack of social network	7
Bullied	7
Experience of racial harassment	4

of cases, and only a tiny proportion of children had no significant adult (an adult besides a parent who helps care for the child, such as an aunt or God-parent) (3%). That said, there was evidence of abuse – physical, sexual or neglect – and of children living in environments low in warmth and high in criticism (both 8%). In terms of wider relationships, one in 10 children (10%) were found to have poor relations or little contact with peers, a rate reflected in other variables such as isolation, lack of a social network, being bullied (all 7%) and experience of racial harassment (4%).

There was evidence of children displaying antisocial behaviour – including aggression and violence – at home (16%), at school (12%) and in the community (7%) (Table 8.6). A small proportion of children (8%) was involved in petty crime or more serious criminal behaviour, and an even smaller proportion was running away from home or engaging in inappropriate or risky sexual behaviour (both 1%). Nearly half of the sample (45%) had no structured out-of-school activities, while a third (31%) had few or no interests.

Table 8.6: Social and antisocial behaviour by children in the *N*=234 sample

Factor	% of children (*N*=234)
Antisocial behaviour at home	16
Antisocial behaviour at school	12
Antisocial behaviour in the community	7
Involvement in crime	8
Running away from home	1
Inappropriate sexual behaviour	1
Little/no participation in out-of-school activities	45
Not occupied/few interests	31
Bullies other children	5

Just over a quarter (28%) of the children had a health problem of some kind (Table 8.7). Rates of physical illness (14% chronic, 12% temporary acute) were higher than for mental ill-health (4%), but a significant proportion of children (11%) showed evidence of being depressed, stressed or unhappy. Very few had a physical or learning disability (3% and <1% respectively), and the rate of drug misuse was also low (2%).

Various difficulties with education and employment were recorded (Table 8.8). At one end of the age spectrum, 13% of children were below school age but not attending any form of preschool (53% of those eligible); at the opposite end, fewer than 1% of children were unemployed (8% of those aged 16–17 years). Similar proportions had special educational needs (8%) or were excluded or truanting (7%), and about one in five (20%) were judged by parents or professionals as not achieving their potential. Six per cent were recorded as having poor relations with their teachers or employer.

Table 8.7: Physical and psychological health of children in the *N*=234 sample

Factor	% of children (*N*=234)
Physical or psychological health problem	28
Chronic physical health problem	14
Temporary acute physical health problem	12
Mental health problem (chronic or temporary acute)	4
Depressed, stressed or unhappy	11
Physical disability	3
Learning disability	<1
Drug misuse	2

Table 8.8: Education and employment of children in the *N*=234 sample

Factor	% of children (*N*=234)
Under school age and not in preschool	13
Unemployed	<1
Special educational needs	8
School exclusion/truancy	7
Not achieving potential	20
Poor relations with teacher/employer	6

The vast majority of children (82%) lived in low-income households (Table 8.9). In most cases this was because the family was dependent on state benefits (72%). Two thirds (67%) of children came from families with money problems, including large debts, and in a third of cases (36%) the family's income was judged by the research team to be insufficient for meeting basic needs.

Table 8.9: Income and living standards for children in the *N*=234 sample

Factor	% of children (*N*=234)
Low-income household	82
Family dependent on benefits	72
Money problems	67
Insufficient income to afford basic requirements	36

In terms of service use, over two thirds (69%) of children lived in a family that had received help from social services in the previous 12 months (Table 8.10). Unsuccessful requests for help were recorded in 3% of cases. Nearly one in 10 (8%) children were deemed not to have been protected, and 11% were found to have a poor relationship or little contact with the relevant professionals. Just over two fifths (43%) lived in families that used the local leisure centre.

Table 8.10: Service use by children and families in the *N*=234 sample

Factor	% of children (*N*=234)
Approached social services in last 12 months	63
Received help from social services in last 12 months	69
Unsuccessful request for help from social services in last 12 months	3
Child not protected	8
Poor relations/no contact with relevant professionals	11
Used local leisure centre	43

Children in need

As expected, the children deemed to be 'in need' – those with evidence of actual impairment to their health or development – showed disproportionately high rates of health, behaviour and educational difficulties (Table 8.11).[1] This can be demonstrated by highlighting the factors on which the children in need were significantly different from other children (the sections that follow on rights, poverty, QoL and social exclusion take the same approach). Over half (52%) had a health problem of some kind, with particularly high rates of chronic physical health (22%) and chronic or temporary acute mental illness (12%). A third (34%) of the children displayed behaviour problems, aggression or violence at home and those involved in crime (17%) were also overrepresented. Nearly a third (31%) of children in need were judged not to be achieving their potential, with a significant proportion (18%) truanting or excluded from school. The prevalence of factors that increase the risk of impaired health and development was also disproportionately high. For example, 15% of children lived in low-warmth, high-criticism environments, half (51%) had a poor relationship or no contact with their fathers and four fifths (78%) lived in households with money problems. It is reasonable to suppose that the quality of these children's environment and their treatment by adults were affecting their well-being.

Many of these features are evident in the case of Leyla, aged 13.[2] She was traumatised from having been sexually assaulted a year previously. She also displayed aggressive behaviour and was not reaching her potential educationally. These factors are evidence of actual impairment to her health and development.

Table 8.11: Factors distinguishing the children in need

Factor	% of children in need	% of children not in need
Poor relationship/no contact with father	51**	32
Low-warmth/high-criticism environment	15*	3
Bullied	13*	4
Poor relations/no contact with peers	22**	3
Isolated	12*	3
Antisocial behaviour at home	34**	5
Antisocial behaviour in the community	17**	2
Antisocial behaviour at school	27**	4
Involvement in crime	17**	2
Chronic physical health problem	22*	7
Depressed, stressed or unhappy	24**	4
Physical or psychological health problem	52**	13
School exclusion/truancy	18**	<1
Not achieving potential	31*	12
Money problems	78*	60
Poor relations/no contact with professionals	24*	5

Note: Significance: * = <0.01, ** = <0.001.

In addition, factors relating to her treatment and environment were arguably contributing to this impairment. She often had to look after her younger brothers and sisters, which was inappropriate given her age. Her parents had limited parenting skills, relying on presents to demonstrate love, and she had to compete for their affection with seven siblings. Her home was also chronically overcrowded. By contrast, Tamsin, a five-year-old girl, was not judged to be in need despite having some difficulties. She had a minor kidney complaint but was receiving adequate treatment. She had no behaviour problems and was doing reasonably well at school. There were factors that, if left unchecked, were thought likely to cause impairment. Her mother struggled to advocate on her behalf because she did not speak good English, and this sometimes made it difficult to obtain adequate medication. The family was also materially deprived, for example they needed a new fridge and wardrobe. However, there was no evidence of actual impairment to the child's health or development.

Children with violated rights

As anticipated, many of the children whose rights were deemed to have been violated showed signs of having been maltreated by a third party (Table 8.12). The failure to *protect* was apparent in the disproportionately high rates of abuse (17%), low–warmth/high–criticism environment (12%) and living in a family that had fled war or oppression (44%). There was also evidence of negligence by the statutory agencies in relation to material *provision* for children. For example, two thirds (65%) lived in state housing that was overcrowded and a fifth (20%) had no contact or poor relations with the relevant professionals.

Table 8.12: Factors distinguishing the children with violated rights

Factor	% of children with violated rights	% of children with rights intact
Who child lives with	54* [with 2 parents]	33 [with 2 parents]
Forced by war/oppression to leave country	44**	10
Overcrowded accommodation	65**	19
Abuse (physical, sexual, neglect)	17**	2
Special educational needs	14*	2
Money problems	78*	59
Approached social services in last 12 months	81**	51
Helped by social services in last 12 months	83**	60
Poor relations/no contact with professionals	20*	4

Note: Significance: * = <0.01, ** = <0.001.

The relatively high prevalence of children with violated rights who had approached social services (81%) or actually received such help (83%) indicates that in many cases the agency response was deemed to have failed to protect or provide for the child adequately or that the agency was not judged to elicit or heed the child's views – they defaulted on the duty to enable *participation*. This is also one explanation for the disproportionately high rate (14%) of children with special educational needs. Finally, it is not immediately clear why over half (54%) of the children with violated rights lived in two-parent families, although further scrutiny of the cases suggests that some have witnessed or suffered abuse by an adult male.

Typical of children with violated rights was Kristin, aged 13. Following a road accident in which she broke her leg, negligence by the hospital (as reported by a parent) made her condition worse. She had not received any compensation. This was interpreted as a failure by the responsible authority to uphold the child's right to adequate healthcare. In contrast, Mahmood, although a victim of crime, was not judged to have had his rights seriously violated. Aged seven, he had been attacked by other children – a violation of his rights to protection – but the police had dealt with the situation appropriately. He had also been temporarily blinded by bleach in the bath, but this was regarded as an accident rather than negligence by any third party. His rights to adequate provision were being upheld; for example, his family provided good support, he was enabled to participate in activities such as swimming, and he had received counselling in relation to attachment problems. In relation to participation, there was evidence that he was being enabled to communicate in matters concerning him, for example he received special help at school with reading and writing.

Children in poverty

To a large degree the profile of the children judged to be in poverty is predictable (Table 8.13). Nearly all (95%) came from low-income households, and in most cases (91%) the family was benefit-dependent. In nearly three quarters (74%) of cases there were money problems and in just under half (49%) there was insufficient income to afford basic requirements. Thus, the children in poverty were disproportionately likely to have low income and poor living standards. In addition, some groups of children appeared to be especially vulnerable to poverty, notably those whose families had been forced to leave their home country (38%). It is also evident that children from poor families were disproportionately likely to have received help from social services in the previous year (77%).

Table 8.13: Factors distinguishing the children in poverty

Factor	% of children in poverty	% of children not in poverty
Forced by war/oppression to leave country	38**	3
Lack of social network	11*	1
Low income	95**	61
Benefit-dependent	91**	41
Money problems	74*	56
Insufficient income for basic requirements	49**	17
Helped by social services in the last 12 months	77*	55

Note: Significance: * = <0.01, ** = <0.001.

Several of these factors are apparent in the case of Jamila, aged four. She lived in a benefit-dependent lone-parent household (indicating low income) and there was evidence of serious money problems (indicating poor living standards). For example, her mother owed money to friends and had recently received £200 from social services to purchase basic items of furniture. An example of a case where poverty was not evident is Katie, aged 11. Her father worked full time and the family enjoyed high material living standards. There was no evidence of low income.

Children with a poor quality of life

The children who were deemed to have a poor QoL were significantly different to the other children in several aspects of their objective circumstances (Table 8.14). There was no evidence of loving relationships in three fifths (60%) of cases and half (52%) had a physical or psychological health complaint. A similar proportion (50%) did not really have any interests or hobbies, and even more (62%) enjoyed few or no extra-curricular activities. The children came disproportionately from families that were unhappy in their homes (64%) or in the neighbourhood (64%) and that had financial insecurities – nearly four fifths (78%) had money problems. Many appeared to be struggling generally; for instance, a third (33%) of the children were judged not to be achieving their potential. The children deemed to have a poor QoL were also distinctive in relation to their subjective outlook, with a third (34%) recorded as being depressed, stressed or unhappy. Evidence of antisocial behaviour at home (43%) and school (33%) could be also interpreted as evidence of distress in the absence of any diagnosed disorder.[3]

Several of these features are displayed in the case of Amelia, aged six. Objectively her circumstances were dire. She lived in a chronically overcrowded flat, sharing

Table 8.14: Factors distinguishing the children with a poor QoL

Factor	% of children with a poor QoL	% of children with a decent QoL
Poor relations/no contact with father	59*	33
Lack of loving relationships	60**	31
Antisocial behaviour at home	43**	8
Antisocial behaviour at school	33**	6
Not occupied/few interests	50*	26
Depressed, stressed or unhappy	34**	4
Physical or psychological health problem	52**	21

Note: Significance: * = <0.01, ** = <0.001.

a bedroom with two siblings, and often went without essential items due to the family's lack of money. Her health was poor, for instance she had serious eczema, and as well as being isolated from her peers she did not enjoy any leisure opportunities. She struggled at school because of her dyslexia and speech problems. There were also indications that her subjective outlook was quite negative; in particular, she was reported as being traumatised following a serious house fire – this included bedwetting and regular nightmares – and she also displayed occasional aggressive or violent behaviour – arguably indicative of distress or frustration. By contrast, Jose was considered to have a good QoL. Aged 10, he lived in a spacious house and his family enjoyed a reasonable standard of living. He had many friends and enjoyed various extra-curricular activities, including sport and music. He was described by his mother as 'happy and sociable'.

Children who were socially excluded

Because only 13 children were deemed to be socially excluded many of the differences between them and the other children on selected variables are not statistically significant. Even so, the figures suggest that, as anticipated, the socially excluded children are disproportionately likely to have weakened or ruptured social ties (Table 8.15).

Starting with the *economic* sphere, all of those eligible (100%) were not in preschool (cf 47% for non–excluded children), a fifth (21%) were excluded or truanting from school (cf 6%), and in the majority of cases there were difficulties

Table 8.15: Factors distinguishing the children who were socially excluded

Factor	% of socially excluded children	% of children not socially excluded
Substandard accommodation	43*	20
Frequent movement	62***	9
Poor relations/no contact with mother	21**	5
Poor relations/no contact with peers	55***	7
Isolated	43***	4
Lack of social network	36***	5
Few/no out-of-school activities	75*	42
Under school age but not in preschool	100***	47
School exclusion/truancy	21*	6
Insufficient income for basic requirements	67*	35
Poor relations/no contact with professionals	67***	9

Notes: Significance: <0.05 *, <0.01 **, <0.001 ***.
All of the *p* values are based on chi-square tests in which more than 25% of cells in the cross-tabulation had an expected value of less than five. The factors selected here are those that relate directly to social exclusion.

connected with low income or poor living standards: for instance, two thirds (67%) lived in families that had insufficient income for basic necessities (cf 35%), and two fifths (43%) lived in substandard accommodation (cf 20%). In the *interpersonal* sphere, a disproportionately high number had poor relations or no contact with their mothers (21% cf 5%) or peers (55% cf 7%), and about two fifths were described as isolated (43% cf 4%) or lacking a social network (36% cf 5%). In the *social/civil* sphere, the vast majority of excluded children (75%) were not participating in out-of-school activities (cf 42%), while in the *political/civic* sphere there were disproportionately high rates of frequent movement (62% cf 9%) and poor relations or no contact with the relevant professionals (67% cf 9%).

It is worth giving two contrasting examples of social exclusion because of the impact of age on the judgements made (in the case of very young and highly dependent children greater account was taken of the parents' situation). Ciara, aged 20 months, was from a benefit-dependent family with poor living conditions (for example the girl did not have her own bed). This was interpreted as exclusion from the economic sphere. She also had weak social ties in the interpersonal sphere, for instance she lacked contact with peers and was described by her mother as 'lonely'. In relation to the social/civil sphere, she did not attend any form of preschool, and in the political/civic sphere she and her mother lived an unsettled existence because of her violent father's threats to abduct her. (Subsequently, when her father was released from prison, the family left the area.) A somewhat different case was Paul, aged 17. He had been excluded from school and lived in a benefit-dependent family (the economic sphere). He had spent spells in prison, where his mother could not afford to visit him, and family relationships were generally strained and violent (interpersonal). He demonstrated no interest or involvement in activities in the community besides crime (social/civil). He did not cooperate with the agencies seeking to help him, for instance he missed appointments frequently, and he had poor relations with teachers who, he alleged, singled him out on grounds of race (political/civic). An example of full inclusion is Emir, aged five. He attended school (the economic sphere) and lived at home with his mother (the interpersonal sphere). He and his family participated in activities in the community, for instance at the leisure centre, and were linked into relevant services such as the Citizens' Advice Bureau (the social/civil sphere). They were also settled in the area having lived there for five years (the political/civic sphere).

Relationship between the conditions and risk factors

It is clear from the preceding analysis that the conditions have many characteristics in common. For example, feeling depressed or unhappy distinguishes children in need from those who are not in need; it is also a significant factor differentiating between children with a decent and a poor QoL. Similarly, living in overcrowded accommodation is a significant factor for both violated rights and poverty. At the same time, each condition is distinctive in terms of its overall character: no two concepts share an identical set of distinguishing features. (Factors that were not significantly different were not included in the tables.)

Following on from this, this chapter now explores the notion that the concepts are complex and cannot be captured by any single risk factor. This is important because there is a tendency with all of the concepts to argue that children with any particular factor have the condition; for example, to assume that low income equals poverty, or that unemployment represents a poor QoL or social exclusion. Thus, each condition was correlated with all 60 factors, regardless of whether they were thought in advance to be indicators of the concept in question. The results revealed highly significant correlations ($p<0.01$) between each concept measure and a range of factors. Table 8.16 shows the strongest correlation for each condition. The factors identified are as might have been expected, given the way that the concepts have been defined and operationalised. However, the fact that they are only moderately strong suggests that no single factor acts as a suitable surrogate measure for any concept.

Table 8.16: Strongest correlations with risk factors for each condition

Condition	Factor	Phi correlation coefficient ($p<0.01$)
In need	Child health problem	0.421
Rights violated	Overcrowding	0.460
In poverty	Benefit-dependent	0.537
Poor QoL	Unhappiness	0.404
Socially excluded	Frequent movement	0.408[a]

Note: [a] With this correlation the expected count was fewer than 5 in over 20% of cells.

There are two main reasons why the associations are not stronger. The first is that not every child who scores on a factor that relates to a condition actually *has* that condition. Taking the above factors as examples, the proportion of children who display them but nevertheless do not exhibit the condition in question ranges from 22% (benefit-dependence) to 69% (frequent movement) (Table 8.17).

Table 8.17: Children with risk factors who are not affected by a related condition

Condition	Factor	% without condition
In need	Child health problem	29
Rights violated	Overcrowding	28
In poverty	Benefit-dependent	22
Poor QoL	Unhappiness	28
Socially excluded	Frequent movement	69

At face value this pattern seems counterintuitive, but in each case there are logical explanations. In relation to need, the problem in question might not have been deemed serious enough to be impairing and there might be countervailing factors; in other words, seen in context the problem is not causing impairment. It may also have been that the need was being met by the provision of appropriate services. In relation to rights, the selected measure focused on *serious* violations only, so that some events or situations that would constitute infringements on another rights measure were filtered out. Moreover, undesirable events or circumstances would not be interpreted as rights violations if: the child was at least partly responsible for it; or the perpetrator had made amends/been prevented from reoffending; or the situation created by the violation no longer pertained; or if there was clear evidence that the agency responsible had fulfilled or was in the process of fulfilling its duties. With poverty it has already been noted that some families have a low income but decent living standards, while others live in squalor but have reasonable incomes (Chapter Four). The discrepancy with QoL can be explained by the fact that children's subjective feelings may be unconnected to their current objective situation – they may be naturally anxious or sensitive or perhaps their distress is caused by past events, as with refugees experiencing trauma long after escaping a civil war. As for social exclusion, no factor renders a child de facto socially excluded; it is the combination of factors that is all-important. Indeed, in a challenge to common assumptions, *none* of the children who were unemployed or excluded/truanting from school were deemed to be socially excluded.

The second reason why the associations between certain factors and conditions are not stronger is that some children will be judged to have the condition by virtue of displaying factors besides those in question. To illustrate this, Table 8.18 shows the correlation coefficients for selected factors where all or most of

Table 8.18: Factors connected with a condition but where the correlation is weak

Condition	Factor	Proportion with condition	Phi correlation coefficient ($p<0.01$)
In need	Mental health problem	10/10 = 100%	0.275[a]
Violated rights	Abuse	16/19 = 84%	0.253
In poverty	Left hostel in last year	12/12 = 100%	0.198[a]
Poor QoL	Running away	3/3 = 100%	0.209[a]
Socially excluded	No significant adult	2/7 = 29%	0.166[a]

Note: [a] With these correlations the expected count was fewer than 5 in over 20% of cells in the cross-tabulation.

the children with the factor have the condition concerned. For example, all 10 children with a mental health problem are in need, but the correlation between this and need is only 0.275 ($p<0.01$). This is because not all children in need suffer mental ill–health.

It is evident from this analysis in this section that each condition is the product of a combination of factors. For research and policy purposes, however, it is helpful to identify which sets of factors in the lives of children are associated with and predictive of each condition. To answer this question it was necessary to use logistic regression, a statistical technique that helps to identify the factors that are strongly, significantly and independently predictive of a given condition (see Appendix B). Table 8.19 summarises the results. It identifies the critical factors for each condition (column 2), giving the odds ratio for each one (column 3) and the proportion of children with the condition according to the number of critical factors that they have (columns 4 and 5).

To illustrate what the figures mean, the strongest predictor of being a child in need is displaying antisocial behaviour (behaviour problems, aggression or violence) at school. This has an Exp(B) coefficient of 7.30, suggesting that the odds of being a child in need are about seven times higher for these children than for those whose behaviour is better. The two other factors – physical or psychological health problem and poor relations or no contact with peers – are also important predictors. Summing the coefficients in the Exp(B) column gives odds of over 19 to one if all three criteria are met: that is, of 19 children who have the three factors it would be expected that all but one are in need. Moreover, whereas only a fifth (21%) of children displaying none of the three factors are in need, the figure increases as other factors are added so that over half (59%) of those with one factor are in need, rising to 94% for children with two factors and 100% for those with all three. Thus, children with none of the factors have only a 0.21 chance of being in need, whereas those with two factors will almost certainly be in need (0.94).

In terms of general points emerging from this analysis, the first is that broadly the predictive factors were deemed at the outset to relate directly to the condition in question (see Appendix C). (The exceptions are as follows: *need* – poor relations/no contact with peers; *rights* – approached social services for help in past 12 months; and *poverty* – forced by war/oppression to leave home country.) For example, it was anticipated that dependence on benefits would indicate poverty, and that feeling depressed, stressed or unhappy would be associated with a poor QoL. A second point is that at least two factors are predictive of each condition; for instance, being forced by war or oppression to leave one's home country is predictive of having violated rights, but so too are living in overcrowded accommodation and experiencing abuse. The third and, arguably, most important point is that the factors are different for each condition; the only one that occurs in two places is being forced to leave one's home country (rights and poverty).

Table 8.19: Factors predictive of the five conditions

Condition	Factors	Exp(B) (<0.05)	% of children with condition where no factors apply	% of children with condition where all factors apply
In need[a]	(1) Antisocial behaviour at school	7.30	21	100
	(2) Physical/psychological health problem	7.14		
	(3) Poor relations/no contact with peers	5.21		
	Total	19.65		
Violated rights	(1) Abuse (physical, sexual, neglect)	250.00	4	100
	(2) Overcrowded accommodation	41.70		
	(3) Forced to leave home country	30.30		
	(4) Approached social services in past 12 months	7.35		
	Total	329.35		
In poverty[a]	(1) Forced to leave home country	9.52	19	96
	(2) Benefit-dependent	6.37		
	Total	15.89		
Poor QoL[a]	(1) Depressed, stressed or unhappy	9.43	13	82
	(2) Antisocial behaviour at home	7.09		
	Total	16.52		
Socially excluded[b]	n/a	n/a	n/a	n/a

Notes:

[a] There is a problem with multi-collinearity for need, poverty and QoL as the independent factors correlate significantly at $p<0.01$ (although the correlations are all weak).

[b] It was not possible to conduct a logistic regression for social exclusion because of the small numbers involved (only 13 children were deemed to be excluded).

Conclusion

This chapter has set out the prevalence of the five conditions for a cross-section of children living in a deprived inner-London community. The analysis offers further support for the second hypothesis that the study set out to test. It shows that the number and identity of children affected by each condition is different, and by comparing the profiles of children with each condition against that of the rest of the sample it has also clarified ways in which the five conditions resemble but are distinct from one another. The last section reinforced the point, demonstrating that different sets of risk factors are independently predictive of each condition, and it also showed why single factors are unsuitable as proxy indicators of the conditions. For example, it is misleading to say that a child automatically has a poor QoL because she feels depressed or unhappy; considerations such as context/antecedents, countervailing factors, the seriousness of the difficulties in question and the efficacy of coping strategies or services all come into play. Equally, sexual abuse in itself is a poor surrogate of violated rights because most rights infringements stem from some other failure on the part of a third party. The next chapter draws on some of these findings as it looks at how the conditions are related.

Notes

[1] Tables 8.11 through to 8.14 only list the factors that were significant at $p<0.01$ (many are $p<0.001$). In a few places – usually where relatively few factors reached this level – reference is made in the text to factors that were significant at $p<0.05$. Factors are listed in the same order as they appeared in Tables 8.3 to 8.10.

[2] All names of children in the book have been changed to help preserve anonymity.

[3] Differences were also evident with a number of other factors relating to relationships, health and living standards, but the small numbers involved meant that they could not be regarded as significant. For example, 15% of children with a poor QoL had a mental health problem (compared with 1% of the other children). This appeared to be significant ($p<0.001$) but the chi-square test was invalid: more than 20% of cells in the cross-tabulation had an expected count of less than five.

NINE

Relationships between the conditions

Two-way relationships between the conditions

This chapter continues to use the data analysed in Chapter Eight to examine relationships between the five conditions (or types of *ill-being*). The starting point is the proposition that the five conditions would be significantly and positively correlated. The analysis shows that this is only partially the case. In the N=234 sample, four of the associations between the conditions are highly significant ($p<0.01$), but all are weak (*phi* coefficient <0.3) apart from that between need and quality of life (QoL) (0.470) (Table 9.1). These findings are surprising in two respects. One is that some pairs of conditions are not positively correlated. For example, the relationship between poor living standards and various health and behaviour difficulties would have suggested that need and poverty are related. The other slight surprise is that none of the conditions are strongly correlated.

Table 9.1: Correlations between the five conditions (N=234 sample)

	Need	Rights	Poverty	QoL	Social exclusion
Need		–	–	–	–
Rights	0.126*		–	–	–
Poverty	0.086	0.191***		–	–
QoL	0.470***	0.136**	0.016		–
Social exclusion	0.247***	0.004	0.043	0.201***	

Note: Significance: <0.10 *, <0.05 **, <0.01 ***.

The weakness of these correlations is reflected in the fact that when relative risk ratios (RRRs) were calculated, only 10 of the 20 scores were significant ($p<0.05$) (Table 9.2).[1] Of these, most were relatively small; scoring positively against one concept did not render a child much more likely to be affected by a second condition. For example, a child whose rights were judged to be violated was approximately 1.4 times more likely to be in poverty than a child whose rights were intact (RRR1=1.354, $p<0.05$). There were exceptions to the rule: to name one, a child in need was over six times more likely to have a poor QoL than one with good health and development (RRR1=6.066, $p<0.05$).

A closer analysis of overlap between the conditions reveals why this pattern arises. Although overlap exists between all five conditions, the most is between

Table 9.2: Relative risk ratios for the five conditions (*N*=234 sample)

	Need	Rights	Poverty	QoL	Social exclusion
Need		1.368	1.255	3.040**	2.377**
Rights	1.339		1.649**	1.419**	1.022
Poverty	1.152	1.354**		1.030	1.148
QoL	6.066**	1.631**	1.062		2.658**
Social exclusion	9.310**	1.036	1.450	4.296**	

Notes: Significance <0.10 *, <0.05 **, <0.01 ***

All figures refer to the likelihood of a child affected by the condition in the column also being affected by the condition in the row. The figures below the shaded line are known as RRR1 and those above as RRR2. So, a child in need is over nine times more likely to be socially excluded than a child who is not in need (RRR1 = 9.310**), while having a poor QoL does not necessarily make a child more likely to be poor (RRR2 = 1.030).

violated rights and poverty (68 children or 30% of the sample) (Table 9.3). This indicates that significant numbers of children have condition X but not condition Y. For instance, 49% (44/87) of children in need were judged to have intact rights, and 54% (51/95) of those with violated rights were not considered to be in need (see Appendix D for all two-by-two tables). A more sophisticated understanding of how the conditions are related can be gained by examining the pattern of five-way combinations.

Table 9.3: Summary of overlap between five conditions (*N*=234 sample)

	Need	Rights	Poverty	QoL	Social exclusion
Need		–	–	–	–
Rights	44 (20%)		–	–	–
Poverty	55 (26%)	68 (30%)		–	–
QoL	43 (19%)	29 (13%)	32 (14%)		–
Social exclusion	12 (5%)	6 (3%)	9 (4%)	8 (4%)	

Note: The raw figures refer to the actual number of children affected by both conditions, while the percentages indicate the proportion of children in the sample so affected.

Five-way relationships between the conditions

Potentially there are 32 five-way combinations of the concepts (2 to the power 5). This is illustrated in Table 9.4, where '1' indicates the presence of a condition and '0' its absence. For example, combination 10 represents children who are in need, poor and socially excluded; they do not have violated rights or a poor QoL.

Out of the 32 possible combinations, 12 did not occur at all, while those that did ranged in prevalence from just under one in five children (18%) – those affected

Table 9.4: The 32 potential five-way relationships between the conditions

Combination number	In need	Violated rights	In poverty	Poor QoL	Socially excluded
1	1	1	1	1	1
2	1	0	1	1	1
3	0	1	1	1	1
4	0	0	1	1	1
5	1	1	0	1	1
6	1	0	0	1	1
7	0	1	0	1	1
8	0	0	0	1	1
9	1	1	1	0	1
10	1	0	1	0	1
11	0	1	1	0	1
12	0	0	1	0	1
13	1	1	0	0	1
14	1	0	0	0	1
15	0	1	0	0	1
16	0	0	0	0	1
17	1	1	1	1	0
18	1	0	1	1	0
19	0	1	1	1	0
20	0	0	1	1	0
21	1	1	0	1	0
22	1	0	0	1	0
23	0	1	0	1	0
24	0	0	0	1	0
25	1	1	1	0	0
26	1	0	1	0	0
27	0	1	1	0	0
28	0	0	1	0	0
29	1	1	0	0	0
30	1	0	0	0	0
31	0	1	0	0	0
32	0	0	0	0	0

Note: '1' indicates the presence of a condition and '0' its absence.

by none of the conditions, or poverty only (combinations 32 and 28 respectively) – to less than 1% – for example, the children who were judged to be in need and socially excluded but who were otherwise functioning satisfactorily (combination 14). Nearly nine in 10 (87%) children were in the top 10 combinations (Table 9.5 and Appendix D).

Table 9.5: The 10 most common five-way combinations (N=234 sample)

Rank	Number of combination	Pattern[a]	%	Cumulative %
=1	32	00000	18	18
=1	28	00100	18	36
3	27	01100	14	50
=4	31	01000	7	57
=4	17	11110	7	64
=4	25	11100	7	71
7	26	10100	5	76
=8	18	10110	4	80
=8	22	10010	4	84
10	30	10000	3	87

Note: [a] The five digits refer to 'in need', 'violated rights', 'poverty', 'poor QoL' and 'social exclusion' (in that order). The codes are 1=condition present, and 0=condition absent. So children in group 00100 are in poverty but unaffected by any other condition.

In order to help understand better how the conditions fit together and, more specifically, to appreciate why they are not as closely related as is commonly thought, the situations of children in each of the six most common five-way combinations (starting with the largest group) are now described. These are deemed sufficient to illustrate the findings that were discovered using quantitative methods and presented earlier in this chapter; they cover nearly three quarters (71%) of children in the sample (for further examples see Appendix D). The number of the relevant five-way combination is given in brackets and tallies with column 2 of Table 9.5.

No condition (combination 32)

Nearly one in five children (18%) were unaffected by any of the five conditions. Ferran, aged 13, lived with his mother. *Need*: He was a normal, healthy, moody teenager. He could have been doing better at school but he showed no signs of any real difficulties. *Rights*: He was being *provided* with love and care by his family and also enabled to do various activities. His family had been helped by the relevant agencies when necessary (mainly the doctor and the police). His father did not make any maintenance payments, but this was not a serious rights infringement.

As regards *participation*, Ferran's good relationship with his mother indicated that there was some cooperation between them when making decisions, and his mother's limited English had not affected her ability to advocate for him. *Poverty*: The family had constant money problems but the mother worked part time and so the family did not receive basic social assistance. *QoL*: Ferran was healthy, had a caring and affectionate relationship with his mother, and enjoyed drama and football. He had friends through attendance at church and was described as being happy at school. *Social exclusion*: Ferran was in school and there was no evidence of low income or poor living standards. He had good relations with his mother and many friends. He was involved in various activities in the community and the family had received appropriate help from agencies. They were settled in the area, having lived there for several years.

Poverty only (combination 28)

The same proportion of children (18%) were in poverty but unaffected by any of the other conditions. Robert, aged eight, was living with his mother and older sibling. *Need*: His health and development were both normal. *Rights*: His rights to *protection* were being upheld because social services were acting to ensure that his mother did not carry out her threat to harm him. For example, they attempted to secure for him a nursery place. The mother had also separated from a violent man. Robert was *provided* for, with social services responding positively to the mother's repeated requests for money to pay for basic items. There was no evidence of Robert being prevented from *participating* in decisions affecting him, and it might be surmised that he would have been agreeable to his mother's violent partner leaving. *Poverty*: His mother was not in paid employment and the family was dependent on basic social assistance. She frequently required emergency money from charity and social services to get by, and also had rent arrears. *QoL*: Although Robert's objective circumstances were not particularly auspicious, there was no evidence – direct or otherwise – of him being distressed, unhappy or anxious. *Social exclusion*: Robert was excluded economically in that his mother was dependent on benefits and required money from agencies for basic items. Otherwise he was relatively well integrated. He lived with his mother and sibling, was linked into social services and receiving appropriate help, and there was no indication of frequent house moves or poor relationships with professionals.

Violated rights and poverty (combination 27)

One in seven children (14%) were poor and experiencing the violation of their rights only. Nadia, aged 12, lived with her parents and three younger siblings. *Need*: She was healthy, well behaved and doing well at school. *Rights*: The family lived in chronically overcrowded accommodation (four children to one bedroom) but there was no evidence of the housing agency taking remedial action.[2] On these grounds, Nadia's rights to privacy (*protection*) and decent living standards (*provision*) were deemed to be violated. *Poverty*: Neither parent was in paid work, so the family relied on social assistance. As well as having inadequate housing the family struggled financially, especially as the children were increasingly wanting expensive designer-label clothes. *QoL*: Nadia enjoyed swimming and was described as 'happy and settled'. *Social exclusion*: Although her family was economically excluded, she was integrated in other respects: she lived with her parents and siblings, was active in the community (Arabic classes and the leisure centre), remained connected with the relevant services and had lived on the estate for over two years.

Violated rights only (combination 31)

One in 14 children (7%) were experiencing the violation of their rights but otherwise doing reasonably well. Sarah, aged 10, lived with her mother and three half-siblings. *Need*: She did not have any health problems, and although she could be quiet and withdrawn the school had no concerns about her. *Rights*: She had to share a bedroom with all three half-siblings (two girls aged 13 and 14 years and an eight-year-old boy) and so her rights to privacy (*protection*) and adequate living standards (*provision*) were judged to be violated. *Poverty*: There was no explicit evidence at the time of low income, despite the mother having required emergency money and Christmas hampers from social services in the past.[3] *QoL*: Although Sarah's housing situation was poor, there was no indication that she felt distressed or unhappy. *Social exclusion*: In terms of living standards the family was excluded. However, Sarah lived with her family and there was no evidence of her having poor relations/no contact with peers. The family had lived in the same place for 10 years, so their living situation was stable.

In need, violated rights, poverty and poor QoL (combination 17)

The same proportion of children (7%) was affected by rights infringements but also in need, poor and having a poor QoL. Nadif, aged six, lived with his parents and older sister. *Need*: He had special educational needs and was struggling at school. He was not thriving in general. *Rights*: He often stayed out late at night, which made him vulnerable given his young age. In addition, his father was severely mentally ill (a 'dangerous schizophrenic' according to the social work file) and had hit and possibly sexually abused the child's sibling. Nadif himself was hit and verbally abused by his mother. This constant exposure to danger violated his rights to *protection*. His rights to *provision* were also breached on several counts. He was prevented from playing outside as a result of a dispute with the neighbour, and neither his parents nor social services had secured sufficient money for him to go on school trips. Agencies had also failed to rehouse the father or to provide the child with counselling. Nadif's ability to *participate* in decisions affecting him was limited. No agency had created a clear opportunity for him to express his opinions, and his parents could not advocate on his behalf because they spoke little English. *Poverty*: Because the parents were unemployed and dependent on basic social assistance they could not afford large items or leisure activities for the children. *QoL*: The difficulties already noted were spoiling Nadif's QoL – strained home situation, lack of fun, learning difficulties and so forth. Agency files described Nadif as being 'under terrible pressure' and the family reported feeling 'unhappy' with where they lived. *Social exclusion*: The only reason that this child was not considered to be socially excluded is that was family had lived on the estate for nearly 10 years and were thus relatively integrated in the political/civic sense. Otherwise he was cut off from society economically (although he attended mainstream school), had poor relations with his parents, was prevented from taking part in activities where he lived or through the school and received little support from agencies.

In need, violated rights and poverty (combination 25)

Again, 7% of children were in need, poor and experiencing the violation of their rights. Tahir, aged seven, lived with his mother and four siblings. *Need*: He was struggling at school because English was his second language. *Rights*: Tahir and his family had been forced in the previous 12 months to leave their home country (Sudan) because of war. They were awaiting a decision about their asylum status. His father was still there but the family had lost contact with him. These circumstances violated Tahir's rights both to *protection* and to *participation* – he had no choice over this important event in his life. In addition, the family lived in extremely overcrowded accommodation provided by the state, and had had their utilities disconnected (a violation of their right to *provision* of basic services). *Poverty*: The family lived on a very low income, and the mother was not receiving certain benefits because of her immigration status. The shortage of money was making life very difficult. *QoL*: In spite of Tahir's educational difficulties and overcrowded accommodation, there was no evidence of him being unhappy. He had a strong bond with his mother, while Arabic and English classes provided some enrichment. *Social exclusion*: The family's low income and poor living standards mean that Tahir was considered to be excluded from the economic sphere, and the fact that they had moved twice in the previous few months – from Sudan to the UK, and from a bed-and-breakfast hostel to the estate – means that he was counted as excluded in the political/civic sphere. However, he was reasonably integrated in the interpersonal sphere since he lived with his mother and siblings, and he was integrated in the social/civil sphere by virtue of participating in various activities in the community – notably language classes and swimming – and being connected to appropriate services – the doctor, social services and housing.

Conclusion

The main findings of this chapter are that the conditions (or type of ill-being) are not as closely related as is often thought. All two-way correlations were weak with one exception (need and QoL = 0.470, $p < 0.01$), and most of the relative risk ratios were also low, indicating that in most cases children with one condition are *not* disproportionately likely to have another. The reasons for these disjunctions are elaborated in the case studies and show how each concept taps different aspects of children's lives. In that respect the data reflect some of the arguments made in Chapter Seven about relationships between the conditions. What are the implications of these findings for policy and practice in children's services? Do the contrasting perspectives offered by each concept underpin different approaches to intervening in the lives of children and families? How does a policy based on upholding children's rights differ from a policy geared towards meeting children's needs? Does tackling social exclusion also help to eradicate poverty? Are there insights originating from a QoL framework that the other perspectives overlook? The next two chapters explore such questions and in doing so examine the third aim of the study.

Notes

[1] RRRs are calculated as follows. In a hypothetical scenario, 30 out of 40 individuals with condition X have condition Y, and 20 out of 60 individuals without condition X also have condition Y. An individual with condition X is therefore just over two times more likely to have condition Y than one who does not have condition X: $(30/40) / (20/60) = 2.273$.

[2] The term 'housing agency' is used as a generic term to refer to the public body responsible for letting and maintaining dwellings.

[3] Explicit evidence of low income was required on the grounds that money problems and poor living standards do not necessarily indicate receipt of an income insufficient to afford required goods; the money might be used frivolously or the family's outgoings might be unavoidably high (for example paying off debts or buying special equipment if a family member has a serious disability).

Part Three
Implications for children's services

TEN

Matching conditions and service styles

Service styles

One of the main contentions of this book is that the way in which children's well-being is conceptualised will shape the service response to which it gives rise. The aim here, therefore, is not to detail what quantities of which service are required to match particular problems in order to achieve specified outcomes. To do this would require in-depth descriptions of specific interventions. Rather, the purpose of this chapter is to deduce the contrasting styles of service that the five conditions (or types of ill-being) require – in other words, the features that services should have logically if they are to have the potential to be effective in addressing a designated condition.

Of course, no archetypal intervention exists for any of the five conditions. Policy and practice tend to exhibit a mix of approaches (see Chapter One). However, drawing on the distinguishing features of each of the concepts (Chapters Two to Seven) and their empirical manifestations (Chapters Eight and Nine) it is possible for each concept to distil out the kinds of features that would characterise a 'pure' service; that is, one that is geared solely towards addressing the condition in question. These are described here in terms of who the service is for, what it does, how it is delivered and why it has those features. Numerous examples from existing provision are given, but where the service response in reality deviates from the pure service this is also noted. Thus, the chapter draws out from actual policy and practice the features that betray the conceptualisation of child well-being with which they are primarily concerned. It is important to stress at the outset that no service style is advocated over others; instead, the analysis is intended as an heuristic device to illustrate how concept drives – or should drive – service style.

Meeting need

Need-orientated interventions should be aimed at children whose health or development is actually impaired or likely to become so without remedial assistance. Potentially this means that a range of children might be targeted, since need can be a product of difficulties in any area of a child's life – living environment, health, identity, relationships and so on (eg DH et al, 2000). In reality, other factors besides evidence of actual or likely developmental impairment shape the identification of and response to need. Often, assistance may be forthcoming because professionals conclude that the child or family has no other source of help, or because of an emergency, or because the client is able to articulate their need and push for it to be addressed. Indeed, while help is arguably more forthcoming for expert-defined (normative) need, there has been a reaction against this in health and social services, and a trend towards basing treatment decisions on patients' assessments of their needs rather than purely on professional diagnosis (eg Foreman, 1996). Other factors that affect whether or not the need is recognised or addressed include the resources at a provider's disposal, where the child or family lives, even whether or not the practitioner is feeling well disposed to the case in question. In short, needs-led provision tends to be characterised by considerable flexibility or discretion; paradoxically, this means that often it is not driven by need at all and that other factors instead are more influential.

It is also the case in children's services that practitioners' perceptions of need often correspond with their agency's existing eligibility criteria, a consequence of which is that some needs may be overlooked. A focus on the presenting problem or on particular administrative categories, or the inclination to attach disproportionate weight to specified areas of expertise, also contributes to some needs receiving more attention than others, and a mismatch between the seriousness of need and service receipt (eg DH, 2001b). For example, the police may focus on a young offender's behaviour and pay less attention to the educational or relational problems at its root.

So what do need-orientated services tend to look like? Interventions designed to meet need can include material and non-material goods and assistance in all areas of a child's life – healthcare and nutrition, advice on relationships, money, furniture and so on. Often what is provided may be fairly simple, in other words things that are essential to basic survival and well-being. An identical need may be met by different satisfiers, depending on the circumstances; for example, a brick house and a mud hut both meet the need for shelter, and there are various possible ways of preventing and treating child maltreatment (eg Little and Mount, 1999; Barlow et al, 2006).

When it comes to the 'how' of delivery, two features stand out in services that are truly needs-led. The first is a focus on outcome and a desire to move children towards healthy development; meeting the need produces a good outcome ('needs met', or less need than before or than might have been expected given known trajectories of children with the need in question). This requires that, as far as possible, services are based on scientific evidence of what works. The concern with averting *likely* impairment means that needs-led services for children tend to embrace techniques that prevent or intervene early in damaging causal chains. A second feature is that need-orientated services allow for interventions to be tailored to each child's situation. They lean towards having a personalised, caring element, rather than being 'one size fits all'.

Why do needs-led services demonstrate the features described here? The purpose of such interventions is to meet children's needs so that they can enjoy normal healthy development. Assistance should generally only be provided if (a) without some kind of intervention the child concerned will suffer harm, and (b) the specified intervention will prevent or alleviate this harm. This judgement tends to depend to some extent on a rounded appraisal of the child's life; truly need-based service responses are generally nuanced and carefully considered rather than knee-jerk reactions to presenting problems. Of course, several other factors underpin the use of need to inform service provision. First is a concern with social justice and the aim of providing for each individual according to their needs (eg Miller, 1976). Second is the way that need can act as a guide to allocating limited resources, with selected priorities attracting extra investment (eg Percy-Smith, 1996). Third, the perceived requirement in market economies to ration welfare provision in the context of rising demand encourages a focus on the most needy. Fourth, since 'needs met' provides one measure of service effectiveness, need is a helpful yardstick for measuring value for money, that is, how to achieve the maximum benefit from minimum expenditure. A fifth advantage of need as an organising concept for children's services – in capitalist societies at least – is its apparent 'conservative' nature (see Chapter Two) and the opening it affords agencies to means-test help for families. Sixth, need prompts an inquiry into the root causes of a difficulty, an attractive feature for proponents of evidence-based practice. For example, a practitioner seeking to meet the needs of a child with, say, behaviour problems, must establish the aetiology of the problem – perhaps adult depression linked to poor parenting – before fashioning an appropriate intervention. Arguably, this contrasts with some of the other conceptual approaches described later in this chapter, in which there is may be a tendency to 'know' the solution implicitly without fully understanding – or seeing the need to understand – the problem.

Upholding rights

Moral rights are held to apply to all people, irrespective of age, gender, ethnicity, actions and so on. The children's rights movement is an attempt to ensure that the standards of treatment regarded as acceptable for adults are also recognised and enshrined in law for children. When these standards are translated into legal rights, the rules then apply to *any child* who comes within their orbit. For those who enjoy such rights, receipt of assistance is usually an entitlement; it is not conditional on particular contributions or behaviour.

This said, rights-based measures arguably betray a fundamentally negative view of human nature, focusing on the evils it can instigate or be complicit to. Thus, attention is generally focused on groups of children who are perceived as experiencing or vulnerable to exploitation or unfair treatment of some form, for example those from minority ethnic groups, disabled children, sweatshop labourers or child soldiers. Such groups are regarded as disproportionately likely to have been defaulted against – in the sense of responsible individuals or organisations failing to intervene or forbear appropriately – and also unlikely to be able to defend themselves.

It should be noted, however, that not all children and families enjoy the same legal rights. Some benefits and freedoms are attached to being a citizen or member of the community or state (eg Marshall, 1950), and because some residents do not enjoy these they may be treated differently (often less well, and without the perpetrators incurring any penalty). Some legal entitlements are conditional on the potential recipient's behaviour and contributions (for example forms of social assistance for the unemployed).

Rights-orientated interventions tend to be characterised by procedures and sets of standards intended to constrain the conduct of individuals and organisations insofar as it affects others. Moral rights can easily be dismissed as unrealistic aspirations (see Chapter Three), so efforts are made to turn them into sharply defined legal entitlements, with parallel duties and liabilities clearly specified and measures in place to enforce them (eg Nickel, 1987). Consequently, the compliance of signatory nation states with the UN Convention on the Rights of the Child (CRC) is likely to be monitored more in terms of outputs – such as the number of facilities for children with learning difficulties – rather than outcomes (for example academic attainment) (see Chapter Three; also Kilkelly, 2006). The rules and procedures specify duties of assistance and forbearance (for individuals and organisations) and cover aspects of provision (material goods), protection (preventing interference with personal integrity) and participation (enabling the exercise of individual liberties).

The emphasis when implementing such interventions tends to be on consistency and rigour. Claimants need not prove their eligibility, desert or neediness (so preserving their dignity) and different individuals should be treated equally, so that those with similar complaints get near-identical responses. Provision of this nature if often promoted by way of what might be regarded as fairly blunt instruments for getting third parties to behave in a way that respects children's rights. Moral rights are enshrined in charters or conventions and harnessed to motivate and cajole individuals and organisations to attain the standards of behaviour towards others to which everyone should aspire. For example, there are many campaign groups pressing for stronger adherence by governments and local providers to the CRC (for example the Children's Rights Alliance of England). In relation to legal rights, typical mechanisms are demanding compliance with detailed regulations and penalising or 'shaming' defaulters, perhaps through litigation. This galvanises duty-holders to act appropriately. A famous case in the US in 1969, for example, saw the American Supreme Court uphold school students' legal right to freedom of expression by supporting their choice to wear black armbands in protest about the Vietnam War (*Tinker v Des Moines School District* [1969], cited in Freeman, 1995).

The choice and style of rights-orientated interventions of the kind just described are underpinned in part by a philosophical belief in the importance of constraints or rules that enable individuals to pursue their own idea of the good (Plant, 1991). Another way of saying this is that people are of equal worth and should therefore be treated equally, or fairly (see above). Thus, children's rights are based on the view that children are not so much weak, vulnerable and in need of assistance, but rather active participants who are capable but needing to be set free. Child liberationists articulate this most explicitly, portraying childhood as an oppressed state more than a developmental phase (Fox-Harding, 1991). The content of entitlements can be explained by the various philosophical justifications for holding certain goods and liberties to be 'rights' (see Chapter Three).

There are also practical reasons for favouring a rights-based approach, the first being that potentially rights 'trump' other considerations affecting how children and families are treated – desert, affordability, administrative convenience and so on (Chapter Three). This force derives from the mandatory parallel duties attached to rights claims; should entitlements be withheld or infringed, these provide a basis for complaint that even high priority goals do not. A second practical reason for adopting a rights framework in policy and practice is that it spares individuals the stigmatisation and loss of self-worth associated with having to grovel, beg or perform in order to obtain their due (Nickel, 1987). Third, and perhaps from a more cynical standpoint, is the fact that rights-based provision may protect the *service provider* against claims of negligence; so long as the duty-holder adhered to the rules, the aggrieved party will struggle to get any recompense (even if their suffering is, arguably, the fault of the duty-holder). Addressing the problem (or need) in question can easily become a secondary concern. A fourth explanation given for the popularity of rights-based measures, this time from a socialist perspective, is that they perform the function of propping up a flawed economic system (capitalism); more specifically, entitlements to a modicum of material welfare help to maintain a healthy and compliant workforce (eg Campbell, 1983).

Tackling poverty

Initiatives to alleviate poverty are generally targeted at children in low-income families and/or those with poor living standards. Low income is defined in various ways, for instance less than 50% of the average income in the country concerned or dependence on basic social assistance (see Chapter Four). Attempts to target families with poor living standards often result in the selection of 'poor neighbourhoods', that is, areas with high scores on deprivation indices. Certain segments of the poor may also be specifically targeted. For example, strings are sometimes attached to assistance so that families are only helped if they have made certain contributions (financial or otherwise), or if they behave in a respectable manner, or if they demonstrate motivation. Essentially this is about identifying the *deserving* poor. Help may also be focused on the worst off or, somewhat perversely, on those families whose hardship is not particularly severe (since they are easiest to lift out of poverty, which looks good in official statistics).

Interventions designed to tackle child poverty generally, or at least logically, do one or more of three things: increase the amount of money that a family or young person receives (income); reduce the amount of money that a household pays out voluntarily or involuntarily (expenditure); and improve living standards, for example by providing better-quality housing, services and leisure facilities. The means of pursuing each of these goals varies, as the following demonstrates.

Starting with the first of these goals, the income of many families in poverty can be increased by enhancing the rates at which state benefits are paid. Efforts may also focus on moving unemployed young people and parents into paid work. This may require the removal of barriers to employment, whether by equipping potential employees with new skills, or by providing better childcare facilities, or by using tax credits and top-up benefits to ensure that take-home pay is sufficiently greater than basic social assistance to 'make work pay'. Initiatives may have a coercive element, for example deliberately suppressing the value of unemployment compensation so that it acts as an incentive for people to seek jobs, or withdrawing assistance from those who are considered able but unwilling to work. Lastly, there are various means of encouraging saving, for example Credit Unions or cheap and accessible bank accounts. Both have the added advantage of helping families to avoid the high interest rates charged by many informal moneylenders.

Moving on to the second approach, one way of reducing a household's outgoings is to cut the proportion of their gross income that goes on tax. This can be achieved by boosting tax allowances (the amount of a person's gross income that is not taxed), reducing the rate at which income is taxed (for example from 25% to 10%) and changing tax bands (the level of income at which tax rates become operative). Another avenue, usually pursued now with some controversy, involves advising hard-pressed families on how to stretch their meagre resources, perhaps through cookery classes, smoking cessation sessions or lessons in budgeting. There is also evidence that targeting state benefits at *mothers* has a positive effect on children's living standards because they are more likely than men to ensure that the family's basic requirements are met before spending money on luxuries (eg Goode et al, 1998).

Besides increasing families' disposable income, living standards may also be enhanced (the third type of poverty alleviation) by repairing substandard housing and by improving access to good-quality shops, leisure facilities and other services – dentists, hospitals, libraries and so forth. Packages of interventions that are targeted at specific areas are a popular method of doing this, at least in the UK where, since the 1960s, there has been a series of such programmes, from Community Development Projects to the more recent Health Action Zones. Implemented well, these strategies can reduce the amounts that poor families must spend on heating, transport and food and attract local investment, which creates employment; however, they also have considerable weaknesses, not least that most poor children live outside poor areas (Gordon, 2000b).

The motivation of policy-makers and campaigners for tackling child poverty is essentially twofold: one, poverty is an affront to human dignity and indicative of the socially unjust distribution of wealth in society; and two, economic hardship is intimately bound up with poor health, crime and the breakdown of relationships. Thus, tackling poverty is a means both of helping to make society fairer and also of averting wider social problems. Interventions to tackle poverty are therefore selected partly on the understanding that they will help to break the two-way connections between low income and poor living standards. It is known, for example, that families with a higher income can afford better-quality housing, food and clothes, not to mention holidays and toys for their children (eg Lloyd, 2006). In turn, improving the access of people in poverty to healthcare, supermarkets, parks and so forth enables them to stay healthier and find work or cut down on unnecessary expenditure. Of course, the policy response to poverty is also shaped by moral values and political expedience; for instance, it may be decided not to introduce large increases in social assistance rates because this is considered likely to encourage idleness and to alienate some better-off taxpayers.

Enhancing the quality of life

Measures to improve quality of life (QoL) are often less targeted than those intended to combat the other conditions. In other words, they are more concerned with whole populations than with discrete subgroups. For example, environmental projects and the provision of certain leisure facilities potentially benefit everyone. This said, some groups may be singled out for attention, including families whose objective conditions are poor (perhaps because they live in substandard housing or in a high-crime area) and children who doctors or teachers identify as distressed or unhappy (whether in relation to external circumstances or because of their general disposition). But what do QoL-orientated services entail?

The multifaceted nature of QoL (Chapter Five) means that there are many ways in which it can be enhanced. Assuming that some of the ingredients of a 'good life' are universal (at least at a general level), four aspects of policy and practice are particularly relevant. First is improvement of the natural and built environment, including housing, air quality and landscape aesthetics. Services here might take the form of targeted area initiatives, comprising measures to tackle crime and violence to make the streets safer, and projects such as building parks and playgrounds on previously derelict land (eg Chaskin, 2006). Second is anything that contributes to the development and sustenance of healthy and fulfilling relationships between children and their family, friends or the wider community. For example, there are interventions that provide opportunities for children and families to meet, such as toddler groups, church activities, youth clubs, sports teams and amateur theatre companies. In the UK, at least, the not-for-profit and community sectors play a major role in such provision. Mediation may help parents and neighbours to resolve conflicts, and various fiscal, social, ceremonial and legal measures can encourage extended families to work at their relationships and provide children with a strong support network (eg Baker, 1996). A third common means of enhancing QoL entails improving the provision of those things that go beyond the functional and serve to enrich life – art, music, sport, spiritual experiences and so forth. Also under this heading are services that improve access to the countryside, entertainments and various other sources of enrichment – youth hostels, discounted admission rates to museums for children, school trips and extra-curricular clubs, for example. Fourth are attempts to improve a child's physical and mental health, in particular their ability to function without pain, how they feel about life and their ability to appreciate it. Especially pertinent here are child and adolescent mental health services, the provision of special equipment for children with disabilities, and hospices for children with chronic illness.

Some aspects of orthodox children's services might be interpreted as addressing the subjective component of QoL. Thus, the concern with eliciting and heeding individuals' preferences plays out in the drive towards joint decision-making between families and professionals; for example, Family Group Conferences are intended to empower families with problems to take control of their situation and formulate solutions (eg Brown, 2002). Applying the same idea at an aggregate level, the greater involvement of children in the design and delivery of services is increasingly encouraged in order to increase a sense of community involvement and develop empathic relationships between providers and clients (Marks and Shah, 2005).

Also relevant here are efforts to improve children's personal resources so that they gain greater benefit from their objective circumstances (Lane, 1996). In particular, education is critical in enhancing children's cognitive complexity, and in training them to appreciate beauty or exposing them to spiritual and other uplifting experiences. Much moral and religious teaching in school seeks to foster a questioning attitude towards western materialism and the individualist ethos; it encourages pupils to be content with less and to place greater value on friendships and qualities such as tolerance. In this vein, Huppert (2005) calls for greater emphasis in schools on the social, emotional, creative and physical aspects of development as well as on academic achievement, a point also made by Layard (2005) in his call for emotional intelligence to be taught in schools. There are signs in recent educational policy developments in the UK that these calls are being acted on.

A QoL perspective is also driving a growing movement to focus more on relationships in service provision. Drawing on research showing the greater salience for well-being of partnership, friendship and community vis-à-vis income (Lane, 2000; Frey and Stutzer, 2002), Layard (2005, p ix) argues for 'a shift in public policy to a new perspective, where people's feelings are treated as paramount'. Jordan (2006a, p 42) concurs, arguing that the so-called 'well-being agenda' 'could redirect attention to the neglected features of human services – relationships, rather than technical expertise' (see also Jordan, 2006b).

It is worth reflecting a little on why QoL-orientated services take the form they do. In acknowledgement of the objective and subjective elements of QoL, the interventions described here are intended to shape children's circumstances and how they feel about them. That said, efforts tend to focus on objective circumstances. This is because while every child has different preferences, there are many areas in which their utility or happiness is likely to be *consonant* with their interests – the need for food and shelter, the freedom to form friendships, the capacity to develop talents and so on. As Dasgupta (1993, p 5) puts it,

> Something that is in a person's interest can hardly fail to influence his state of mind. What a person does, what he achieves – more generally, what he is capable of achieving – are things that, while plainly not the sole determinant of his welfare [utility], are clearly one set of ingredients of his welfare [utility].

The wide-ranging nature of QoL-orientated provision also reflects holistic and ecological perspectives – the idea that different aspects of life are closely interwoven and that children's environment and social relations have significant ramifications for their well-being. For example, improving access to play parks may help young children to meet their peers more and enjoy improved health.

It is also apparent that some efforts to enhance QoL have different goals than do responses to the other four conditions; instead of being geared towards rectifying difficulties, they seek to elevate the level of children's existence. (With the other four concepts the respective policy aims are addressing impaired health or development [need], righting wrongs [rights], combating material hardship [poverty] or inserting the detached back into mainstream society [social exclusion].) This difference is largely because a child's QoL can always be improved (however good it is), whereas once a child's needs are met they cannot be met any *more*, just as a child who is not in poverty cannot be made *less* in poverty. This explains why many QoL-orientated services potentially apply to all children and not just the afflicted or miserable.

Combating social exclusion

Although social exclusion technically concerns the fairly catastrophic detachment of individuals from society (Chapter Six), policy-makers tend to focus their attention on children and families 'at risk' of exclusion – those whose social ties in one or more spheres of participation are attenuated or ruptured. Precisely who is targeted depends on how 'inclusion' and 'exclusion' are interpreted. In the UK it often appears to be young people and families who lack morals (allegedly), work or money respectively (Levitas, 2000, p 362) – after the moral underclass (MUD), social integrationist (SID) and redistributionist (RED) discourses of exclusion described in Chapter Six. In other countries the populations targeted may be different, depending on the economy, culture and style of welfare provision. For example, in a society with high employment people who are dependent on benefits during their active life may be heavily stigmatised; the same category might be tolerated in a society experiencing entrenched structural unemployment (Paugam, 1996b). The targeting of interventions spatially – 'zone initiatives' – has also proved popular in the UK (Percy-Smith, 2000a), and it is arguable that by differentiating between people's circumstances (owing to a dynamic perspective) a social exclusion perspective leads to more refined and better-targeted policies (Hills, 2002).

As will be seen, the nature of provision for excluded populations varies according to who is targeted, but it may be stated that, theoretically at least, any measure that forges, repairs or helps to sustain a child's social ties – to the labour market (or other productive activity), to friends and family, to the wider community and to civic and political institutions – may be considered to help combat social exclusion. Many anti-exclusion measures are often multipronged and involve multiagency responses in the areas of health, education and community regeneration; this reflects the notion that social exclusion is 'a complex phenomenon that requires complex policy interventions' (Percy-Smith, 2000b, p 16). That said, it is also common to find initiatives that focus on one or other of the main social ties – the precise focus depends on the underlying interpretation of inclusion/exclusion. So, the MUD perspective gives rise to techniques for making young people and families integrate in the civic or political sense. Many of these *penalise* or display intolerance of exclusion; for example, there are various punishments in the UK for even fairly low-level antisocial behaviour, while punitive social assistance rates – or tying receipt of benefits to responsibilities such as seeking work – are used to discourage idleness. Moral education is aimed in part at curbing sexual promiscuity among young people. Citizenship modules in school curricula and the kind of correctional courses that young offenders sometimes receive are about helping children to understand other people's views, to respect major institutions and to take responsibility for their actions. Minority ethnic community groups may be denied certain public funds unless they forgo customs considered to be offensive or anachronistic in British society, and some are required to pledge allegiance to their country of residence. Turning to a SID perspective, where the main priority is participation in productive activity, there are numerous means of keeping children in education, training or work. These include: provision in mainstream schools for children with learning or behavioural difficulties; legal injunctions and fines for parents who condone their offspring's truancy; financial and other incentives for schools not to exclude pupils; and training schemes for school leavers aged 16-17 years.

Anti-discrimination measures are designed in part to pre-empt any tendency to exclude young people from work on the basis of disability or ethnicity (Gordon and Spicker, 1999). Meanwhile, protagonists of the RED viewpoint advocate action against child poverty (discussed earlier in the chapter).

There are other perspectives too regarding how to combat social exclusion. As already illustrated in relation to QoL, helping children and parents to stay integrated in social networks can take many forms; of particular relevance here, however, are measures to maintain contact between children cared for away from home and their families, and 'contact centres' for children to meet with absent parents in cases where a breakdown of the parental relationship was acrimonious. Both play a pivotal role in sustaining vulnerable children's familial ties (Bullock et al, 1998a; Kroll, 2000). Geographic exclusion can be addressed by better transport links, or by providing new facilities and services in cut-off neighbourhoods.

Standing back for a moment, it is apparent that four themes run through these approaches to combating social exclusion. First, all address *risk factors* of social exclusion. For example, low attainment, poor health and a substandard physical environment all make it difficult for children to participate in certain activities – whether by making them unemployable, or less able to sustain social relationships, or incapable of obtaining access to activities in the community. Thus, it might be argued that a better understanding of process enables a social exclusion perspective to inform a more active welfare state aimed at preventing social exclusion as opposed to a more passive orientation that responds to social exclusion (Hills, 2002). Second, many initiatives are coercive; they attempt to 'reinsert' people into specific spheres of activity or behaviour patterns, often in ways that the individuals would not necessarily choose. This might involve forcing unemployed youth into tedious or poorly paid jobs (Levitas, 1998), or expecting immigrants to assimilate into the dominant ethnic culture (Williams, 1998), or placing young rough sleepers in group-living accommodation (Cheetham and Fuller, 1998). A third observation is that most approaches focus on the excluded rather than the excluder(s) – what Veit-Wilson (1998) refers to as the *weak* and *strong* models respectively; the former encompasses attempts to alter the handicapping characteristics of the excluded and to enhance their integration into the dominant society, while the latter centres on restraining the excluding force. The weak model arguably informs policy in the UK, but the strong version has been evident in attempts in Sweden to tackle inequality (Byrne, 1999). Fourth, an emphasis on combating social exclusion draws attention to aspects of deprivation beyond cash and material living standards and therefore leads to a richer policy mix.

What informs these efforts in policy and practice circles to combat social exclusion? Essentially they rest on a conviction that healthy social ties are important not only for individuals but also for society as a whole (see Chapter Six). Certainly individual children whose social ties are weakened or ruptured often suffer as a result; the links between educational difficulties, poor health, relationship problems and antisocial behaviour, for example, are well established. And cumulatively, the effects of severed social ties are deemed to undermine the cohesiveness of a society by eroding any sense of interdependence and mutual responsibility. Young people may lose the motivation to respect other people's interests and liberties, and with it any expectation that they will be treated fairly. The activities involved in forging, mending and sustaining social ties are therefore intended to prevent social disorder.

Application to policy and practice

The key points from the previous discussion are summarised in Table 10.1. What happens if these ideas are applied to one of the outcomes desired by children's services in most western developed countries (eg DfES, 2003), namely health?

How would that outcome be interpreted from the five different conceptual perspectives, and how would those perspectives inform different service responses? What follows highlights the differences between approaches but also, hopefully, indicates that all are valuable in their own right and, together, help create a rich policy mix. (This is not to deny that there are tensions between them; indeed these are explored in Chapter Eleven.)

A need perspective, therefore, would focus on achieving reasonable physical or psychological health measured in terms of mobility, pain, mood and so on. The emphasis would be on evidence-based prevention and/or treatment.

A rights perspective would, arguably, be more concerned with process and ensuring, for example, that the individuals concerned receive appropriate treatment from suitably qualified staff, experience reasonable waiting times and are enabled to contribute to decisions about their treatment. Accordingly the practice response would be to ensure that procedures are in place for selecting and implementing tried-and-tested treatments (and for providing redress where there is negligence in this respect), and to secure adequate resources and maintaining systems to reduce waiting lists. Attention would also be paid to developing rigorous processes for staff recruitment and obtaining patient's opinions (both before and following their treatment).

From a poverty perspective the main concerns as regards the outcome of health would be that individuals can afford adequate nutrition and medicine and to live in housing that does not cause or exacerbate medical problems, and that they are not barred from healthcare by cost. Budgeting and cooking skills lessons might be one route taken, together with advocating for social assistance and related state benefits to be related to the costs of maintaining a healthy lifestyle. Financial assistance with healthcare might be offered in the form of exemptions from doctors' charges.

A social exclusion perspective might also cover these elements but it would be most concerned that individuals can access healthcare and are tied into primary health services in particular. Strategies to help achieve this might include relocating resources within deprived communities, perhaps in a one-stop shop or via healthcare professionals in schools.

A QoL perspective would add another dimension altogether. Arguably, it would focus attention on helping people to feel fit, healthy and happy (to experience positive well-being and not just the absence of ill-health), on minimising pain and on improving the service user's experience of using health services. The kind of services that would be promoted might not be 'medical' in the strict sense but rather involve the promotion of sports, walking and cycling as well as more general public health initiatives (for example to reduce pollution) and alternative therapies. Hospice and other forms of pain control would play an important role, as would the notions of providing unobtrusive treatment in pleasant settings and 'service with a smile'.

Table 10.1: The style of potentially effective interventions

	Need	Rights	Poverty	QoL	Social exclusion
Who the service is for	Technically children whose health or development is impaired or likely to become so, although other considerations affect the profile of those who receive assistance	Technically *all* children, although attention inevitably focuses on those who are vulnerable to or victims of exploitation and unfair or inappropriate treatment	Generally children and families who are in low-income families and/or those with poor living standards, although certain segments of the poor may be specially targeted	Potentially everyone but with particular attention to those who are judged to have poor objective circumstances or who show signs of being distressed or unhappy	Technically children and families whose social ties in one or more spheres of participation are attenuated or ruptured, but emphasis depends on how inclusion is interpreted
What it does	Material and non-material goods in all areas of children's lives, often at a fairly simple level	Often characterised by procedures and standards intended to constrain the conduct of individuals and organisations insofar as it affects others	Increase income, reduce outgoings and/or improve living standards	Enhance the natural and built environment, develop and sustain healthy and fulfilling relationships, improve provision of enriching activities, promote physical and mental health and encourage an individual's capacity to appreciate life and shape their lives	Forge, repair or help to sustain an individual's social ties – to productive activity, to friends and family, to the wider community and to civic or political institutions – but depends again on how inclusion is interpreted

continued

Table 10.1: *(continued)*

	Need	Rights	Poverty	QoL	Social exclusion
How it is delivered	Orientated towards improving health and development outcomes, based on evidence of what works in breaking causal chains, and often tailored to the individual	Often through charters, campaigns, and litigation designed to cajole, motivate and sometimes shame third parties to act towards others appropriately and fairly	Various, including raising social assistance rates and moving people into paid work (to increase income), boosting tax allowances and promoting budgeting (to reduce expenditure) and repairing substandard housing or regenerating poor areas (to improve living standards)	A wide range of services and processes not only to change people's situations but also to change their appraisal of those situations	By addressing risk factors of exclusion and coercing the excluded to become reinserted into society
Why it has those features	Underpinned by often competing notions of rationing and social justice	Rights have a certain force and so can 'trump' other considerations affecting how children and families are treated, also they preserve the dignity of rights-holders	Underpinned by the notion of social justice and wanting to make society fairer but also by the concern to avert wider social problems associated with poverty	Reflects an holistic appreciation of life in that all aspects (internal/external, objective/subjective etc) contribute to a sense of well-being; also the view that flourishing is different from/more than the absence of well-being	Aimed at promoting social cohesion and preventing social disorder; this goal is seen as superseding other goals (eg individual choice)

Targeting conditions

It is one thing to identify the style of services required to remedy the various conditions identified; it is quite another to ensure that they reach their target – that needs-led interventions get to children in need and so on. There are several reasons why children with a condition may not receive an appropriate service. One is a conscious decision by policy-makers or service providers to focus more on one condition than another, for example to address need rather than poor QoL. Another explanation is that one condition is taken to represent the *whole* problem, so that, for example, a decision to focus on social exclusion is taken on the grounds that this will encompass all children requiring assistance. A further possibility is that services are poorly targeted and miss their intended beneficiaries.

The potential implications of such scenarios can be illustrated using data from the study on which this book is based. Table 10.2 shows the number of children in the N=234 sample described in Chapter Eight who would *not* receive an intervention if at any one time only one of the five conditions were targeted. The condition that receives attention from services (X) is presented in the rows. It is apparent that in every case, interventions to address condition X *only* would fail to reach some of the children with condition Y (indicated in the columns). For example, interventions that accurately target children in need in the community would miss over half (52%) of the children affected by *any* condition and a similar proportion (56%) of those whose rights are seriously violated. Focusing on socially excluded children on the estates would involve missing the vast majority (86%) of children in need, and even more (92%) of those in poverty. In reality, neither scenario is likely – for the simple reason that such precise targeting is never going to happen. However, it does illustrate the potentially enormous *practical* significance of the

Table 10.2: Proportion of children not helped by targeted services for particular conditions

Condition targeted (X)	Proportion of children affected by Y condition who would not receive help (%)						
	In need	Rights violation	Poverty	Poor QoL	Social exclusion	Any condition	All children
In need	0	56	57	18	15	52	61
Rights violation	50	0	47	47	62	49	58
Poverty	34	27	0	38	30	26	39
Poor QoL	50	72	75	0	38	72	77
Social exclusion	86	97	92	87	0	93	94
Base (N)	87	97	138	54	14	192	234

outcome of debates that, at face value, appear purely semantic and theoretical (for example 'should policy be driven by need or social exclusion?' and 'should rights inform provision or is a focus on improving children's QoL more appropriate?').

Conclusions

This chapter has set the scene for testing in Chapter Eleven the third general hypothesis in the study, namely that services aimed at addressing some conditions are ineffective in relation to others, and that while contradictions exist they can be minimised by a better understanding of the concepts. It is clear from the discussion on effectiveness (the first part of this chapter) that services aimed at addressing each of the five conditions require different emphases. These emphases follow logically from the unique perspective of each conceptual approach, and traces of them are evident in existing provision for children. It is also evident, from the analysis of targeting (the second part of this chapter), that the pattern of conditions that is addressed has significant ramifications for the number of children helped and for the proportion of those with other conditions who miss out. How is this information useful? At least four options might be considered.

First, having selected a conceptual framework – and thus identified the condition(s) to address and the children who require assistance – a policy-maker or practitioner will have a good idea of what style interventions require if they are to be effective. For example, if the goal is to lift children out of poverty, the intervention should focus on improving income and living standards rather than on providing counselling (which is likely to be more effective in enhancing QoL). If the goal is to combat social exclusion then the focus should be on forging and repairing social ties rather than on addressing developmental deficits (which will make a greater contribution to meeting need). And so on.

Second, armed with knowledge about the style of services required by different conceptual approaches, a researcher can begin to analyse systematically existing provision and assess its likely ability to address different conditions. A small start has been made in this chapter, albeit only on a broad canvas. For instance, a proliferation of procedures and guidelines for practitioners may indicate progress in upholding children's rights but it is likely to have less impact on levels of need measured in terms of the prevalence of certain health or behavioural difficulties. Whether or not this is deemed to be a problem depends on what strategic decisions have been taken about the purpose of children's services (see Chapter Twelve).

Third, the discussion of service styles suggests that even if services are mis-targeted – so that resources are wasted and intended beneficiaries lose out – all is not lost: some benefit is *still* likely to accrue to unintended recipients. This is partly because aspects of the service styles are shared; for example the rights and QoL perspectives both promote the value of soliciting children's views. It is also because some provision is generally beneficial and certainly unlikely to do harm by any yardstick. For example, need-orientated services might help to prevent children who are poor but not in need from developing impaired health or development, or even help to alleviate their poverty. Group sessions for a young person who is not in need may nevertheless enhance his self-esteem and a social network that would help him to find work and so earn a decent wage, protecting him from poverty. The history of public health measures also shows that services can be ineffective and poorly targeted but have an unexpected positive effect. Maximising the capacity for such serendipitous situations to occur is discussed in Chapter Twelve.

Fourth, if it proves difficult to identify the intended recipients of services (those with condition X) – because of a lack of suitable information, for example – it is possible to do the next best thing and identify condition Y, which, if targeted accurately, would involve missing the least children with condition X. Table 10.3 sets out how this would work on the basis of the study data. For example, identifying children in need is the way to pick up the largest proportion of socially excluded children (it misses just 15% of those cases). Of course, this does not show the proportion of children in need who are *not* socially excluded but who would end up receiving interventions designed to combat social exclusion (86%). Significantly, the worst alternative target condition is social exclusion, essentially because its prevalence is so low (using the measure applied here).

Table 10.3: Best and worst proxy conditions to target

Target condition	Best proxy target	% cases missed	Worst proxy target	% cases missed
In need	Rights violations	34	Social exclusion	86
Rights violations	Poverty	27	Social exclusion	97
Poverty	Rights violations	47	Social exclusion	92
Poor QoL	Need	18	Social exclusion	87
Social exclusion	Need	15	Rights violations	62

In summary, knowing that the conditions are related but discrete, and that a different style of intervention is required for each one, policy-makers should consider carefully which condition(s) they wish to target and then ensure that the right children receive interventions that are capable of being effective in tackling their condition(s). Of course, reality is more complicated than this. In particular, and as will be apparent from the discussion in the first part of this chapter, the five broad styles of policy and practice have the potential to contradict one another. What this means specifically, and how it can be avoided in the pursuit of a more congruent pattern of service, is considered in the next chapter.

ELEVEN

Developing congruent children's services

Potential contradictions between service styles

It is evident from the previous chapter that while the service responses required to address the five conditions (or type of ill-being) may help to foster a rich service or policy mix, and so arguably increase the chances of improving child well-being, they also exist in tension and potentially contradict one another. Initiatives to address one condition may inadvertently impair efforts to tackle another, thereby creating or perpetuating problems. Moreover, they will almost certainly use resources to generate apparently successful outputs and outcomes, which, measured in terms of another condition, are actually of limited value, even damaging. The first part of this chapter therefore takes services for each condition in turn and discusses possible contradictions as they affect children and families who receive the service.

Services to meet need

Services to meet children's need exist in tension with rights-driven responses in at least four respects. First, the flexibility or discretion that is innate to responses to unmet need tends to generate guidance (rather than rules) that can be interpreted such that someone who technically is not entitled to assistance receives it (and vice versa) – a point made by Donnison (1982) in relation to state benefits. From a rights perspective this might be perceived as an insecure basis for distributing welfare resources to children and families, because it allows proper forbearance and assistance to be withheld at discretion.

Second, because a needs approach is inclined to treat children as passive objects, it generally draws more on the evidence of 'what works' than does a rights-orientated response, which views children as social actors and therefore pays greater attention to user opinion. In medicine, for example, children with chronic illnesses may have their right to influence decisions about receipt of drugs or surgery overridden by well-meaning adults on the basis of research studies supporting proven interventions. Although it might be argued that this is in the patients' best interests, such an approach is vulnerable to criticisms of being authoritarian or paternalistic.

Third, whereas a needs approach is more inclined to provide limited services *for* children and families, and to expect that this will be sufficient and welcomed, rights protagonists tend to be concerned with countering structural problems and so empowering clients to lead more autonomous lives (Barnes, 1998). This might be characterised as the difference between, say, a disabled young person attending a special day centre because that is what agencies offer, and the same child being enabled via improved transport and anti-discrimination practices to secure paid work. The former rests on the view of service recipients as passive subjects who are necessarily dependent on the expertise and benevolence of professionals. The latter, rights-based approach, holds that vulnerable children and families are often poorly served and entitled both to a higher standard of provision and also to a greater say in decisions that affect them. This tension has its roots in the one of the differences between sociological and developmental psychology perspectives, where the former focuses more on political power relations and the latter concerns local and individual interactions, which are more apolitical (Mayall, 2002).

Fourth, the nuanced nature of needs-led responses means that agencies may not intervene in the case of, say, an infant who is smacked by a parent if there is evidence that the incident was a one-off or took place in a generally warm and loving environment. A need perspective encourages consideration of the context and prompts intervention when (a) there is actual or likely harm and (b) something can be done to ameliorate or prevent that harm. Thus, an expert in the aetiology of developmental impairment might contend that such occurrences rarely cause lasting damage (eg Zielinski and Bradshaw, 2006), and that removing the child from their home or taking action against the perpetrator would be even more harmful. Support at home for the child and family might be offered as an alternative. From a rights perspective, by contrast, it might be argued that this constitutes negligence because it leaves the wrongdoer unpunished and the child vulnerable to further abuse. Again, these tensions might be traced back to differences between developmental psychology and sociology as regards their view of children: the former is concerned more with future development (how small people become big people) rather than with the present experience, and so encourages decision-making with one eye on likely implications; it is also more aware of differences between individuals and the factors that lead to good and bad outcomes, thereby informing nuanced interventions, whereas the more rights-oriented sociological perspective focuses on commonality and what binds children together as a social group distinct from adults (Woodhead, 1997; Mayall, 2002) – hence the blunter interventions that it informs, as described in Chapter Ten.

In relation to poverty, there is little reason to think that needs-led services will harm either a family's income or their living standards. There are reasons, however, to believe that needs-led services may not contribute greatly to children's quality of life (QoL) (beyond ensuring a modicum of material well-being). The first is that what is sufficient to meet a child's needs may not necessarily enhance that child's QoL; indeed, in some instances it may actually cause it to deteriorate. Some need-satisfiers are not particularly desirable for those who receive them, indeed some are extremely unpleasant; examples include harsh disciplinary regimes to remedy young people's behavioural problems or the use of distressing therapy sessions to cure phobias or heal emotional scars. Connected with this point is the fact that QoL concerns a higher level of well-being than need-satisfaction. This is reflected in the way that health-related QoL measures often capture patients' *feelings* as well as their physical functioning (Farquhar, 1995; Bowling, 1997; Skevington and Gillison, 2006). Similarly, in international development the focus of basic needs strategies on eliminating malnutrition, disease and illiteracy (see Chapter One) contrasts with wealthy nations' avowed pursuit of comfort and enrichment (Streeten et al, 1981; Seabrook, 1999). Indeed, it is partly because the merits of the need-satisfier are crucial to QoL that health and social care have tended to be organised more around a conservative concept like need, leaving the market to deal with wants and desires. It is also because keeping things from getting worse is considered to be morally preferable (measure for measure) to making things better (Goodin, 1988).

A second reason why need-orientated services may not enhance QoL is that, at least in their purest sense, they are geared towards enabling individuals to achieve agency per se rather than to act out a particular life plan (see Chapter Two). Thus, those items that are required in order to pursue specific personal goals must be regarded as 'wants', not needs. For example, regular and excessive alcohol consumption and thrill-seeking activities might be 'essential' activities for some young people, but policy-makers concerned with 'children in need' are unlikely to invest in such provision. Aspects of services that do help children to enjoy or obtain what they want are arguably more QoL-focused, for example a local football team or a holiday club. In a UK children's services context the tension may be captured in the way that an emphasis on achievement of specific targets, outcomes and behavioural changes, supported by managerial monitoring of efficiency and cost-effectiveness, overrides the notions of affection and positive regard as drivers of direct work with children and young people. For example, Jordan (2006a) notes how in the preliminary evaluation of the preschool programme Sure Start the relational aspect – measurably improved bonding between mothers and young children – was almost seen as a by-product of the focus on behavioural and learning outcomes that were targets of the initiative, even though it was central in terms of children's well-being.

Third, the by-products of need-satisfaction may have a detrimental impact on individuals' QoL. In the industrialised western world the process of producing ever more sophisticated need-satisfiers and of generating them in large quantities arguably contributes to various modern malaises, such as air pollution and global warming. Evidence of links between these environmental problems and respiratory and skin complaints suggests that some children's QoL suffers as a result (Quilgars and Wallace, 2002).

Initiatives to meet need may also render the individuals who are assisted vulnerable to social exclusion. For example, teaching children with behavioural or learning difficulties in a non-mainstream school or special unit is potentially stigmatising and can isolate them from their friends and communities (Cullingford, 1999; Rabiee et al, 2005). Similarly, before the UK 1948 Children Act came into force it was common for relationships between children in care and their parents to be severed; this was largely a product of active policies to rescue poor children from 'worthless and incompetent' parents and of assuring them spiritual salvation (Parker, 1990, p 25). In other words, the act of meeting the children's need for safety and nurturing – as it was perceived – contributed to their exclusion from family life. From a more right-wing perspective, it has even been argued that state support for unemployed or antisocial young people perpetuates their exclusion from society by failing to encourage them to enter the labour market or to conform to behavioural norms (eg Murray, 1990), although evidence for this actually happening is scant.[1]

Services to uphold rights

One characteristic of rights-based provision is the use of rules and regulations to shape the behaviour of duty-holders. A danger of this approach is that children with obvious needs are overlooked, either because their situation does not fit specified eligibility criteria for certain entitlements, or because addressing their difficulties lies beyond the explicit duty of the provider. In other words, respect for due process – and, often, attributing blame when duties are not fulfilled – may take precedence over rectifying deficits of care and meeting clients' needs. The rigidity that often characterises a rights-orientated approach also militates against delivering packages of support that meet children's needs for affection, warmth, self-esteem and so on (eg Jordan, 2006a). Indeed, Smith (1997) argues that regulations in the UK aimed at protecting children against abuses of power are in danger in some cases of turning foster and residential carers into 'technicians' who must perform certain tasks, so squeezing out some of the experiential qualities – responsiveness, comfort, appreciation and so forth – that help meet the aforementioned needs. A further way in which respect for rights may generate or prolong need is by allowing the wishes of service users to dictate the intervention. There is a danger that vulnerable children are encouraged to make decisions about their education and family life without sufficient professional guidance concerning their best interests (Thomas and O'Kane, 2000; Thomas, 2002). Rights-orientated services also have the potential to exacerbate child poverty, for similar reasons to those mentioned in relation to need. Thus, a family in material hardship might be refused state funds because their circumstances do not match the specified eligibility criteria.

Children's QoL also risks being damaged – or at least it may not be enhanced – by interventions aimed at protecting children's rights. At least four reasons for this may be given. First, because of the somewhat bureaucratic culture that a rights perspective can promote (see earlier in this chapter), assistance may end up being quite sanitised. Stated bluntly, what is sufficient to fulfil formal requirements and to allow a supervisor to tick the relevant box on a check sheet need not involve any enthusiasm or kind words on the part of the person providing the service. Such relational elements matter far more when viewed from a QoL perspective

(Layard, 2005; Jordan, 2006a, 2006b). Second, whereas rights are intended primarily to guard children against what is *bad* for them, measures to enhance QoL are more concerned with providing what is *good* (Bullock et al, 1994). This tension may be characterised as the difference between a child in residential care being entitled to protection from abuse, which is important and contributes to a better QoL for that child, and being enabled to enjoy foreign holidays or sports activities, which enriches that child's life. This is partly connected to the rather conservative character of many legal rights – a product of the assumption that ascribing to somebody a duty implies that its execution is possible. Third, a feature of rights is that they help to resist the utilitarian temptation to trade in the interests of a small number of people in order to secure a greater sum of the lesser interests of many people (Waldron, 1984). They serve autonomous individuals, not wider society. One contention, therefore, might be that they stand in the way of significant improvements to children's QoL. For example, the quality of many children's lives would be vastly improved if school bullies were excluded or punished more severely, but the children doing the bullying share rights to education and to physical protection that guard against more draconian interventions. Fourth, because rights-based interventions are often invoked in acrimonious disputes or other sensitive situations, they have a greater likelihood than services driven by the other concepts of causing children distress, such as when efforts to promote participation in decision-making result in a child being expected to choose which parent to live with following a marriage break-up.

The previous example is also relevant in relation to tensions between rights-based provision attempts to combat social exclusion, as it illustrates the capacity of confrontational and litigious service responses to weaken children's social ties. Applied in the context of a family, such interventions can easily set child against parent (eg Cooper, 1998). Other aspects of a rights-orientated approach may also undermine a child's integration in various spheres of activity. Thus, affirmative action to counter discrimination may involve separating disabled children from their peers (as in the previously mentioned examples concerning education), while young people encouraged to think in terms of their rights rather than their responsibilities could conceivably be tempted then not to participate in certain collective endeavours – from contributing their labour and volunteering in the community to obeying the law.

Services to tackle poverty

As a rule, alleviating poverty by raising low incomes and improving inadequate living standards is unlikely to generate need. That said, some interventions – notably those aimed at reducing a family's expenditure – may inadvertently impair children's health and development. For example, encouraging families to cut back on food and heating could increase the risk of malnutrition and disease (especially for very young children) since some of the items that poor families are sometimes criticised for buying – food that is high in calories and low in nutrition, for example – are actually the most cost-efficient way of meeting their needs. Similarly, a lack of leisure activities is often associated with young people displaying behavioural and learning difficulties. It is also difficult to imagine how anti-poverty measures could infringe children's rights, unless of course they are coercive; for instance making a teenage mother choose between the options of low-paid work or losing benefits arguably denies her the right to exercise real influence over her lifecourse.

It is easier to envisage how efforts to tackle poverty can cause children's QoL to deteriorate, at least in the immediate and short term. For example, unemployed young people who are coerced into paid work may experience working conditions that they consider unpleasant or find that the new responsibility results in stress and less time for recreation. Similarly, advice on budgeting may cause families in poverty to buy less appetising food and reduce their use of substances such as tobacco and alcohol, or stop them from enjoying certain kinds of entertainment. Area-based regeneration projects may also have a negative impact on children; while helping some local residents to climb out of financial hardship, often at the same time they reduce the amount of green playing space and increase traffic and pollution.

There may also be instances in which tackling poverty increases the risk of social exclusion. Anti-poverty initiatives that require cuts in personal expenditure are likely to jeopardise a family's social ties. This is because participation in most spheres of activity costs money – for smart work clothes, for buying drinks and tickets when out with friends, for telephone calls and travel if volunteering for a community project, for gifts on special family occasions and so on. In addition, it might be argued that increasing social assistance rates makes it easier for young people to survive reasonably comfortably *outside* the labour market, so diminishing the incentive provided by punitive benefit rates to find and keep employment (with its associated benefits in terms of social networks). Esping-Andersen (1990) calls this process 'decommodification' as it makes it easier for an individual not to have to sell their labour: it lessens the extent to which they are a labour market commodity.

Services to enhance quality of life

As a rule, efforts to improve children's QoL are unlikely to generate need. Indeed, needs-led responses may actually be enhanced by attention to QoL issues. For instance, a systematic review of studies to see if doctor–patient relationships have a therapeutic effect irrespective of any prescribed drug or treatment found that a warm, friendly and reassuring manner is more effective than formal consultations without reassurance (Di Blasi et al, 2001). That said, there could still be a tension between the two approaches. The importance of the subjective perspective to QoL makes practitioners more inclined to heed the views of service users, one consequence of which can be harm to the child (noted earlier in this chapter).

Policies aimed at improving children's QoL are also unlikely to increase the risk of poverty or impede its eradication. They may have a counterproductive effect in relation to social exclusion, however, particularly if concerns about the *quality* of activity in certain spheres prevent the relevant social tie from being forged or repaired. For instance, hazardous work conditions are often used as a pretext for campaigning against child labour (which plays an important economic role in some societies), and social workers may resist returning a separated child home to her family if they consider her carers to be abusive or if the home is an insufficiently stimulating environment.

Services to combat social exclusion

It is possible to imagine scenarios in which policies to promote inclusion actually increase children's vulnerability to developmental impairment (need) or frustrate attempts to address it. For instance, a truanting child encouraged to attend school may become the victim of bullying, while efforts to force children to improve their behaviour – perhaps by threatening their parents with prison – may actually exacerbate family conflict and other risk factors that contribute to the impairment. However, these situations are likely to be rare. More likely, perhaps, is the coercive nature of many policies to combat exclusion also violating the rights of individuals. So, young people who refuse the offer of a job or who behave antisocially may be threatened with the withdrawal of entitlements to social assistance. Similarly, patients who are obese or smokers might be required to sign contracts stating that they may only receive health treatment if they diet or quit cigarettes. Making state support conditional in this way goes against the grain of granting assistance as an entitlement. These contradictions arise because whereas rights are about being free to do certain things, inclusion often entails obligations – the expectation that individuals (including children) will participate in the community and market as consumers, taxpayers, workers, carers, altruistic volunteers and so on (eg Plant, 1990; Scott, 1994; Stewart, 1995). Put another way, inclusion is *performed* as much as or even more than it is *claimed*.

A further reason why efforts to combat exclusion are connected with violated rights is that some policies aimed at fostering inclusion actually legitimate prevailing inequalities. The kind of 'workfare' programmes used to insert school leavers into jobs that are often poorly paid and even dangerous could be cited as examples of this – what Sen (2000, p 28) calls 'inclusion on bad terms'. In other words, inclusion-oriented policies can divert attention away from the radical change required to protect individuals' rights (Barry, 1998). Fostering inclusion may also link children into spheres of activity where rights abuses are endemic, such as an abusive family; social workers face a constant struggle to balance vulnerable children's right to protection and their simultaneous right (and that of their parents) to a family life.

In relation to poverty, some initiatives to combat social exclusion require unemployed parents to take low-paid work – so including them in the labour market but leaving them still with insufficient income to afford some basic necessities for their children and therefore in or at risk of poverty (eg Levitas, 1996). This is partly because paid work generally reduces the amount of means-tested benefit to which individuals are entitled, but also because the individuals concerned become liable to pay tax and may forfeit income earned through the grey economy. Disjunctions like this arise largely because inclusion initiatives strive primarily to haul the excluded 'on board the vessel' – to lift people above a certain threshold and into the mass of society. That is the outcome of concern. Anti-poverty measures, by contrast, are more likely to be concerned with reducing the economic distance between citizens (whether excluded or included). They also tend to focus on income and material living standards, whereas to combat exclusion it is necessary to address relational factors – to look at 'impoverished lives, and not just at depleted wallets' (Sen, 2000, p 3). Effectively the two approaches have different roots: concern with *equality* promotes the avoidance of poverty, while the goal of *fraternity* fuels attempts to prevent exclusion from the community (p 24).

Finally, a focus on exclusion tends to evoke concern about the *existence* rather than about the *quality* of a social tie. Stated bluntly, the goal first and foremost is to ensure that a preschool child is at nursery or playgroup; it is not with how they are treated there or if the facility is clean and well equipped. Similarly, living with family or being part of other social networks counts for far more in the inclusion–exclusion equation than does whether those relationships are nurturing. Nor does it matter that much if the inclusion is coerced, as with a young person who prefers to sleep rough but who is forced to live in a hostel; yet when inclusion is compelled it is less likely to promote a sense of well-being (Gore and Figueiredo, 1997).

Avoiding contradictions between service styles

In an ideal world, services for any one of the five conditions discussed here would neither increase the risk of the other conditions nor frustrate attempts to alleviate any of them. Thus, efforts to meet children's needs would not violate children's rights, social exclusion would be combated without impeding anti-poverty measures aimed at the same families and so on. More than that, a service for one condition would positively help to address the others. So, needs-led services would be a means of protecting children's rights, which in turn would enhance the beneficiaries' QoL. How feasible is this scenario?

The evidence is mixed. The findings from the analysis in Chapters Seven and Nine showed that, conceptually and empirically, the five conditions are less closely related than is widely assumed and, as a consequence, they give rise to different service styles or emphases (Chapter Ten). For example, many children in poverty are not socially excluded, just as not every socially excluded child is poor, and services to tackle poverty are not necessarily the same as those designed to combat social exclusion. Previous studies and a mixture of original quantitative and qualitative analysis of data in the present study for children living on the inner-London estate have been used in this book to help explain these disjunctions. It is also clear from the discussion in this chapter that, continuing the same example, initiatives to tackle poverty may contribute to exclusion, just as efforts to combat social exclusion may leave poverty untouched. Further empirical work is required to validate some of the patterns described here, but effectively they support part one of the study's third hypothesis, namely that services aimed at addressing some conditions are ineffective in relation to others.

On the other hand, Chapters Seven and Nine demonstrated that, in some cases, the five conditions *are* connected; that is, children with condition X are disproportionately likely to have or develop condition Y. For example, children in need were found to be disproportionately likely to have a poor QoL. Analyses from previous studies and a number of case studies drawn from the dataset described in this book were used to identify some of the causal links that account for such patterns. The implication of this work is that where such a relationship exists, dealing with one condition has the potential to address the other condition, or at least not to cause or perpetuate it: if X causes Y, and X is addressed, then Y will also be addressed (at least in part). This statement is supported by the discussion in Chapter Ten, particularly around applying the idea to children's health, and earlier in this chapter; although it was possible to identify many potential contradictions between efforts to deal with different conditions, in some cases few or no such contradictions were found. For example, tackling poverty or enhancing QoL is unlikely to generate need. Even contradictions that were thought possible were not necessarily considered to be common.

Taking these points together there is good reason to think that the other part of the third hypothesis also holds: that contradictions between services for different conditions can be minimised by a better understanding of the concepts. For example, services to meet children's needs should be able to complement and even aid initiatives to enhance children's QoL (and vice versa: improving children's QoL should not interfere with – and may even contribute to – their needs being met). But realising this potential depends on knowing what the differences between the concepts are and how they are related. One practical strategy, then, for illuminating these possibilities is to draw on the findings contained in the book and set out some straightforward statements in the following approximate form with a view to guiding policies in children's services for the five conditions:

> In order to tackle [condition X] for a person without giving them [condition Y] or hindering attempts to treat their [condition Y] it is necessary to do [service style for condition X] and at the same also do [service style that prevents/addresses condition Y].

This idea is developed in Chapter Twelve, so for now three examples illustrate how such statements might work:

- *Need and rights:* In order to treat a child's illness (need) without causing or perpetuating the violation of their rights to participation, it is necessary to consult them beforehand, provide them with information and obtain their consent prior to administering the treatment.
- *Social exclusion and poverty:* In order to protect an unemployed young person against social exclusion without forcing them into or prolonging their poverty, it is necessary to help them to get a job for which the net income (wages minus tax and forfeited benefits) is adequate for a low cost but acceptable budget.
- *QoL and rights:* In order to enhance recreational facilities so that children can enjoy playing outside more (QoL), while at the same time upholding children's rights to protection, it is necessary to ensure that equipment in a new adventure playground complies with safety regulations, and that all activities there are supervised by a responsible adult.

Of course, this approach seems rather formal and, perhaps, somewhat contrived. A more informal approach that could nevertheless be instructive would simply be to reflect on these ideas when undertaking planning and clinical casework.

Towards congruent children's services

It is clear from this and the previous chapter that the emphases of services for children have far-reaching ramifications for child well-being. This is particularly apparent when examined through the lenses of need, rights, poverty, QoL and social exclusion. If all, or at least two or more, of these five distinct but related conditions are to be addressed satisfactorily, a *congruent* pattern of services (or service mix) is required. Chapter Twelve considers the factors that influence which conditions the service mix is orientated towards. The remainder of this chapter considers, at a conceptual level, the discrete features of a service mix.

The term 'congruence' is used to mean accordant or fitting together, as in a mosaic of triangles. A congruent set of services might be considered to have four features. First, interventions are fashioned or designed so that they have the potential to be effective in alleviating or preventing a specified condition. Second, those interventions are targeted accurately; that is, they reach children with the condition in question. Third, the interventions do not bring about − or hinder efforts to alleviate − *other* conditions, whether for the child with the original condition or for other children; they complement one another. Fourth, where possible, interventions aimed at alleviating or preventing one condition also help to address another, thereby achieving some degree of synergy.

Figure 11.1 expresses these ideas visually. It shows two discrete but related conditions (X and Y). Children in segment *a* have X only, children in *b* have X and Y, children in *c* have Y only and children in *d* have neither X nor Y. The *effectiveness* of services designed to address X or Y is measured according to how children are moved between *a*, *b*, *c* and *d*. So, the most effective services for condition X move children from *a* and *b* to *c* or *d*. The accuracy of *targeting* refers to how far

Figure 11.1: Venn diagram of services for two overlapping conditions

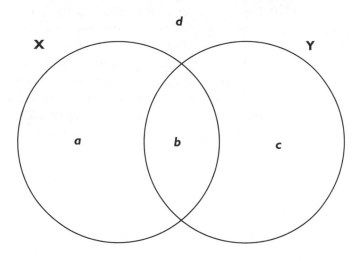

services addressing X are only received by children with X (the same with Y). Thus, completely accurate targeting means that services for X only go to children in *a* and *b*, while total mis-targeting is when services for X go to children in *c* and *d*. Partial mis-targeting is when services for X go to either *a* or *b* (but not both). Of course, a service can be totally effective and also well targeted but have negative side-effects. A service for condition X may shift children from *a* and *b* to *d* but in the process move children from *d* to *c* or hinder attempts to move children out of *c*. It is therefore desirable that services are *complementary* (in the sense of adding to or completing something). Fully complementary services not only address the target condition successfully, but also avoid increasing the risk of – or hindering efforts to address – other conditions. They complete rather than contradict other preventive and remedial activity. In Figure 11.1 services for X would alleviate or eradicate X and avoid creating – or frustrating measures to deal with – Y. Ideally there would also be evidence of *synergy*. This term is generally used to describe the working together of two or more drugs, muscles, machines and so forth to produce an effect that is greater than the sum of the individual parts. It is used here to describe a service that in the course of addressing condition X helps to alleviate or to prevent the development of condition Y. Based on Figure 11.1, a service designed to address condition X would demonstrate synergy – or be 'synergistic' – if it moved children from *b* to *d*: as well as addressing X it aids the efforts of services tackling Y.[2]

How does the study described in this book contribute towards a congruent pattern of services? First, it sets out different ways of defining and measuring the five conditions: unmet need, violated rights, poverty, poor QoL and social exclusion (Chapters Two to Seven). Achieving greater understanding about the contours of each condition provides a platform for determining the style of interventions that stand to be effective (Chapter Ten). Second, by devising simple dichotomous measures (Chapter Eight and Appendix A) and by charting, in one particular community, the prevalence of and overlap between the conditions (Chapters Eight and Nine), the book helps service planners and practitioners to identify those children with certain conditions. This information assists with the proper targeting of services at both aggregate and individual levels (Chapter Ten). Enhanced versions of the prototype measures used for this study, applied in clinical settings and then aggregated or adopted in epidemiological-style surveys, would allow this task to be undertaken more accurately. Third, the book has drawn attention to primary and secondary evidence of the disjunction between conditions, in other words how children may have one but not another (Chapters Seven and Nine), and issued warnings about the way in which services can contribute to this pattern (see the first half of this chapter). Fourth, the book provides evidence of how the conditions often co-occur, so that children with condition X often have condition Y and vice versa (those without X often do not have Y) (Chapters Seven and Nine). The present chapter develops this thinking by offering pointers as to how complementary and synergistic services can address two or more conditions simultaneously. The final chapter links these ideas back to the research and policy context described in Chapter One.

Notes

[1] Although apparently voluntary withdrawal from society does not count as social exclusion given the definition in Chapter Six, the attenuation of social ties arguably increases the risk of exclusion and so is included in the examples here and elsewhere in the chapter.

[2] Synergy is different from complementarity in two respects: (1) it is about alleviating or eradicating conditions, not just preventing their emergence or not hindering other efforts to address a condition; and (2) it is usually achieved when two (or more) sets of services are working on the *same* people who have two (or more) conditions.

TWELVE

Conclusions

The study reported in this book has looked at child well-being in terms of unmet need, violated rights, poverty, poor quality of life (QoL) and social exclusion. Owing to a confluence of several factors, including moral imperatives, legislation and scientific evidence, all five concepts appear currently as policy objectives in children's services in the UK and other western developed countries. In many respects this is welcome; it should be evident by this juncture in the book that there is value in looking at children's lives through different lenses. At the same time, varied terminology and multiple initiatives bring with them the danger of confusion. There is a risk of using different words to refer to the same phenomenon, whether in discussions between researchers, policy-makers and practitioners, or across administrative and disciplinary divides. There is also the potential for policy-makers to speak with a forked tongue; that is, of devising and enacting initiatives that are inherently contradictory. Moreover, unless a concept is properly understood, how can its empirical formulation be measured and addressed? And unless the objective of services is made explicit, how can their effectiveness be assessed?

There is considerable research into each of the concepts individually, showing that although some broad consensus has been reached concerning the contours of each, their definitions remain contested and they continue to be measured in numerous ways. Partly because of this, however, conceptual and empirical research into the links between them, and the implications of this for services, is scant by comparison. In particular, it has not been possible to find an epidemiology-style survey that examines different perspectives on the well-being of normative samples of children living in the community. More specific gaps in the literature were identified in Chapters Two to Six.

Given this context the contributions of the book can be grouped under three headings corresponding to the study's aims: first, the clarification of how the concepts are defined and measured, and an exploration of how they are related; second, an empirical analysis of the prevalence of the conditions among children representative of a particular community, and an elucidation of the patterns of overlap between them; and third, an attempt to chart theoretically and practically the implications of the ideas and findings for children's services.

Defining the concepts, and relationships between them

The first aim of the study was to identify the defining characteristics of the five concepts and to explore the relationships between them. Chapters Two to Six described how the five concepts are traditionally defined and measured. They showed that there are various approaches to doing this but that it is possible for each one to identify broad conceptual parameters or an underlying narrative or discourse. An account was also given of how the strengths and weaknesses of different measures shaped how the concepts are operationalised in this study.

Chapter Seven then identified the distinguishing features of each concept, using information from Chapters Two to Six to summarise them in terms of seven dividing lines. For example, whereas the antecedents of need are irrelevant to whether or not it exists and unmet needs may reflect personal deficiency or structural injustice, a rights violation can only derive from an act of omission or commission by a third party. Rights cover a range of topics, from housing and health to freedom of speech, but poverty focuses more narrowly on income and living standards. Poverty concerns the wherewithal to lead a minimally adequate life, whereas QoL goes beyond functionality to include enrichment. In contrast to QoL, taste and choice are of little bearing in the case of social exclusion; the existence of a social tie is more important than its quality. And unlike need, which is measured in terms of health and development and having the capacity to act (agency), social exclusion is concerned with degrees of participation or integration.

In addition, Chapter Seven used analyses from previous studies to compare the empirical formulations of the concepts. This is novel, in that most previous work has looked more at links between *components* of the concepts. The conditions were found to be overlapping but not coterminous, with some connections more likely to occur than others. This may be illustrated in relation to (a) need and rights and (b) poverty and social exclusion. Thus, unmet need and violated rights often go together in the sense that respect for rights is conducive to need-satisfaction, and meeting need is to some extent a prerequisite for the exercise of rights to liberty and respect for property rights. However, upholding rights to liberty may expose children to harm, and litigious or reactive responses to alleged rights abuses may overlook or perpetuate need. Equally, there is evidence of rights being violated for a 'higher end' (to meet need), and one-off actions may constitute a violation of rights without causing need (because context and consequences are important considerations with the latter). The relationship between poverty and social exclusion is also interesting. Certainly poverty is associated with attenuated or severed social ties, for example antisocial behaviour, unemployment and being unable to participate in certain social activities. Equally, financial hardship can foster support networks and increase the likelihood of people being linked into some services. Low-paid jobs make it possible to be poor but attached to the labour market, and, despite lurid tabloid headlines, few poor families inhabit a feckless, crime-ridden culture distinct from the rest of society or live in geographically excluded neighbourhoods. Nor is everyone who is excluded necessarily poor. They may have encountered barriers besides low income, for example discrimination, while a lack of paid work (detachment from the labour market) can be compensated for by alternative sources of income and goods (perhaps through the 'grey economy').

Taken together these points support the first hypothesis: the five concepts are related but not as closely as is widely assumed. They do have characteristics in common, and some definitions of concept X are closer than others to definitions of concept Y, but they can also be distinguished from one another in significant ways. A clear message is that all five concepts contribute a unique perspective on a child's well-being, and that one will draw attention to features that another one misses. The analysis also suggests that individuals can have one condition but not another, and that understanding these patterns will assist with developing an appropriate service response. These points were explored further in Parts Two and Three of the book respectively.

Prevalence of the conditions, and overlap between them

The second aim of the study was to measure the prevalence among children in the community of the conditions to which the concepts refer, and to compare the overlap between them. Based on the analysis in Chapters Two to Six, five dichotomous tests (one per concept) were applied to data on 234 children living on a moderately deprived and ethnically diverse inner-London housing estate.

Prevalence of the conditions

Out of necessity a novel approach was taken to operationalising several of the concepts (Chapter Eight and Appendix A). The results reported in Chapter Eight support part of the second hypothesis, namely that the prevalence of the conditions varies considerably. The drawbacks – even logical implausibility – of using single factor proxy measures for several of the concepts were also exposed. These points are now elaborated, taking each of the five concepts in turn.

Starting with need, standard approaches to measurement involve calculating the demand for services or ascertaining what people want. Here, information about expert-defined need was gathered for all areas of each child's life, an approach grounded in theories of need drawn from political philosophy and evidence from child psychology regarding the essential requirements for healthy child development. A child was only deemed to be 'in need' if their health or development was *actually* impaired. This definition is based partly on the England and Wales 1989 Children Act but also resonates strongly with the basic needs of physical health and autonomy noted by Doyal and Gough (1991) and correlates strongly (0.8, $p<0.01$) with the measure designed to capture that definition (see Appendix A). Two fifths (39%) of the children were affected in this way.

The literature is coy about measuring rights violations, betraying a lack of common ground about methods and numbers. Reading between the lines of much that is written, one finds the assumption that the rights of children as defined by certain social characteristics, administrative categories or contexts are breached de facto. In an attempt to generate a more meaningful figure, the study reported in this book applied a measure specifying the content of children's rights and how they might be violated. The approach drew on philosophical work and international legislation for the content, and case law for the principles that guided decisions (Chapter Three). When the decisions were aggregated, two fifths of children (42%) were judged to be experiencing serious rights violations. In addition, a comparison of the rights measure with a possible proxy such as 'abuse' revealed a correlation of just 0.253 ($p<0.01$) (Chapter Nine), reinforcing the point that this concept – like the others – is complex and cannot be captured by a single factor.

The measure used in the study for poverty is unremarkable insofar as many studies have combined low income and poor living standards and applied such a measure to representative community samples. (Most have also done it far better, with the advantage of using specific poverty-related data.) However, what the present study adds is some comparative data for alternative indicators. For example, using the selected measure, under two thirds (61%) of children were poor, but looked at in terms of poor living standards alone, this rose to four fifths (80%). In addition, the study makes it possible to explore how close different measures are, for example the selected measure correlates moderately strongly (0.517, $p<0.01$) with dependence on basic social assistance (see Appendix A). Clearly the choice of indicator has a significant bearing on poverty rates and on *who* is deemed to be poor.

QoL is measured in terms of poor objective circumstances and a negative subjective appraisal of circumstances. Although many health-related indices combine the same features, here the measure is applied to a community sample rather than to a clinical population. Just under a quarter (23%) of children were identified in this way. Further, as with poverty the comparisons of prevalence rates using different indicators are illuminating. For example, the vast majority (84%) of children had poor material circumstances, but only one third (33%) lacked extra-curricular activities. Similarly, only a third (32%) of the children scoring on the selected measure were reported by parents or agency professionals to show signs of unhappiness. Clearly, using a lack of enrichment or unhappiness as the main QoL measure would have produced a very different picture.

The study reported in this book broke new ground by measuring the prevalence of social exclusion for a sample of children representative of a particular community. Drawing on theories concerning the essential features of the concept (eg Room, 1999) and empirical studies that chart adults' participation in several spheres of activity (eg Burchardt et al, 1999), it measured children's participation in the economic, interpersonal, civil and political spheres. Six per cent of the sample was excluded in all four areas. Again, it is instructive to look at alternative indicators. For example, prevalence rates for the three interpretations of exclusion identified by Levitas (1998) could be as follows: a lack of integration in the labour market 1%; the underclass 8%; and economic hardship 61%.[1]

Overlap between the conditions

The other part of the second hypothesis (not mentioned earlier) was that there is greater overlap between some conditions than others but that none subsumes another. This was informed by the discussion in Chapter Seven, but further reason to think it probable was provided by subsequent empirical findings in Chapter Eight. Here, the statistical analysis showed that each condition is distinctive in terms of overall character. The critical distinguishing factors in children's lives were largely as anticipated; for example antisocial behaviour and health problems were highly predictive of a child being in need, while abuse and being forced to flee war or oppression were highly predictive of children having violated rights.

The results on overlap (Chapter Nine) also supported the hypothesis but, more significantly, revealed less overlap generally than might have been expected given widespread – and often unspoken – assumptions in social research and policy. For example, being 'in need' and having violated rights are generally treated as different ways of referring to the same thing. Yet only 44 children (20%) were deemed to be in need and to have their rights violated, compared with 43 (19%) who were in need but whose rights were intact, and 51 (23%) who were not in need but whose rights were violated. The fact that all of the correlations between conditions were weak – apart from a moderately strong association between need and QoL (0.470, $p<0.01$) – reinforces the message, as does the fact that most of the relative risk ratios were low: children with condition X were not much more likely to have condition Y than children who did *not* have X. For instance, children whose rights were judged to have been violated were only 1.3 times more likely than other children to be poor.[2]

Chapter Nine also used quantitative analysis and qualitative case studies of children in the sample to explain some of the more counterintuitive patterns regarding disjunctions. This chimed with much of the earlier discussion (especially Chapter Seven), showing, for example, that children may have their rights to privacy violated without it affecting their health and development (they are not in need), and that children from poor households often participate in several spheres of activity (they are not socially excluded) and enjoy a decent QoL.

Implications for children's services

The third aim of the study was to consider the implications of the findings for policy and practice in children's services. Although there is an extensive literature on children's services, much work in recent years has focused on the relationship between child protection and family support, the process of service delivery and the nature and effectiveness of specific interventions (eg Axford et al, 2005; Scott and Ward, 2005; McAuley et al, 2006a). It was therefore considered timely to focus specifically on the wider conceptual framework in which children's services operate and on how different kinds of provision fit together. In attempting to redress this balance, then, the book has made five main contributions, which are now outlined. Together they support the third hypothesis, namely that services aimed at addressing some conditions can be ineffective in relation to others, and that while contradictions exist they can be minimised by a better understanding of the concepts.

A theory of congruent services

The first contribution has been to set out some theoretical ideas about the components of a congruent service response to discrete but related conditions: (a) the selection of effective interventions that are (b) accurately targeted, which (c) complement each other and (d) achieve a degree of synergy (Chapter Eleven).

The style of services

The second contribution of the book has been to identify the features that an intervention must have *logically* if it is to have the potential to be effective in addressing a specified condition (Chapter Ten). For each of the five conditions, these features were described in terms of who the service is for, what the service does, how the service is delivered and why the service has these features. For example, services for need may include material and non-material provision, although the precise nature of the need–satisfiers will vary with different settings. Rights-orientated interventions are aimed primarily at children and families who are disproportionately subject to poor treatment, with assistance not conditional on what people have or have not done. Among the main strategies for tackling poverty are increasing rates of state social assistance (and any statutory minimum wage), tackling debt, teaching budgeting skills and improving housing and local facilities. QoL interventions seek to enrich people's lives, whereas efforts to combat social exclusion are driven by a belief in the value of social ties both for the individual concerned and for the wider society.

These perspectives should inform the evaluation of services, because they pinpoint what services for different conditions are trying to achieve and how likely they are to be effective against different criteria. For instance, it is perhaps naive to expect that giving a chronically ill child choice about what treatment they receive will improve their health (need), but it represents an opportunity for them to exercise their rights and may yield some benefits in terms of their level of life satisfaction (QoL). Similarly, efforts to integrate an unemployed young person into the labour market might be more appropriately evaluated in terms of participation in mainstream society (social exclusion) than by reference to income and living standards (poverty). Perhaps the value of new child protection procedures and regulations should be assessed according to how far organisations and individuals abide by them (rights) rather than in terms of improvement to the children's health, behaviour or educational attainment (need).

Such an approach not only encourages policy-makers and practitioners to specify more precisely the desired outcomes of an intervention, it also makes evaluations more realistic. Some desired results will be very difficult to achieve with some kinds of intervention. For example, it is arguably easier for a practitioner to help a child reintegrate into school (and thereby tackle social exclusion) than it is to make that child happy (improving QoL). This is because the latter outcome depends largely on an individual's subjective appraisal of their circumstances. Similarly, adherence to certain regulations might protect a client's rights but there is no guarantee that it will help meet their needs; freewill, accidents and genetic make-up may conspire to undo any good work done by professionals. Evaluating services in terms of what they can realistically achieve means acknowledging both the value of applying different yardsticks, and also the limits of certain services.

The fit between services

The third contribution of this book has been to demonstrate how ideas and findings from the study can be used practically to improve the targeting, complementarity and synergy of children's services interventions (Chapter Eleven). One way it has done this is by highlighting the implications of helping children with one condition at the expense of others. For example, assisting children in need in the community in question means that nearly a fifth (18%) of those with a poor QoL would be overlooked (using the measures employed here). Similarly, if services for children in need were to go to children in poverty, one third (35%) of children in need would not be reached and three fifths (58%) of those who *did* receive the need-orientated intervention would not need it (they are poor but not in need). This latter point is particularly important given the common use of socioeconomic indicators as proxy measures for child need.

Another way that the book has sought to inform service development is by highlighting potential points of conflict or tension between services (Chapter Eleven). Take need and social exclusion, for instance. Initiatives to combat exclusion by maintaining children's ties to certain spheres of activity may impair those children's health or development, perhaps because of abusive relationships in their families or hazardous working conditions. Equally, some approaches to meeting need may exclude children – as is the case, arguably, with the segregation of some children with special educational needs. A further contribution is to identify potential synergies between interventions that have different ends in view. For instance, allowing children some choice over how they are helped both upholds their rights to participation and also helps to enhance their level of satisfaction (QoL). Since it is most common to have a service mix that is informed by more than one concept, there is much value in seeking complementarity and synergy.

Practical applications

The study's fourth contribution is therefore practical. The four elements of a service mix as identified earlier – effectiveness, targeting, complementarity and synergy – can be brought together in a simple statement for any of the 10 two-way combinations (see also Chapter Eleven). This has the potential to help guide the thinking of policy-makers and managers when they are fashioning and implementing children's services. For example, when designing a congruent service response to need and poverty the main things to bear in mind would be the following (the source of the information is in square brackets at the end of each paragraph):

(a) *Effectiveness*: Services to meet need can include material and non-material provision (often of a basic nature). The precise nature of the need-satisfiers will vary with different settings. However, they should be tailored to individual circumstances and rooted in scientific evidence of what works with an emphasis on early intervention. Anti-poverty measures seek to increase a young person's or family's income, to reduce their expenditure or to improve their living standards. The primary ways of tackling poverty are by increasing rates of state social assistance, getting the unemployed into paid work, tackling debt, cutting tax liabilities, teaching budgeting skills and improving housing and local facilities. [From Chapter Ten.]

(b) *Targeting*: Two fifths of children (39%) in the sample were in need. They were identified by a measure of actual impairment to health or development. Three fifths (61%) of the children were in poverty. They were identified using a measure that combines low income and poor living standards. A quarter of the children (26%) were in need and in poverty. Another quarter of the sample (26%) was neither in need nor poor. The interventions for need and poverty summarised in (a) above should be targeted accordingly. [From Chapters Eight and Nine.]

(c) *Complementarity*: A young person should not be required to take paid work or cut back on expenditure if it will make them physically ill or stressed or impair their health or development in other ways. [From Chapter Eleven.]

(d) *Synergy*: Meeting a child's needs, for example by tackling a disability, conduct disorder or illness, may help that child and their family to avoid or move out of poverty because they find a decently paid job or move out of substandard housing. Improving a family's income or living standards may help to enhance the child's health and development. [From Chapters Seven and Eleven.]

Deciding what to do

The fifth contribution of the study in relation to children's services is to illuminate decisions regarding the mix and balance of provision. Arguably, the ideal scenario would be that all five conditions are addressed. However, resource limitations and the potential for contradictions between services driven by different concepts of child well-being require choices about orientation (whether explicit or de facto). Should efforts be concentrated on meeting need or on protecting rights (or both)? Can QoL be enhanced at the same time as tackling social exclusion? Answers to such questions inform the decision to intervene with some children and not others; in other words, to orientate the service mix towards some conditions more than others.

As already indicated, these decisions are made and adjusted by policy-makers and managers continuously, whether consciously or not. They are also influenced by moral concerns, legal imperatives, pragmatic considerations, scientific evidence and public opinion or consumer views. By attempting to highlight the different possible consequences of such decisions, this book endeavours to help those involved to think more systematically about what *should* be done and, within that, what is *possible*. For instance, while there are sound arguments for helping children in need, for instance, there are also reasons *not* to intervene despite evidence of need, just as it is defensible to assist children who are not in need (Table 12.1). Thus, moral beliefs may determine that a vulnerable child receives help to achieve healthy development, but this may prove difficult if resources are stretched. Equally, evidence of the value of primary supports and requests from families for help may underpin a decision to assist children whose health or development are satisfactory and unlikely to deteriorate.

Evaluation of the research

The results of any study must be considered in relation to the strengths and weaknesses of the research. The study reported in this book may be evaluated in respect of five features. First are the sample and method. A strength of the study is that data were collected for a sample of children representative of those living in the selected community (including 161 children from families that did not respond to the survey). Many studies, by contrast, focus on discrete groups of children defined by a particular characteristic or administrative category, which is suitable for some purposes but inadequate if the aim is to assess the nature and level of well-being in the child population. A significant proportion of the sample came from groups regarded as 'difficult to reach' in social research terms, notably minority ethnic groups and families seeking asylum. Interviewing parents and carers provided information from someone with immediate knowledge of the child's circumstances, while data from the agency files added detail and provided a check on the accuracy of the interview account. A weakness of the study, however, is that the sample does not resemble the UK child population and nor does it include children living in any kind of institution (see Chapter Eight and Appendix A). This restricts the wider applicability of the findings and makes it difficult to provide policy-makers with definitive figures regarding the prevalence and overlap of the conditions (although the results may apply to other similar neighbourhoods).

Second, the book seeks to provide relatively succinct and straightforward accounts of the various ways in which each of the concepts has been defined and measured. The advantages and disadvantages of these approaches are highlighted. In the process, the book tries to simplify some complex ideas and brings together

Table 12.1: Factors that shape decisions about providing services for children in need

Factor	(a) Reason for helping children in need	(b) Reason for not helping children in need	(c) Reason for helping children who are *not in need*
(1) Moral concerns	Children are inherently vulnerable and it is incumbent on adults/society to ensure that they achieve and maintain reasonable standards of health and development	Assistance forfeited/not earned (eg poor behaviour or failure to pay tax)	Treatment of child unacceptable, even though child has emerged unscathed (eg one-off act of violence by parent), or certain interventions considered good practice even though it is unclear how the child's health and development will benefit (eg support to express opinion)
(2) Legal imperatives	Statutory agencies required to provide services for children whose health or development is actually impaired or likely to become so without remedial assistance	Rules do not allow it (eg housing for asylum-seeking families)	Child has broken law (eg one-off crime and needs solicitor at police station)
(3) Scientific evidence	Accumulation and interaction of risk factors over time predisposes some children to social and psychological problems, but proven interventions can break these chains of effect	Condition is terminal (eg cancer) or treatment would exacerbate problem (eg removing child from family)	Primary prevention programme with entire population (eg measles, mumps and rubella vaccinations)
(4) Pragmatic considerations	Focusing on children in need is cost-effective because it means that services can be rationed and targeted	Lack of resources (eg only helping most serious cases, referring case to alternative agency)	Resources or service happen to be available (eg places at family centre)
(5) Public opinion/ consumer views	Children and families often ask for and appreciate support	Assistance refused or not sought (eg wary of service provider, under pressure from partner, alternative support available)	Family requests help, siblings of child in need helped, or child 'progresses through the ranks' (eg attended playgroup and now attends after-school club)

literature from a range of disciplines that extends beyond the traditional boundaries of much children's services research – political philosophy, development economics, medicine and environmental studies. Notwithstanding these strengths, much has been written about each concept and it was impossible to do justice to every development and shade of opinion regarding their meaning and measurement. Connected to this, the study is largely bound by an Anglo-Saxon and 'Third Way' perspective on welfare provision, particularly as regards to the service examples in Chapters Ten and Eleven.

A third strength is that the theoretical and empirical perspectives are linked by operationalising each of the concepts in relation to children. A series of dichotomous measures is applied for each condition and the results are compared. Because there is transparency about the components of the measures it is possible for others to criticise, adopt or change them as they choose. For rights, devising an empirical test and applying it to a population is a fairly novel approach, if difficult and not entirely successful; work in that area has tended to be more theoretical, legal and often polemic. The attempt to measure quantitatively the prevalence of social exclusion for children is also innovative (see also Lloyd, 2006). At the same time, the reanalysis of data collected for a separate study meant that it was not possible to apply ideal tests for the five conditions. Some decisions were consistently difficult in spite of the guidance (see Axford, 2003). This was partly because of insufficient source information. For example, more data on the *causes* of problems – in particular whether the state or another individual were to blame – would have helped with measuring rights. Similarly, extra detail about children's non-school activities and their general levels of happiness would have assisted with making judgements about their QoL, and more depth regarding children's relations with peers and professionals would have made it easier to apply the measure of social exclusion. In short, compromises were required.

Fourth, the way in which the five approaches to conceptualising child well-being are related is explored theoretically and empirically. This is valuable since they are often discussed together or referred to in the same breath without being compared. The process of comparing the concepts and conditions was handicapped, however, by a lack of directly relevant literature. Few studies have examined explicitly the relationships between either the concepts or the conditions. Consequently, it was necessary to read between the lines somewhat and rely on linking *components* of the conditions – essentially treating them as proxy measures – rather than comparing the conditions per se. For example, the relationship between QoL and social exclusion was explored in part using research findings about the emotional health (QoL) of children excluded from school (exclusion) (Chapter Seven). This approach is not entirely satisfactory but it was a case of making best use of the material available.

Fifth, the book examines the implications for services of the characteristics of the five concepts and the relationship between the conditions to which they refer. It proposes a simple theoretical framework for assessing the extent to which services for discrete but related conditions are congruent. It identifies the different styles of intervention required for tackling each condition. This helps with monitoring and evaluating the effectiveness and value of different interventions because it specifies which indicators are relevant. The study also highlights potential contradictions between services that are responding to different conditions and introduces methods to help with (a) avoiding these contradictions when designing and implementing services, or (b) deciding which condition is a priority if contradictions cannot be resolved. All this said, the book has paid insufficient attention to services. In particular, the service data were not suitable for robust empirical work on the connections between the conditions and different interventions. This was partly because the study was a snapshot; assessments of the effectiveness, synergy and complementarity of the service responses would require the analysis of follow-up data.

Taking the research forwards

Clearly the method for the study discussed in this book could be strengthened (see Appendix A). There is also a case for undertaking analysis using alternative measures of the five concepts or with a longitudinal dimension (see Axford, 2003). However, arguably the main area requiring further study concerns patterns of service provision. The analysis should focus on the extent to which there is evidence of effectiveness, accurate targeting, complementarity and synergy in relation to the five concepts. This would indicate the orientation of individual interventions and the service mix generally. A reasonable hypothesis is that the 'centre of gravity' of children's services shifts depending on the relative strength of the factors that shape policy. For example, moral concerns and the consumer perspective are arguably inclined to make services more rights-orientated, whereas the pragmatic and scientific influences favour a needs-led approach. Particular attention would be paid to how far the appropriate kind of intervention reaches children with certain conditions. Do children in need receive need-orientated interventions? And what proportion of them get help? Following that, outcomes could be measured in terms of the five conditions. This would indicate whether the service response was better at tackling some conditions than others. For example, it might become apparent that children's rights are being protected, but that many children still have a poor QoL. Pursuing these avenues would also improve the understanding of whether services to improve child well-being are contradicting one another or working in tandem.

Conclusion

This book began by observing the growth of concern in children's services with child well-being and arguing that this risks overlooking the fact that child 'ill-being' has long been a cause for concern, albeit conceptualised in several different ways, including unmet need, violated rights, poverty, poor QoL and social exclusion. Each condition has its distinguishing features (Chapters Two to Seven) but overlaps with the others to varying degrees (Chapters Seven and Nine). Because they are different, the services required to tackle each one also require different orientations, despite the synergy that sometimes exists between them (Chapters Ten and Eleven). Used carefully, therefore, *all five* concepts can act as useful lenses through which to view and understand children's well-being, and so, hopefully, inform improved services. By implication, it is unhelpful if different concepts become the preserve of particular professions, or if policy-makers (and managers and researchers) abandon one in favour of another. It may not be possible for children's services provision to be driven by all five simultaneously because of the tensions that exist between them, and if the overriding focus is on improving children's health and development – as it is in many service settings – then arguably need is king. But together the different ways of conceptualising child well-being potentially help to inform a rich service mix, and to lose any perspective is to see a little less clearly. There is still much work to be done in terms of defining and measuring the conditions and in order to understand better the requirements of services for tackling them. However, the ideas and findings presented here have made a contribution to the field and may be used practically. It is the contention of this book that developing these ideas and pursuing the avenues for further research identified earlier will help to improve outcomes – however they are defined – for vulnerable children and their families.

Notes

[1] The dataset contains various possible indicators for each of the three interpretations. The proxy variables selected here for illustrative purposes are 'unemployed', 'petty crime' and 'poverty' respectively (see Appendix A).

[2] There are a handful of exceptions, for example children in need were over nine times more likely than other children to be socially excluded (relative risk ratio = 9.310, $p<0.05$).

Appendix A
Method

The dataset

Since practical constraints meant that it was not possible to collect primary data of the nature and volume required, an existing source was sought instead. A range of options were assessed against five considerations. First, the dataset needed to have children as the unit of analysis, with information relating to them directly. Second, it was considered desirable to have information on children of all ages, that is 0–17 years (in line with the England and Wales 1989 Children Act). Third, data were sought that pertain to a cross-section of children living in the community, since this would provide insights into the extent of and relationship between the conditions in society. Fourth, it was evident that examining children living in a discrete neighbourhood would have significant merits (particularly for measuring QoL and social exclusion). Fifth, there should be data on risk and protective factors in all areas of the child's life, and also some evidence of contact with and use of services (the latter is valuable for judging the violation of a child's rights).

In light of these criteria it was decided not to use datasets that:

- are based on households or that assign children the classification given to the reference person;
- focus on a subset of children in specified school years, or draw the divide between children and adults at 15/16 years, or track a cohort of children born in a particular week;
- only include children in contact with service agencies;
- are restricted to a national picture; or
- focus exclusively on either child development (thereby omitting information on interventions) or process (most such studies are weak on child development).

Instead, it was decided to reanalyse data from phase one of *Children Supported and Unsupported in the Community* – a study funded by the UK Department of Health and conducted by Dartington Social Research Unit (Axford et al, 2003). This was an exploratory study aimed at providing evidence on the nature of need among children in the community, the extent to which they and their families use children's services and how these agencies, together with coping strategies, affect children's development. An added advantage of this source was that the author was joint lead researcher on the study and therefore very familiar with the data from having been closely involved in all stages of the work.

The dataset contains information on 689 children and their families living on a moderately deprived and ethnically diverse inner-city housing estate in London. This represents 62% of the 1,116 children estimated to have lived on the estate at the time. Tests indicate that although the sample is not representative of children in England and Wales, it is representative of all children on the estate (measured in terms of age, first language and number of children resident). Data were collected in the period April-July 1998 and covered the child's situation at the time as well as providing a retrospective view of the previous year. In most cases (528 children) the main source was the child's principal carer, from whom information was gathered by way of one-hour semi-structured interviews. The sample was boosted by 161 other children from the estate; data on these children were collected from social services and education welfare files using a separate schedule. The two data collection instruments covered the same topics:

- risk and protective factors in different areas of the child's life;[1]
- coping strategies used by the child and their family to address difficulties; and
- interactions with a number of children's services agencies.

Details of the study aims and method are now provided.

The study from which data are drawn

The study *Children Supported and Unsupported in the Community* was funded by the UK Department of Health and conducted by Dartington Social Research Unit between 1998 and 2003. Data were collected from two sites: one in inner-city London (1998 and 2000/01), the other a small town in Devon (2001). This book uses data from the first phase of data collection in the London site (London 1). Reports on the full study and on work in each site are available from the Research Unit (Axford et al, 1999, 2001, 2003). This Appendix focuses on London 1.

Study aims

The study had five aims:

(1) to gather from representative community samples empirical evidence on patterns of need in all areas of the child's life;
(2) to explore why some children come to the attention of children's services while others do not;
(3) to chart patterns of service take-up and manner of contact;
(4) to analyse strategies used by families to cope with children's needs and to draw out messages to inform the planning of children's services; and

(5)   to compare outcomes for different patterns of need, taking into account different combinations and amounts of services and the presence and operation of coping strategies.

Study site

A neighbourhood in a London borough was selected based on the Research Unit's links with local health, education and social services departments. It was felt that this opportunistic approach would ease access to administrative data held by the agencies and that the evidence emerging from the study stood a good chance of being used to benefit the community concerned. Using Office for National Statistics (ONS) classifications (see Wallace and Denham, 1996) the borough counts as 'Inner-London' and, according to 1991 Census data, ranked 12th out of 366 districts in England on the *Townsend Deprivation Index* (Gordon and Forrest, 1995).

Within the borough the focus was on a well-defined estate comprising eight enumeration districts (six from one ward and two from another). The estate comprises 1,461 flats and maisonettes in high- and low-rise developments, and lies between a motorway and a railway line. In terms of provision for children and families there are easy-access, low-intensity social services alongside traditional health and education interventions.

Representativeness of the study site

It is evident from Table A1 that the study site was not representative of the sociodemographic profile of the national child population. For example, the proportion of people from a minority ethnic group was much higher in the study site (48%) than in England and Wales as a whole (8%).[2] Similarly, a quarter of the children (26%) lived in lone-parent households compared with a tenth (10%) nationally. Clearly these discrepancies present challenges for applying the results to broader populations.

Sampling technique

A Census approach was taken to building a sample in that the study sought to obtain information on every household in the study site with resident children. This was done by way of (a) a community survey and (b) an examination of local children's services' agency files. There were two stages to the survey. In the first, the estate was screened to identify households with children. Data were collected on the number of children resident, the ages of those children and the family's first language. As well as identifying participants for the study, this provided one check on whether or not the final sample was representative of the community. In the second stage of the survey interviews were conducted with the principal

Table A1: Sociodemographic data for the study site and for England and Wales[a]

	Study site %	England and Wales %
Minority ethnic group	48	8
Unemployed as a proportion of economically active	25	9
Adults suffering long-term limiting illness	18	15
Owner-occupied households	13	69
Children in lone-parent households[b]	26	10

Notes:

[a] Based on 1991 Census information. The study site data are based on Small Area Statistics. The eight enumeration districts on which they are based are not precisely coterminous with the neighbourhood.
[b] This figure is for children aged 0–15 years only.

carer in the household.[3] In relation to the agency files, data were sought on any child living on the estate during the fieldwork period (April-July 1998).

Several strategies were pursued in order to secure a good response rate in the survey. First, households were visited at different times of the day and week; in some cases up to 20 attempts were made to find someone at home. Second, where it was available, up-to-date information about residency was obtained from the local housing office. Third, attention was paid to the length and content of data collection instruments and to interviewer training. Fourth, advance publicity, conversations with local professionals and cash incentives (£5 per interview) were used to inform local people about the study and to allay any concerns that they might have had.

Response rate

The response rate for screening was very high (99%): information was unavailable for just 16 out of the 1,461 households. Two fifths of the dwellings (*N*=581) contained children. Interviews were obtained in 265 of these (46%), producing information on 528 children. The work on social services and education welfare files generated data on 301 children: this included 145 who were also in the community survey sample, and 161 additional cases. Altogether, then, data were gathered on 689 children, or three fifths (62%) of the 1,116 children estimated from screening to be living on the estate.

Sociodemographic profile of the sample

The sample split almost evenly between boys (49%) and girls (51%) and the age profile mirrored that for the national child population (Table A2). Exactly half of the children lived with a lone parent, and over two fifths (43%) were in two-parent households. Overall there were 1.95 children per household. In most cases there were no more than three children resident, but 22% of the sample lived in households with four or more children. The majority of the children's families had been resident in the area for two or more years, but a quarter (24%) had lived there for less time, with 7% resident for under six months. Almost every child (97%) lived in rented accommodation, and two thirds (66%) came from families that were dependent on benefits. As for ethnicity, in 57% of cases English was the second language in the child's household, with the main first languages (after English) being Arabic (20%), Somali (5%), Spanish (4%) and Farsi and Eritrean (both 3%). A quarter of the children (24%) lived in families that had been forced to flee their home country by war or oppression.

Representativeness of the sample

Notwithstanding the difficulties of obtaining comparable data, Table A2 contrasts selected sociodemographic characteristics for the $N=689$ sample with the children in both the London borough in which the work took place and the country as a whole. The sample resembles the profile of the borough and the country on several characteristics, but especially age and the proportion of households where adults are unemployed. Otherwise it is quite different, particularly in relation to rates of overcrowding, tenure and households headed by a lone parent.

The sample is representative, however, of the children living on the estate where the study took place. This was ascertained by using screening data to compare the households on whom data were obtained from the principal carer or agency files (the $N=689$ sample) with those where children were resident but no such data were gathered.[4] Table A3 shows that, broadly speaking, the sample resembles all households with children in terms of number of children resident, the ages of those children, and whether or not the family's first language is English. Families with three or more children resident or children aged 6-11 years are slightly overrepresented, while children aged over 16 years are underrepresented ($p<0.05$).

Data sources

As has already been mentioned, data were collected from two main sources: interviews with the child's principal carer, and agency files. The rationale for this was threefold.

First, it allowed a rich picture of each child's situation and past experiences to be assembled. For example, the carer accounts proved particularly strong on the child's living situation, health and behaviour, while the case files offered helpful insights into the primary reason for contact with the agency, the immediate outputs of the intervention and, in some cases, the historical background to a family's difficulties.

Table A2: A comparison of the study site, the borough and the national picture

Characteristic	Study area (April–July 1998)	Borough (1991 Census)	National picture
Age			
0–4	29%	33%	28%[c]
5–9	28%	27%	29%
10–15	33%	30%	33%
16–17	9%	10%	10%
Children per household	1.95	1.7	1.48[d]
Overcrowded households	27%[a]	5%	3%[e]
Unemployment	21%[b]	26%	24%[f]
Children living in lone-parent families	50%	21%	20%[g]
Rented accommodation	97%	61%	33%[h]

[a] Proportion of households in *N*=689 sample that were overcrowded (defined as >1.5 people per room, not including kitchen and bathroom).
[b] Proportion of households in *N*=689 sample where one or both carers are unemployed.
[c] UK 1997.
[d] Great Britain 1996–97.
[e] England 1996–97.
[f] Great Britain 1993.
[g] Great Britain 1995–96.
[h] UK 1996–97.

Sources: RBKC (1993); CSO (1994); ONS (1997, 1998)

Second, where data were available from two sources it was possible to assess the accuracy of reporting by carers and practitioners. Triangulating different sources in this way helped to build confidence in the data. However, while accounts were usually complementary, with one fleshing out a point to which the other merely alluded, occasionally they were contradictory. When this happened the interview version was selected. This was partly because parents are more likely to have intimate knowledge of their child's situation. It was also because agency records tend to be assembled to obtain information about the presenting problem, and because most families' contact with children's services is fleeting.

Third, collecting data from agency files helped to boost the size of the sample. Thus, the profile of the overall sample was as follows. For the majority of children (*N*=528), data were collected from parents and/or other carers talking about their children. Further information was gathered from social services (*N*=277) and education welfare (the service responsible for monitoring and addressing periods of unauthorised absence from school) (*N*=45). The overlap between these sources is set out in Table A4. For example, there was information on 130 children from

Table A3: Representativeness of households in the *N*=689 sample[a]

	Households in *N*=689 sample (%)	Households with children not in sample (%)	All households with children (%)
Number of children			
1	46	49	47
2	27	34	29
3+	28	18	24
p=0.029			
Children aged 0–5 years			
Yes	52	45	49
No	48	56	51
p=0.143			
Children aged 6–11 years			
Yes	52	42	49
No	48	58	51
p=0.033			
Children aged 12–16 years			
Yes	40	37	39
No	61	63	61
p=0.570			
Children aged 17 years			
Yes	8	18	12
No	92	82	89
p=0.001			
First language English			
Yes	45	40	43
No	55	61	57
p=0.273			

Note: [a] All figures are column percentages, for example 46% of households in the *N*=689 sample have one child only. Due to rounding up, the figures do not always add up to 100%. The *p* values were calculated using the chi-square test for two or more unrelated samples (see Bryman and Cramer, 1997, pp 124-7).

both interviews and social services records (row 4), and for 10 children information was available from these *plus* education welfare (row 7).

Data collection instruments

The London 1 wave of data collection used two data collection instruments: a parent interview schedule for the community survey, and an agency schedule for gathering information from case files. Both sought to elicit information on

Table A4: Sources of data

	Source	Number of children	%
1	Interview (I)	383	56
2	Social services department (SSD)	131	19
3	Education welfare officer (EWO)	24	3
4	I + SSD	130	19
5	I + EWO	5	1
6	SSD + EWO	6	1
7	I + SSD + EWO	10	1
Total		689	100

all children (0-17 years) resident in a household, as well as on the parents/carers and, to a lesser extent, other relatives. The focus was on the child's situation in the period April–July 1998, although information was also collected about developments over the previous year.

The parent schedule covered four areas:

• sociodemographic characteristics (including financial situation);
• risk and protective factors in six domains (living situation, family and social relationships, social and antisocial behaviour, physical and psychological health, education/employment, and financial situation);
• coping strategies; and
• service take-up.

There was a mixture of structured questions designed to produce objective information on the child's situation, and more open-ended questions aimed at eliciting carers' views about their lives and the lives of their children. Data collection needs were prioritised so that a standard interview could be completed in one hour.

The instrument used for collecting data from agency files comprised the same broad sections but required the researcher to record data in a mostly qualitative format using an aide memoire to ensure that the main constructs were covered. The instrument borrowed heavily from a qualitative method designed by Dartington Social Research Unit (1999) for collecting administrative data.

Data collection process

The community survey took place between April and July 1998. All interviews were conducted in the homes of respondents by researchers (10 in total) trained to use the interview schedule. Where necessary, interpreters were used in the languages of Arabic, Somali, Spanish and Portuguese. Data were collected from agency files by two researchers in September 1999.

Ethics

Potential ethical concerns surrounding the study were addressed in line with recommended good practice (eg DH, 2001c; SRA, 2002). The first main issue was informed participant consent. Respondents were required to complete a consent form prior to being interviewed. This dealt with the treatment of data revealed during an interview as well as access to records held by children's services agencies. Participants were told how the information would be stored, what it would be used for and by whom, and that they would have a right to see the information gathered about them.

The second issue concerned the advantages and disadvantages for subjects of participating in the research. It was argued that participation in the study was voluntary, and that in time the data collected should help to improve children's services and so benefit some of the participants and/or their families. Where a respondent appeared to be in need of support from children's services the interviewers were permitted to make a referral to the relevant agency (via the lead researchers and with the respondent's consent). In addition, each participant in the community survey was given £5 as a token of thanks for their participation.

The third main area covered in the ethics assessment was confidentiality. All data were recorded anonymously, and completed carer and agency schedules were stored under lock and key at the offices of the Research Unit. Only staff associated with the study had access to the data.

Devising and applying the measures

For each of the five main concepts considered in this book it was necessary to devise a dichotomous measure that would discriminate between children with the condition and those without it. In order to take into account different approaches to defining and measuring each concept, 24 measures were used in total – several for each concept (see next section). They were applied to the dataset by hand using a decision-making instrument that was designed to help the coder (the author) identify and then connect logically important pieces of information regarding each child's situation. The data had been transferred from the carer and agency schedules and summarised for each child on a specially designed form. Accompanying guidance written by the author outlined the relevant factors to consider for each concept and the instrument included space for recording the rationale behind each judgement. Samples of the decision-making instrument, a summary form and guidance can be found in the PhD thesis that this book is based on (Axford, 2003, App B).

Just over a third of the children (*N*=234) were judged against the five concepts using this decision-making instrument and the summary forms. A sample of this size was deemed to be sufficiently large for the statistical procedures used in analysis, and, since the decision-making process itself required exhaustive analysis of each case, it would not have been feasible with the given time and resources to apply the measures to all children in the dataset. The demographic profile of the subsample is described in Chapter Eight of this book but here it can be stated that the subsample is broadly representative of the 689 children in terms of demographic characteristics and data sources (Table A5). More specifically, it resembles all 689 children in terms of gender, age, who the child lives with, benefit dependency and leaving a country because of war or oppression. Children living in families where English is not the first language, or that have four or more children resident, or that have lived in the area for 10 or more years are slightly overrepresented ($p<0.05$). The sample is not representative in terms of source, with cases in which data were obtained from files overrepresented ($p<0.001$).

From measures to analysis

Having applied 24 measures to the data (see Table A6 for details) it was necessary to select one measure per concept for the main part of the analysis. The five that were chosen can be summarised as follows:

Need	the child has actual impairment to their health or development (which includes behaviour and education) [need1]
Rights	the child is a victim of a *serious* violation of any of their rights to provision, protection or participation; for example, rape, assault, abuse, war/oppression, victim of official negligence or poor practice [rights2]
Poverty	the child lives in a low-income household *and* has poor living standards (including substandard accommodation, a lack of basic items, few/no leisure opportunities, and money problems) [poverty3]
QoL	the child has poor objective circumstances (including poor living standards, ill-health, fractious relationships and little enrichment) *and* displays a negative subjective outlook (signs of being anxious, unhappy or distressed) [qol3]
Social exclusion	the child's ties to all four of the following spheres are attenuated or ruptured: economic, domestic/interpersonal, social/civil and political/civic [sx6]

Why were these five measures selected out of the 24 possible options? There is statistical support for the choice of *all* of the measures, which correlate highly (>0.7) or moderately (0.4-0.7) with at least one other measure of the same concept (Table A7). Coefficients range from a high of 0.954 ($p<0.01$) between qol3 and qol2 (distress, anxiety or unhappiness) to 0.416 ($p<0.01$) between sx6 and sx3 (ruptured or attenuated links to any two of: work/school, family, community and peers). More importantly, for three of the concepts the choice of measure was mainly theory-driven: poverty is best measured in terms of the living standards that are attainable given available resources; QoL has both

Table A5: Representativeness of the *N*=234 sample[a]

	Children in *N*=234 sample (%)	Other children (%)	Children in *N*=689 sample (%)
Gender			
Male	46	50	49
Female	54	50	51
p=0.308			
Age			
0–4 years	26	31	29
5–9 years	29	28	28
10–15 years	33	33	33
16–17 years	11	8	9
p=0.438			
Who child lives with			
Lone parent	53	49	50
Two parents	42	43	43
Other	5	8	7
p=0.305			
Carer's first language			
English	37	46	43
Not English	63	54	57
p=0.024			
Number of children resident			
1	23	24	24
2	29	26	27
3	23	31	28
4+	26	20	22
p=0.083			
How long family resident in area			
<6 months	10	6	10
6 months–	16	21	19
2 years–	19	19	19
5 years–	22	30	28
10+ years	33	24	27
p=0.028			
Family benefit-dependent			
Yes	68	5	6
No	32	35	34
p=0.457			
Family forced to flee home country by war/oppression			
Yes	26	23	24
No	74	77	76
p=0.481			
Data source			
Interview only	40	59	52
Agency file only	28	21	23
Interview and agency file	32	21	25
p=0.000			

Note: [a] All figures are column percentages, for example, 46% of children in the *N*=234 sample were male. Due to rounding up, the figures do not always add up to 100%. The *p* values were calculated using the chi-square test for two or more unrelated samples (see Bryman and Cramer, 1997, pp 124–7).

objective and *subjective* elements; and since social exclusion involves a somewhat catastrophic rupture of the social link it makes sense to require that all four social ties be at least attenuated. In relation to need and rights, however, scientific and pragmatic reasons accounted for the preferred measures being discarded in favour of alternatives. Using the measure 'impair', which concerns actual and likely impairment to health or development, 84% of the sample were deemed to be 'in need'. Subsequent analysis on other datasets using a firmed-up protocol for measuring impairment (Little et al, 2003) indicates lower levels of need, which can be explained mainly by a previously overgenerous interpretation of 'likely'. In other words, children were identified here as having *likely* impairment when on re-examination impairment was, at most, *possible*. Thus, the actual measure selected for need draws on the first part of the definition of 'in need' given in Chapter Two, namely *actual* impairment to health or development. For rights, it was decided to select the highest possible threshold on the assumption that there would be broad consensus that cases identified using this measure do constitute 'violations'; the data for determining rights violations were not ideal, which is not helpful given that they would be needed to support the contentious claim, using the purist measure from a theoretical perspective, that 81% of children were suffering the violation of their rights. For rights, then, the chosen measure sticks to the principles underpinning the preferred measure ('rights1') but refers only to *serious* violations.

Evaluation of the method

The method has strengths and weaknesses relating to the dataset and the analysis. The first strength is that the dataset contains good-quality information on nearly two thirds (62%) of the children on the estate. The community survey only covered 47% of cases, but this is still reasonable given that the neighbourhood presented characteristics widely recognised as contributing to low response rates in social surveys, notably high population density and significant proportions of economically deprived households, minority ethnic families and tenants (de Vaus, 1996). The sample is also a representative cross-section of local families: on a range of criteria – age, first language and number of children in the household – there were no significant differences between the characteristics of households in the sample and other households with children in the neighbourhood. Nor were there any distinctive characteristics among those families refusing to be interviewed. (Agency data on the 161 children whose parents were *not* interviewed revealed that they did not differ in any significant way demographically from children whose parents consented to be interviewed. There were few cases where a parent's or carer's refusal to participate could obviously be attributed to the child's circumstances.) The sample also includes a significant number of 'difficult-to-research' and potentially excluded groups, such as asylum seekers and recipients of intensive assistance from social services.

Table A6: How the concepts were measured (24 measures)

Concept	Theory	Components	Test	Threshold
Need	A child is in need if their health or development are actually or likely to be impaired (England and Wales 1989 Children Act)	(a) *Actual impairment*: problems with health, behaviour, education or development	need1	Evidence of *actual* impairment to health or development (includes behaviour and education)
		(b) *Likely impairment*: maltreatment, poor parenting or a poor environment	need2	Evidence of circumstances in which impairment to health or development is *likely* (either in existence but not recorded, or likely in the near future unless remedial action is taken)
			impair	Evidence of *actual* or *likely* impairment (or both)
	Doyal and Gough (1991) argue that the two universal *basic* needs are physical health and autonomy. Unmet *intermediate* needs – for adequate protective housing, adequate nutritional food and water, a non-hazardous physical environment etc – will be manifested as unmet basic needs. These in turn result in social harm, namely the fundamental and sustained impairment of social participation	Physical health (a) Physical health problem (b) Physical disability Autonomy (c) Mental health problem (d) Lack of learning/cognitive skills (e) Lack of socially meaningful opportunities	need3	Evidence of impaired *physical health* or restricted *autonomy* (or both)

Note: Measures that are shaded were used in the study.

continued

Table A6: continued

Concept	Theory	Components	Test	Threshold
Rights	Children have rights to protection, provision and participation – the 3 Ps (1991 UN Convention on the Rights of the Child)	(a) Standards under any of the 3 Ps have not been upheld, whether by the state (eg failure of social worker to take account of child's voice) or another person (eg child abused by father)	rights1	A violation of any of the 3 Ps
			rights2	*A serious violation of any of the 3 Ps (eg rape/ assault/abuse, chronic living standards, war/political oppression, victim of official negligence/poor practice)*
		(b) Cases where the breached standard is down to misfortune (eg an accident), genetic make-up (eg illness) or the child's own will (eg deciding not to attend school) do not count	rights3	Two or more of the 3 Ps violated
	Parts of the children's rights literature highlight sociodemographic groups that are arguably discriminated against on a routine basis. The implication is that the rights of all children in these groups are infringed	(a) Minority ethnic groups (b) Travellers (c) Looked-after children (d) Lone-parent families (e) Asylum seekers/immigrants (f) Children with physical/mental disabilities/ SEN (g) Children with caring responsibilities (h) Pregnant teenagers	rights4	Child is a member of any of the listed sociodemographic groups

Note: Measures that are shaded were used in the study.

continued

Table A6: continued

Concept	Theory	Components	Test	Threshold
Poverty	Poverty can be measured directly – in terms of *living standards* – or indirectly – in terms of *income* (Ringen, 1987). Some studies employ a measure of poverty that combines low income *and* poor living standards (eg Peter Townsend's *Poverty in the UK*, 1979).	(a) *Low income*: receipt of social assistance (below most standard poverty measures – 50% average income, budget standards etc) or low wages	poverty1	Evidence of low income, whether *actual* (eg benefit-dependent) or *highly likely* given carer's sociodemographic status (eg unemployed lone parent)
		(b) *Poor living standards*: substandard housing, lack of basics/leisure opportunities, money problems	poverty2	Evidence of poor living standards
	The argument for using a combination is that some people with low incomes have high living standards (eg alternative sources of money/provision) while some people experience material hardship but have decent incomes that they use for other purposes (eg to pay off debts or gamble)		poverty3	Evidence of both low income and poor living standards
	Households dependent on basic social assistance are highly likely to have an income that is less than both the 50% average income line and a low cost but acceptable budget standard (see eg Parker, 1999)	Child lives in a household dependent on basic social assistance or a proportion thereof (eg asylum-seeking families do not receive full social assistance)	poverty4	Evidence that child lives in a household dependent on basic social assistance or a proportion thereof

Note: Measures that are shaded were used in the study.

continued

Table A6: continued

Concept	Theory	Components	Test	Threshold
Quality of life	Quality of life is usually measured in terms of a person's *objective circumstances* and/or their *subjective outlook*. This reflects the substantive good and preference/hedonist conceptions of a 'good life'. The argument for combining the two is that neither a happy peasant nor miserable millionaire can be said to have a poor quality of life	(a) *Objective circumstances*: evidence of poor living standards, ill-health, fractious relationships, little enrichment (eg clubs, outings, parks)	qol1	Child's objective circumstances are poor
			qol2	Child's subjective outlook is negative
		(b) *Subjective outlook*: evidence of distress, anxiety or unhappiness; this could be direct (eg 'child cries a lot') or indirect – in the sense that the child's behaviour is indicative of distress etc (eg 'child withdrawn and panicky')	qol3	Poor objective circumstances and negative subjective outlook
	Quality of life can also be conceived of in terms of the things that *enrich* a person's life, that is, elevate it above the hum-drum of daily existence	No extra-curricular activities (eg clubs, outings, parks)	qol4	Evidence that the child does not enjoy any extra-curricular activities

Note: Measures that are shaded were used in the study.

continued

Table A6: continued

Concept	Theory	Components	Test	Threshold
Social exclusion	Social exclusion can be defined in terms of detachment from mainstream society, usually as a result of the accumulation of multidimensional disadvantage (eg Berghman, 1995; Jordan, 1996; Room, 1999). A child becomes vulnerable to social exclusion when their social links are either *ruptured* (eg separation from family, exclusion from school, permanently at home) or *attenuated* (eg poor relationship with parents, truancy or disaffection with school, only mixing with delinquent peers). How this is measured depends on how inclusion is defined, ie what spheres of activity make up children's participation in society (two options are presented here)	(a) *School/work*: not attending school/work (or other age-appropriate option) or attending but disengaged	sx1	*Ruptured* social links in all four spheres
		(b) *Family*: no/minimal contact or poor relations with family and/or family is an insecure base	sx2	*Attenuated* social links in all four spheres
		(c) *Community*: involvement in community activities minimal or purely antisocial/criminal	sx3	Ruptured or attenuated social links in two or more spheres
		(d) *Peers*: no/minimal contact or poor relations with peers	sx4	Ruptured or attenuated social links in one or more spheres
		(a) *Economic*: low income/poor living standards and/or not at age-appropriate school/work option	sx5	*Ruptured* social links in all four spheres
		(b) *Domestic/interpersonal*: no contact/poor relations with family/peers	sx6	*Attenuated* social links in all four spheres
		(c) *Social/civil*: no activities and/or no connection with appropriate services	sx7	Ruptured or attenuated social links in two or more spheres
		(d) *Political/civic*: frequent movement/temporary unsettled residence/poor relations with teachers, professionals or employers	sx8	Ruptured or attenuated social links in one or more spheres

Note: Measures that are shaded were used in the study.

Table A7: How the selected measures correlate with alternative measures (*N*=234)

Selected test	Alternative tests	Correlation coefficient[a, b]
need1	need2	0.195***
	impair	0.365***
	need3	0.800***
rights2	rights1	0.411***
	rights3	0.451***
	rights4	−0.046
poverty3	poverty1	0.782***
	poverty2	0.647***
	poverty4	0.517***
qol3	qol1	0.246***
	qol2	0.954***
	qol4	0.137**
sx6	sx1	−0.017
	sx2	0.150**
	sx3	0.416***
	sx4	0.254***
	sx5	–
	sx7	0.279***
	sx8	0.081*

[a] The *phi* coefficient is suitable for measuring associations between nominal variables and two-by-two tables. It is calculated as the square root of chi-square divided by *N* and generates a value between 0 and 1. A score between 0 and 0.3 signifies a weak association, 0.4–0.7 is moderate and any value over 0.8 indicates a strong correlation.
[b] Significance levels are indicated by asterisks as follows: $p<0.10$*, $p<0.05$** and $p<0.01$***.

A related weakness, however, is that no adequate data could be obtained from the children's home or the Travellers' site that were located on the estate. Access to the former proved difficult, and the Travellers were unwilling to be interviewed individually. This was particularly unfortunate in relation to the measurement of social exclusion. Further, the somewhat distinctive sociodemographic profile of the estate (Chapter Nine) presents challenges when applying the results since the data cannot be regarded as representative of the situation in England and Wales.

The second advantage of the dataset is that information was derived from different sources. As well as providing information on non-respondents in the community survey this helped to generate more comprehensive accounts of children's lives. The parent/carer accounts were particularly strong on the child's living situation, health and behaviour. Agency records were less comprehensive, partly because practitioners tend to focus on the presenting problem and also because most families' contact with children's services is fleeting. Even so, they contained good information on the reason for coming forward for professional help, the nature of the intervention and, in some cases, the historical background to a family's difficulty. Moreover, while different accounts were occasionally contradictory, one source invariably fleshed out what another alluded to; they complemented each other. For example, in one case the interview ascertained the following information, none of which was recorded on the social services file: the need for refurbishment of the child's home; the reasons for the child's exclusion from school; and the mother's physical health problems. The file was stronger on historical information such as the mother's alcohol misuse and the child's drug misuse.

There are some concerns about the reliability of some of the data, however. In particular, the child's perspective is glaring by its omission. This was a handicap especially when seeking to measure QoL (where subjective feelings are crucial), and more generally it contributes to the inevitable distortion of the child's actual circumstances since the information is filtered via a carer/agency and is thus second- or even third-hand. Checks were made during the fieldwork to ensure that the interview and agency schedules were being completed consistently, and safeguards were in place to minimise the distortion or loss of crucial information. However, such measures are never infallible.

A third strength is that the dataset contained a sufficiently wide array of data that measures could be formulated and applied for each concept. For example, evidence on risk and protective factors in all areas of the children's lives (health/ development, family relations and the wider environment) were used to measure need. The data on how children were treated by third parties (individuals and agencies) were adapted to help with assessing violations of rights. The less comprehensive information on money and living standards was used to create recognisable indicators of poverty. Variables that offer some insight into the child's subjective outlook were combined with qualitative comments about extra-curricular activities to capture QoL. And data on apparently tangential topics such as length of residence were used creatively as proxy indicators for aspects of social exclusion.

Even so, the validity of some of the data might have been higher. The dearth of standardised questions and psychometric scales proved a limitation and may explain why the some of the findings on children's health did not tally with reliable epidemiological sources (levels of emotional problems in particular appeared to be underreported). It is also known that there were instances where respondents misunderstood questions or struggled to give articulate answers, and some difficulties arose from mistranslation. In addition, only two agencies were included as sources; a fuller picture of the neighbourhood and the lives of children living there would have been gained by tapping information from schools, health and voluntary providers.

The fourth benefit of the method concerns the consistency with which the judgements of child well-being were made. Every judgement was reviewed for accuracy and to make sure that all salient information had been considered. In addition, a second opinion was obtained on one in 10 cases (23 children) and discrepancies between judgements highlighted. Some judgements were revised in the light of these checks. When the judgements were inputted onto an SPSS database and the sample was split in half (alternate children), tests using the chi-square statistic for two or more unrelated samples indicated that the decision-making was consistent throughout the sample – the so-called 'split-half test' (see Bryman and Cramer, 1997, pp 124-7). In other words, for each measure the proportion of children in the one half who were affected was compared with the proportion in the other half who also scored positively on the measure. The results are set out in Table A8. None of the *p* values is significant at even 0.10, indicating that there is no significant difference between the two halves of the dataset on any measure. This indicates that every measure was applied consistently.

A related drawback with the method, however, was that the measures were quite complex and therefore time-consuming to apply. Each judgement required that all aspects of the child's situation be considered systematically, and for each measure different pieces of information needed to be linked in a particular sequence. To assist with this, and to improve consistency, it was necessary to tighten the guidance, thereby leaving less room for different interpretations of the same information. Details of some of the nuances of the decision-making are given in the thesis that this book is based on (Axford, 2003, App H). There would also be merits in using factor analysis to help simplify the structure of the measures, and also in checking their internal consistency.

A fifth strength is that the analysis made full use of qualitative *and* quantitative data. The former were crucial for applying the measures to each individual. This was partly because the raw data retained their colour and detail, but also because using paper forms made it easier to examine evidence from multiple sources and to visualise connections. This approach also helped with weighing up the many factors affecting each child (in some respects asking a computer to think like this is much harder). The quantitative data aided the exploration of the aggregate picture. For every child, information on the 60 variables, together with the judgements on all five concept measures, were inputted onto an SPSS database. Subsequent statistical analysis assisted with identifying the prevalence and distinguishing features of the conditions to which the concepts refer, as well as elucidating the relationships between them.

A problem, however, is that although the measures for the present study were formulated to exploit the available data fully, their content was constrained by virtue of reanalysing information collected for another purpose. Future work in this area would therefore benefit from collecting primary data that relate more closely to chosen measures (rather than fitting measures to the available data). In particular:

Table A8: Split-half test on all measures for children in the *N*=234 sample

Measure	Half 1 (%)	Half 2 (%)	*N*=234 sample (%)
need1 *p*=0.562	37	41	39
need2 *p*=0.315	82	77	79
need3 *p*=0.731	43	45	44
impair *p*=0.723	85	83	84
rights1 *p*=0.246	84	78	81
rights2 *p*=0.894	42	41	42
rights3 *p*=0.351	39	45	42
rights4 *p*=0.617	94	92	93
poverty1 *p*=0.623	74	71	73
poverty2 *p*=0.141	84	76	80
poverty3 *p*=0.119	66	56	61
poverty4 *p*=0.508	70	66	68
qol1 *p*=0.287	86	81	84
qol2 *p*=0.791	24	26	25
qol3 *p*=0.791	24	23	23
qol4 *p*=0.741	34	32	33
sx1 *p*=0.318	0	<1	<1
sx2 *p*=0.479	3	4	4
sx3 *p*=0.701	29	27	28
sx4 *p*=0.181	55	46	51

continued

Table A8: *(continued)*

Measure	Half 1 (%)	Half 2 (%)	N=234 sample (%)
sx5[a]	–	–	–
sx6 p=0.987	6	6	6
sx7 p=0.184	50	41	46
sx8 p=0.835	91	91	91

Note: [a] No children scored positively on this measure.

- Psychometric scales and standard questions from national surveys would help with generating more reliable information on sensitive matters such as relationships, domestic violence and abuse, and assist with capturing need (impaired health or development in relation to normative patterns) and QoL (children's emotional state).

- Orthodox poverty indicators based on net disposable household income after housing costs, receipt of benefits (possibly via official records) and the ability to afford socially perceived necessities would assist with identifying *core* poverty.

- Structured social histories based on a list of potentially stressful life events would help with measuring all concepts, but particularly rights (for example, victim of crime, forced to escape war/oppression), QoL (for example, problems with neighbours, sudden health problem) and social exclusion (for example, redundancy, changing school).

- Additional detail on families' interactions with a wider range of children's services would make it easier to judge the violation of rights (how children have been treated given their entitlements) and social exclusion (the tie to basic services). For example, there are numerous providers besides social services, health, education and the police (those included in the study) and for each contact it would be helpful to know: whether the individual or the agency made the initial approach; if an agency rejected requests for assistance; the nature of the intervention; and the benefits and side-effects of the service.

- Obtaining information directly from children about aspects of their lives with which parents/agencies are perhaps less familiar – notably conditions and pay at work, emotional state, peer relations, and participation in recreational activities and civic/political affairs – would help with measuring all concepts, but particularly rights, QoL and social exclusion.

- A longitudinal element is necessary in order to trace historical patterns of continuity and discontinuity in the child's life and also to make accurate prognoses of life trajectories. This information would help with measuring need (*likely* impairment to health or development), QoL (how the present compares with past experiences) and social exclusion (entrenched disadvantage).

Conclusion

Notwithstanding the difficulties encountered, it is evident from this Appendix that it was possible to ascertain the prevalence of all five conditions for a sample of children living in the community. Chapters Eight and Nine in this book present the findings. It is important at this juncture to stress that the empirical part of the study is by no means a definitive statement regarding the prevalence of and relationship between the five concepts. The results will be contested and this is as it should be; others will perhaps show how different measures generate different findings. What can be claimed for the method, however, is that it applies 'good-enough', theory-based measures to reasonably good data on a representative cross-section of children from a discrete community. Anyone repeating these measures with the same children would get broadly similar results.

Notes

[1] *Risk factors* are aspects of an individual or their environment that predispose some children to specific social or psychological problems. *Protective factors* are attributes or circumstances that work in certain contexts to reduce or modify an individual's response to particular combinations of risk and thereby reduce that individual's susceptibility to a range of social or psychological problems.

[2] One quarter (25%) of the children in the sample were living in families that had been forced to flee their home country by war or oppression.

[3] Often stage two followed stage one immediately in that at the screening stage the respondent assented to being interviewed.

[4] The latter figure excluded the 16 households for which no data were obtained.

Appendix B
Logistic regression

What logistic regression does

Logistic regression helps with predicting which of two categories a case is likely to belong to given certain other information (Field, 2000, p 163). The term 'predict' is used in the statistical sense that 'within [a] particular model the variable is strongly, significantly and independently associated with the outcome, and may therefore be viewed as influential in the "pathway" to that outcome' (Ghate and Hazel, 2002, p 293). It does not mean that the presence of a predictor variable automatically leads to the outcome in question, or that the former causes the latter. Logistic regression is suitable when the outcome or 'dependent' variable is categorical, and the predictor or 'independent' variables are categorical or continuous.

Why logistic regression is useful

Although several variables may be significantly associated with a target variable, any one may not have independent predictive power once other factors have been controlled for. In other words, the association may be the product of their mutual association with a third factor. For example, since income tends to increase with age, so anything else that generally increases with age, such as dental decay, can be used with some success to predict income. A possible but wrong conclusion would be to say that not brushing one's teeth might be a good career move (more decay equals higher income). Multivariate analysis reduces the chances of making such an error; it is unlikely that dental decay has any predictive power that cannot be explained in terms of age (Bullock et al, 1998). Logistic regression is a multivariate technique that assists with disentangling which are the key factors that predict a target variable that is *categorical*, and which are statistically associated with the target variable primarily due to a shared underlying factor (Ghate and Hazel, 2002).

How a logistic regression is done

First, correlations are carried out to identify factors that are significantly associated with the outcome variable. Second, those variables are fed into the logistic regression model in SPSS (they can be added all at once or individually). There are various techniques for doing this, but a common one is the 'forward stepwise' approach. This compares the predictive accuracy of the model with and without the predictor variable in question, retaining it if it makes a significant difference to how well the model fits the data. Third, the results are examined, with particular attention to the following:

- The predictive accuracy of the model *without* any predictive variables. SPSS predicts that all cases will fall into the largest category and as such will automatically be correct in more than half of cases. The actual *percentage of correctly predicted cases* is given, together with the *'log likelihood' statistic*, which indicates how much unexplained information remains (this will be lower in subsequent steps if the addition of other variables improves the model's predictive accuracy).
- The predictive accuracy of the model *with* a new predictive variable. The new *log likelihood statistic* indicates the extent to which the addition of a new variable has reduced the amount of unexplained information. The *model chi-square statistic* (and significance level) indicates how much better the model is at predicting the outcome variable. The *classification table* shows what proportion of cases are now predicted accurately. The *Wald statistic* (and significance level) indicates whether or not the new variable is making a significant difference to the model's accuracy. And the *Exp(B) coefficient* (and significance level) indicates the change in odds of the outcome variable occurring as a result of one unit change in the predictor variable. The *classification plot* gives a visual impression of how well the model fits the data.

Fourth, individual cases are examined for (a) their predicted and actual group membership and (b) their predicted probability of being in X outcome category (from 0 to 1 where 0 is no chance and 1 is 100% chance). Particular attention is paid to *false negatives* (cases that did have the outcome variable even though they were predicted not to) and *false positives* (cases that did not have the outcome variable even though they were predicted to). Fifth, residuals – identified by SPSS – are examined to see why they are unusual, that is (a) why they did not fit the model well or (b) why they exerted undue influence on the model. Sixth, where appropriate, a test is applied to see if there is any evidence of multicollinearity (where there is strong correlation between two or more predictors in a regression model) as this can bias the results. If there is it should be noted.

An example of logistic regression in children's services research

Bullock and colleagues (1998) identify the five factors that are highly predictive of separated children being reunited with their families (for example, the child has retained territory in their family home). By summing the Exp(B) coefficients of these factors they obtain odds of 13 to one if all five criteria are met. Of those who have all five factors, 93% returned home within six months of separation, compared with just 13% of those lacking any such factor. In other words, a child who retains a role (1) and territory (2) within his or her family, where the family considers itself a family (3), the social work plan is inclusive (4) and the problems that led to separation are subsequently eased (5), has a very high probability (0.93) of rapid return.

Appendix C
The 60 variables

Table C1 shows how the 60 variables were thought to relate to the five concepts prior to the analysis. They are categorised according to the dimensions of the child's life used in the data collection instruments and in the summary form.

Tables C2-C6 take the same 60 variables and show how they relate to the constructs that make up the measures for each concept that were selected for analysis.

Table C1: The 60 variables by the five concepts

Variable	Need	Rights	Poverty	QoL	Social exclusion
Sociodemographics					
Gender	*	*	*	*	*
Age	*	*	*	*	*
Who child lives with			*		*
Number of residents in household	*	*	*	*	*
English as a second language	*	*	*	*	*
Forced by war/oppression to leave country		*			
Child in house <6 months					*
Frequent movement					*
Living situation					
Overcrowded accommodation		*	*	*	*
Substandard accommodation		*	*	*	*
Safety problems				*	
Fear or experience of antisocial behaviour				*	
Family unhappy in home				*	
Family unhappy in area				*	
Family and social relationships					
Poor relations/no contact with mother					*
Poor relations/no contact with father					*
Poor relations/no contact with relatives/siblings					*
Loving relationships				*	

continued

Table C1 *(continued)*

Variable	Need	Rights	Poverty	QoL	Social exclusion
No significant adult				*	*
Abuse (physical, sexual, neglect)		*			
Low-warmth/high-criticism environment				*	*
Poor relations/no contact with peers				*	*
Isolated				*	*
Lack of social network				*	*
Bullied		*		*	*
Experience of racial harassment		*			
Social and antisocial behaviour					
Antisocial behaviour at home	*			*	
Antisocial behaviour at school	*			*	
Antisocial behaviour in the community	*			*	
Involvement in crime	*			*	
Running away from home	*			*	
Inappropriate sexual behaviour	*			*	
Little/no participation in out-of-school activities			*	*	*
Not occupied/few interests			*	*	
Bullies other children	*			*	*
Physical and psychological health					
Physical or psychological health problem	*			*	
Chronic physical health problem	*			*	
Temporary acute physical health problem	*				
Mental health problem (chronic or temporary acute)	*			*	
Depressed, stressed or unhappy				*	
Physical disability	*				
Learning disability	*				
Drug misuse				*	
Education and employment					
Under school age and not in preschool					*
Unemployed					*
Special educational needs	*				

continued

Table C1 *(continued)*

Variable	Need	Rights	Poverty	QoL	Social exclusion
School exclusion/truancy	*				*
Not achieving potential	*				
Poor relations with teacher/employer					*
Income and living standards					
Low-income household			*		*
Family dependent on benefits			*		*
Money problems			*		*
Insufficient income to afford basic requirements			*	*	*
Service use					
Approached social services in past 12 months					
Received help from social services in past 12 months					
Unsuccessful request for help from social services	*				*
Child not protected	*				
Poor relations/no contact with relevant professionals					*
Used local leisure centre			*	*	*

Table C2: The variables relevant to need (need1)

Element	Variables
Health	Physical or psychological health problem
	Chronic physical health problem
	Temporary acute physical health problem
	Mental health problem (chronic or temporary acute)
	Physical disability
	Learning disability
Behaviour	Antisocial behaviour at home
	Antisocial behaviour at school
	Antisocial behaviour in the community
	Involvement in crime
	Running away from home
	Inappropriate sexual behaviour
	Bullies other children
Education/development	Special educational needs
	School exclusion/truancy
	Not achieving potential

Table C3: The variables relevant to rights (rights2)

Element	Variables
Assault/abuse	Abuse (physical, sexual, neglect)
	Bullied
	Experience of racial harassment
War/oppression	Forced by war/oppression to leave country
Chronic living conditions	Overcrowded accommodation
	Substandard accommodation
Official negligence	Unsuccessful request for help from social services
	Child not protected

Table C4: The variables relevant to poverty (poverty3)

Element	Variables
Low income	Low-income household
	Who child lives with [lone parent]
	Family dependent on benefits
Poor living standards	Money problems
	Insufficient income to afford basic requirements
	Used leisure centre [negative response]
	Overcrowded accommodation
	Substandard accommodation
	Little/no participation in out-of-school activities
	Not occupied/few interests

Table C5:The variables relevant to quality of life (qol3)

Element	Variables
Poor objective circumstances	Overcrowded accommodation
	Substandard accommodation
	Family unhappy in home
	Family unhappy in area
	Safety problems
	Fear or experience of antisocial behaviour
	Low-warmth/high-criticism environment
	No significant adult
	Loving relationships [negative response]
	Poor relations/no contact with peers
	Lack of social network
	Isolated
	Bullied
	Bullies other children
	Little/no participation in out-of-school activities
	Not occupied/few interests
	Insufficient income for basic requirements
	Physical or psychological health problem
	Used local leisure centre [negative response]
Negative subjective outlook	Antisocial behaviour at home
	Antisocial behaviour at school
	Antisocial behaviour in the community
	Involvement in crime
	Running away from home
	Inappropriate sexual behaviour
	Drug misuse
	Depressed, stressed or unhappy

Table C6: The variables relevant to social exclusion (sx6)

Element	Variables
Economic sphere	Family dependent on benefits Money problems Insufficient income to afford basic requirements Who child lives with [lone parent] Overcrowded accommodation Substandard accommodation Low-income household Under school age not in preschool Unemployed School exclusion/truancy
Domestic/interpersonal sphere	Who child lives with [substitute care, independently] Poor relations/no contact with mother Poor relations/no contact with father Poor relations/no contact with relatives/siblings Low-warmth/high-criticism environment No significant adult Poor relations/no contact with peers Lack of social network Isolated Bullied Bullies other children
Social/civil sphere	Little/no participation in out-of-school activities Unsuccessful request for help from social services Used local leisure centre [negative response]
Political/civic sphere	Frequent movement Child in house <6 months Poor relations with teacher/employer Poor relations/no contact with relevant professionals

Appendix D
Additional results

The two-way relationships between the five conditions

Each of the following 10 tables takes a pair of conditions and shows how they are related using data from the *N*=234 sample. For example, Table D1 shows that 44 of the children who were in need had their rights violated (20% of the sample) compared with the other 43 whose rights were intact (19%). Of those who were not in need, 51 nevertheless had violated rights (23% of the sample).

Table D1: Need and rights

	Rights violated	Rights intact	Total
In need	44 (19.8%)	43 (19.4%)	87 (39.2%)
Not in need	51 (23.0%)	84 (37.8%)	135 (60.8%)
Total	95 (42.8%)	127 (57.2%)	222 (100.0%)

Table D2: Need and poverty

	In poverty	Not in poverty	Total
In need	55 (25.5%)	29 (13.4%)	84 (38.9%)
Not in need	75 (34.7%)	57 (26.4%)	132 (61.1%)
Total	130 (60.2%)	86 (39.8%)	216 (100.0%)

Table D3: Need and quality of life

	Poor quality of life	Decent quality of life	Total
In need	43 (19.4%)	44 (19.8%)	87 (39.2%)
Not in need	11 (5.0%)	124 (55.9%)	135 (60.8%)
Total	54 (24.3%)	168 (75.7%)	222 (100.0%)

Table D4: Need and social exclusion

	Socially excluded	Not socially excluded	Total
In need	12 (5.4%)	75 (33.8%)	87 (39.2%)
Not in need	2 (0.9%)	133 (59.9%)	135 (60.8%))
Total	14 (6.3%)	208 (93.7%)	222 (100.0%)

Table D5: Rights and poverty

	In poverty	Not in poverty	Total
Rights violated	68 (30.2%)	26 (11.6%)	94 (41.8%)
Rights intact	70 (31.1%)	61 (27.1%)	131 (58.2%)
Total	138 (61.3%)	87 (38.7%)	225 (100.0%)

Table D6: Rights and quality of life

	Poor quality of life	Decent quality of life	Total
Rights violated	29 (12.6%)	67 (29.0%)	96 (41.6%)
Rights intact	25 (10.8%))	110 (47.6%)	135 (58.4%)
Total	54 (23.4%)	177 (76.6%)	231 (100.0%)

Table D7: Rights and social exclusion

	Socially excluded	Not socially excluded	Total
Rights violated	6 (2.6%)	91 (39.4%)	97 (42.0%)
Rights intact	8 (3.5%)	126 (54.5%)	134 (58.0%)
Total	14 (6.1%)	217 (93.9%)	231 (100.0%)

Table D8: Poverty and quality of life

	Poor quality of life	Decent quality of life	Total
In poverty	32 (14.2%)	106 (47.1%)	138 (61.3%)
Not in poverty	19 (8.4%)	68 (30.2%)	87 (38.7%)
Total	51 (22.7%)	174 (77.3%)	225 (100.0%)

Table D9: Poverty and social exclusion

	Socially excluded	Not socially excluded	Total
In poverty	9 (4.1%)	126 (56.8%)	135 (60.8%)
Not in poverty	4 (1.8%)	83 (37.4%)	87 (39.2%)
Total	13 (5.9%)	209 (94.1%)	222 (100.0%)

Table D10: Quality of life and social exclusion

	Socially excluded	Not socially excluded	Total
Poor quality of life	8 (3.5%)	46 (20.2%)	54 (23.7%)
Decent quality of life	6 (2.6%)	168 (73.7%)	174 (76.3%)
Total	14 (6.1%)	214 (93.9%)	228 (100.0%)

The 32 five-way combinations of the conditions

Table D11 shows the frequency of each of the 32 five-way combinations of the concepts for the children in the N=234 sample. For example, just three children (1.4%) displayed all of the conditions: in need, violated rights, poverty, poor QoL and social exclusion. This was the joint 16th most common combination.

Two-way relationships between the conditions not covered in Chapter Nine

Chapter Nine included qualitative case studies of children affected by the six most common five-way combinations. Together they covered 27 out of the 40 possible two-way relationships shown in Table D12.

This section provides examples from the N=234 sample of the remaining 13 two-way relationships. Each relationship is given the number of its box from Table D12 (so that 'Relationship 2' refers to two-way relationship 2, that is, 'in need but rights intact').

In need but rights intact (relationship 2)

A four-year-old girl living with her mother. *Need*: She was suffering from allergies and a urinary problem. *Rights*: Her home had been burgled recently, thereby infringing her rights to privacy, but this did not count as a *serious* breach of her right to protection.

Rights intact but a poor QoL (relationship 23)

A 16-year-old boy living with his father. *Rights*: This child was subject to inconsistent care and poor boundary-setting (*provision*). Sometimes he had to undertake caring responsibilities for his disabled father. However, these were not deemed to be serious infringements of his rights. Moreover, social services and the education psychology service were working hard to achieve stability for the child and to provide him with diversionary activities such as holiday schemes. They were trying to take the pressure off him by supporting his father. They also sought to involve him in decision-making (*participation*); for example they arranged a meeting of family members, allowed him to veto his father's wish for him to be accommodated (he remained at home) and negotiated with him about his future. *QoL*: The child's parents had separated, and their acrimonious relationship meant that he received poor care. His home environment was characterised by fear and tension, and he had asthma and some caring responsibilities.

Table D11: The 32 five-way combinations (*N*=234 sample)

Combination	Pattern	Frequency	%	Rank
1	11111	3	1.4	=16
2	10111	1	0.5	20
3	01111	2	0.9	=19
4	00111	0	0	=32
5	11011	0	0	=32
6	10011	2	0.9	=19
7	01011	0	0	=32
8	00011	0	0	=32
9	11101	0	0	=32
10	10101	3	1.4	=16
11	01101	0	0	=32
12	00101	0	0	=32
13	11001	0	0	=32
14	10001	2	0.9	=19
15	01001	0	0	=32
16	00001	0	0	=32
17	11110	15	6.9	=5
18	10110	8	3.7	=9
19	01110	3	1.4	=16
20	00110	0	0	=32
21	11010	5	2.3	=12
22	10010	8	3.7	=9
23	01010	0	0	=32
24	00010	4	1.9	13
25	11100	14	6.5	6
26	10100	11	5.1	7
27	01100	31	14.4	3
28	00100	39	18.1	1
29	11000	5	2.3	=12
30	10000	7	3.2	10
31	01000	15	6.9	=5
32	00000	38	17.6	2

Note: The ones and zeros in the second column indicate the presence (1) or absence (0) of the five conditions in the following order: in need; rights violated; poverty; poor QoL; and social exclusion. Thus, '10100' indicates children who were in need and in poverty only.

Table D12: Outline of the 40 possible two-way combinations[a]

	In need		Rights violated		In poverty		Poor QoL		Socially excluded	
In need			1	2	5	6	9	10	13	14
			3	4	7	8	11	12	15	16
Rights violated	–	–			17	18	21	22	25	26
	–	–			19	20	23	24	27	28
In poverty	–	–	–	–			29	30	33	34
	–	–	–	–			31	32	35	36
Poor QoL	–	–	–	–	–	–			37	38
	–	–	–	–	–	–			39	40
Socially excluded	–	–	–	–	–	–	–	–		

Note:

[a] The quadrants are ordered as follows: (a) top left: row and column = yes, (b) top right: row = yes, column = no, (c) bottom left: row = no, column = yes, (d) bottom right: row and column = no. So for need and rights: (1) in need and rights violated, (2) in need but rights not violated, (3) not in need but rights violated (4) not in need and rights intact.

In need but not poor (relationship 6) and not poor but a poor QoL (relationship 31)

A 15-year-old boy living with his parents and three siblings. *Need:* He had hearing problems and was disruptive and violent with a history of theft and assaults. He was unable to read or write. *Poverty:* The family's living standards were poor. They lived in damp, overcrowded accommodation and often required emergency money from social services for food and clothes. However, the child spent little time at home (he has been in prison) and his father was working part time. *QoL:* The child craved attention and approval but his father showed no interest in him. He lived in substandard housing and was struggling to find a sense of identity and purpose. He had poor self-esteem and suicidal thoughts. His behaviour could be interpreted as a cry for help.

Not in need but a poor QoL (relationship 11)

A seven-year-old girl living with her mother. *Need:* She was very bright. *QoL:* However, she had asthma and was not enjoying school. A similar case was that of a 10-year-old girl living with her parents and older sister. *Need:* She was healthy and doing well at school. *QoL:* However, her home was overcrowded and she was upset about her parents' impending separation.

In need and socially excluded (relationship 13), rights violated and socially excluded (relationship 25), poor and socially excluded (relationship 33) and poor QoL and socially excluded (relationship 37)

A 14-year-old boy living with his mother and two siblings. *Need*: He suffered from severe headaches and nosebleeds. *Rights*: The family had been forced to leave his father behind when they fled Uganda as political refugees. The child was being subjected to severe racial harassment in the neighbourhood. The abuse was preventing him from engaging in activities in the community. Compounding this situation was the refusal of the housing agency to grant the family the transfer that they sought. Collectively, these factors suggest that the child's rights to *protection*, *provision* and *participation* were being seriously violated. *Poverty*: Household income was very low: his mother was unemployed and receiving a student grant and benefits. The flat was in a poor state of repair and the family had needed discretionary money from social services for basic items such as carpets. They were struggling financially. *QoL*: The child's housing was in need of improvement, he had health problems and the racial harassment deprived him of fun and friendship. He felt threatened and frightened, and his poor health could have been stress-related. *Social exclusion*: The child was economically excluded by virtue of living in a low-income household. He was isolated from his peers (interpersonal sphere) and prevented by the victimisation from participating in community activities (the social sphere). The family were also very unsettled (political/civic sphere). They had come to the estate six months previously from a bed-and-breakfast hostel and had already had to seek temporary refuge elsewhere when the flat was flooded. They were still anxious to move permanently in order to escape the harassment.

Rights intact but socially excluded (relationship 27) and decent QoL but socially excluded (relationship 39)

A one-year-old girl living with her mother and stepfather. *Rights*: Social services had failed to tell the housing agency about a hole in the wall near the stairs that could have proved dangerous for a small child. Nor had they attempted to supply the child's mother with a much-needed cot and pushchair. These omissions violated the child's right to protection and provision respectively, but were not deemed to meet the criteria for a serious violation. *QoL*: As well as living in substandard housing and lacking basic items, the child was dependent on an isolated mother and therefore lacked fun and contact with peers. However, there was no evidence of her being unhappy. *Social exclusion*: The family was dependent on basic social assistance and unable to afford basic items (economic sphere). The child had no contact with peers or anyone else in the community because her mother was so isolated (interpersonal and social spheres). The family were unsettled and looking to move, having arrived only recently on the estate (political/civic sphere).

Not poor but socially excluded (relationship 35)

A 17-year-old boy living sometimes in prison and sometimes with his mother, sibling and stepsibling. *Poverty*: His mother required money from social services and charity to keep him at home or to visit him in prison. However, there was no explicit evidence of low income, indeed general living standards were good. *Social exclusion*: The child was excluded from school (economic sphere). Family relations were strained and when in prison he saw little of his mother (she could barely afford to visit) (interpersonal sphere). His only activities in the community were crime-related (social sphere). He was leading a transient existence, drifting in and out of prison, and his relations with professionals were poor; he felt that he was subject to racial bullying by teachers at school, and he often missed appointments with children's services agencies (political/civic sphere).

References

Abel–Smith, B. and Townsend, P. (1965) *The Poor and the Poorest*, London, G. Bell and Sons.

Abrahamson, P. (1995) 'Social exclusion in Europe: old wine in new bottles?', *Druzboslovne Razprave*, vol 11, no 19-20, pp 119-36.

Abrahamson, P. (1997) 'Combating poverty and social exclusion in Europe', in Beck, W., van der Maesen, L. and Walker, A. (eds) *The Social Quality of Europe*, Bristol, The Policy Press.

Abrams, F. (2002) *Below the Breadline: Living on the Minimum Wage*, London, Profile Books.

Abrams, M. (1973) 'Subjective social indicators', in Central Statistical Office (eds) *Social Trends 4*, London, HMSO.

Adelman, L., Ashworth, K. and Middleton, S. (2000) 'Child poverty in Britain', in Gordon, D., Adelman, L., Ashworth, K., Bradshaw, J., Levitas, R., Middleton, S., Pantazis, C., Patsios, D., Payne, S., Townsend, P. and Williams, J. (eds) *Poverty and Social Exclusion in Britain*, York, Joseph Rowntree Foundation.

Ahuvia, A. C. (2000) 'The link between economic growth and increased subjective well-being', Paper presented to the Third Conference of the International Society for Quality of Life Studies, Girona, Spain, 20-22 July.

Alcock, P. (1997) *Understanding Poverty* (2nd edition), Basingstoke, Macmillan.

Andrews, F. M. (1974) 'Social indicators or perceived life quality', *Social Indicators Research*, vol 1, no 3, pp 279-99.

Angold, A. (2002) 'Diagnostic interviews with parents and children', in Rutter, M. and Taylor, E. (eds) *Child and Adolescent Psychiatry* (4th edition), Oxford, Blackwell.

Appasamy, P., Guhan, S., Hema, R., Majumdar, M. and Vaidyanathan, A. (1995) 'Social exclusion in respect of basic needs in India', in Rodgers, G., Gore, C. and Figueiredo, J. B. (eds) *Social Exclusion: Rhetoric, Reality, Responses*, Geneva, International Institute for Labour Studies.

Archard, D. (2004) *Children: Rights and Childhood* (2nd edition), London, Routledge.

Argyle, M. (2000) 'Are there national differences in happiness?', Paper presented to the Third Conference of the International Society for Quality of Life Studies, Girona, Spain, 20-22 July.

Armstrong, L. (2001) *It's Not About the Bike: My Journey Back to Life*, London, Yellow Jersey Press.

Ashworth, K., Hill, M. and Walker, R. (1994) 'Patterns of childhood poverty: new challenges for policy', *Journal of Policy Analysis and Management*, 13, no 4, pp 658-80.

Atkinson, A. B. (1995) *Incomes and the Welfare State*, Cambridge, Cambridge University Press.

Atkinson, A. B. (1998) 'Social exclusion, poverty and unemployment', in Atkinson, A. B. and Hills, J. (eds) *Exclusion, Employment and Opportunity*, CASE Paper 4, London, Centre for the Analysis of Social Exclusion, London School of Economics and Political Science.

Atkinson, A. B., Cantillon, B. and Marlier, E. (2002) *Social Indicators: The EU and Social Inclusion*, Oxford, Oxford University Press.

Audit Commission (2005) *Local Quality of Life Indicators: Supporting Local Communities to Become Sustainable*, London, Audit Commission.

Axford, N. (2003) 'Child well-being from different perspectives: defining, measuring and responding to unmet need, violated rights, poverty, poor quality of life and social exclusion', PhD thesis, University of Exeter.

Axford, N. (2007) 'Deciding on the service mix: how conceptions of child well-being inform children's services', Working Paper, Dartington, Dartington Social Research Unit.

Axford, N., Little, M. and Morpeth, L. (1999) *Children Supported and Unsupported in the Community: Work in Progress*, Report submitted to the Department of Health.

Axford, N., Little, M. and Morpeth, L. (2001) *Early Findings from Research and Development Work Designed to Provide an Evidence Base for Children's Services*, Report submitted to the Department of Health.

Axford, N., Little, M. and Morpeth, L. (2003) *Children Supported and Unsupported in the Community*, Report submitted to the Department of Health, Dartington, Dartington Social Research Unit.

Axford, N., Berry, V., Little, M. and Morpeth, L. (eds) (2005) *Forty Years of Research, Policy and Practice in Children's Services: A Festschrift for Roger Bullock*, Chichester, Wiley.

Axford, N., Madge, J., Morpeth, L. and Pring, J. (2004) 'Mapping the data needed to plan integrated services: a case study of children's services in one locality', *Journal of Integrated Care*, vol 12, no 3, pp 3-10.

Bagguley, P. and Mann, K. (1992) 'Idle thieving bastards? Scholarly representations of the "underclass"', *Work, Employment and Society*, vol 6, no 1, pp 113-26.

Baker, N. (ed) (1996) *Building a Relational Society: New Priorities for Public Policy*, Aldershot, Ashgate.

Baldwin, D., Coles, B. and Mitchell, W. (1997) 'The formation of an "underclass" or disparate processes of social exclusion? Evidence from two groupings of "vulnerable youth"', in MacDonald, R. (ed) *Youth, the 'Underclass' and Social Exclusion*, London, Routledge.

Baldwin, S. and Gerard, K. (1990) 'Caring at home for children with mental handicaps', in Baldwin, S., Godfrey, C. and Propper, C. (eds) *Quality of Life: Perspectives and Policies*, London, Routledge.

Balibar, E. (1992) 'Inégalités, fractionnement social, exclusion', in Affichard, J. and de Foucauld, J.-B. (eds) *Justice Sociale et Inégalités*, Paris, Editions Esprit. [Cited in Procacci, 1996, p 12]

Barlow, J., Simkiss, D. and Stewart-Brown, S. (2006) 'Interventions to prevent or ameliorate child physical abuse and neglect: findings from a systematic review of reviews', *Journal of Children's Services*, vol 1, no 3, pp 6-28.

Barnes, M. (1998) 'Whose needs, whose resources? Accessing social care', in Clarke, J. and Langan, M. (eds) *Welfare: Needs, Rights and Risks*, London, Routledge.

Barry, B. (2002) 'Social exclusion, social isolation and the distribution of income', in Hills, J., Le Grand, J. and Piachaud, D. (eds) *Understanding Social Exclusion*, Oxford, Oxford University Press.

Barry, M. (1998) 'Social exclusion and social work: an introduction', in Barry, M. and Hallett, C. (eds) *Social Exclusion and Social Work: Issues of Theory, Policy and Practice*, Lyme Regis, Russell House Publishing.

Bebbington, A. and Miles, J. (1989) 'The background of children who enter local authority care', *British Journal of Social Work*, vol 19, no 1, pp 349-68.

Bell, S., Clark, D., Knapp, M., Layard, Lord, Meacher, Baroness, Priebe, S., Thornicroft, G., Turnberg, Lord and Wright, B. (2006) *The Depression Report: A New Deal for Depression and Anxiety Disorders*, London, London School of Economics and Political Science, The Centre for Economic Performance's Mental Health Policy Group.

Ben-Arieh, A. (1997) 'Introduction: measuring and monitoring the state of children', in Ben-Arieh, A. and Wintersberger, H. (eds) *Monitoring and Measuring the State of Children: Beyond Survival*, Proceedings of an International Workshop, Jerusalem, Israel, 22-25 January 1996, Vienna, European Centre for Social Welfare Policy and Research.

Ben-Arieh, A. and Goerge, R. M. (eds) (2006) *Indicators of Children's Well-being: Understanding their Role, Usage and Policy Influence*, Dordrecht, Kluwer Academic Publishers.

Ben-Arieh, A., Hevener-Kaufman, N., Bowers Andrews, A., Goerge, R. M., Lee, B. J. and Aber, L. J. (2001) *Measuring and Monitoring Children's Well-Being*, Dordrecht, Kluwer Academic Publishers.

Bennett, F. (2005) 'Promoting the health and well-being of children: evidence of need in the UK', in Scott, J. and Ward, H. (eds) *Safeguarding and Promoting the Well-Being of Children, Families and Communities*, London, Jessica Kingsley Publishers.

Berghman, J. (1995) 'Social exclusion in Europe: policy context and analytical framework', in Room, G. (ed) *Beyond the Threshold: The Measurement and Analysis of Social Exclusion*, Bristol, The Policy Press.

Berridge, D. and Brodie, I. (1998) *Children's Homes Revisited*, London, Jessica Kingsley Publishers.

Berry, V. (2007) 'The differential impact of inter-parental conflict and parent–child conflict on children's developmental outcomes', PhD thesis, University of Bath.

Berry Brazelton, T. and Greenspan, S. I. (2000) *The Irreducible Needs of Children: What Every Child Must Have to Grow, Learn, and Flourish*, Cambridge, MA, Perseus Books Group.

Bisset-Johnson, A. (1994) 'What did states really agree to? Qualifications of signatories to the United Nations Convention on the Rights of the Child', *International Journal of Children's Rights*, vol 2, no 4, pp 399-411.

Blackburn, C. (1991) *Poverty and Health: Working with Families*, Milton Keynes, Open University Press.

Blair, T. (1999) 'Beveridge revisited: a welfare state for the 21st century', The 1999 Beveridge Lecture given at Toynbee Hall, London, 18 March, reprinted in Walker, R. (ed) (1999) *Ending Child Poverty: Popular Welfare for the 21st century?*, Bristol, The Policy Press.

Bliss, C. (1996) 'Economics of the environment', in Offer, A. (ed) *In Pursuit of the Quality of Life*, Oxford, Oxford University Press.

Blyth, E. and Milner, J. (eds) (1996) *Exclusion From School: Inter-Professional Issues for Policy and Practice*, London, Routledge.

Bolland, J. M. (2003) 'Hopelessness and risk behaviour among adolescents living in high-poverty inner-city neighbourhoods', *Journal of Adolescence*, vol 26, no 2, pp 145-58.

Bowlby, J. (1951) *Maternal Care and Mental Health*, Geneva, World Health Organization.

Bowling, A. (1995) 'What things are important in people's lives? A survey of the public's judgements to inform scales of health-related quality of life', *Social Science and Medicine*, vol 41, no 10, pp 1447-62.

Bowling, A. (1997) *Measuring Health: A Review of Quality of Life Measurement Scales* (2nd edition), Buckingham, Open University Press.

Bradbury, B. and Jantti, M. (1999) *Child Poverty across Industrialised Nations*, Innocenti Occasional Papers, Economic and Social Policy Series 71, Florence, UNICEF International Child Development Centre.

Bradshaw, J. (1972) 'A taxonomy of social need', in McLachlan, G. (ed) *Problems and Progress in Medical Care*, Oxford, Nuffield Provincial Hospital Trust.

Bradshaw, J. (ed) (1993) *Budget Standards for the United Kingdom*, Aldershot, Avebury.

Bradshaw, J. (1994) 'The conceptualization and measurement of need: a social policy perspective', in Popay, J. and Williams, G. (eds) *Researching the People's Health*, London, Routledge.

Bradshaw, J. (1999) 'Child poverty in comparative perspective', Paper presented to the conference 'Developing Poverty Measures: Research in Europe – Defining and Measuring Poverty', University of Bristol, 1-2 July.

Bradshaw, J. (2000) 'The outcomes of child poverty', Paper presented to the conference 'What Future for Social Security? Cross-National and Multi-Disciplinary Perspectives', University of Stirling, 15-17 June.

Bradshaw, J. (2001) 'Methodologies to measure poverty: more than one is best!', Paper presented to the international symposium 'Poverty: Concepts and Measures', Mexico City, 28-29 March.

Bradshaw, J. (2002) 'Children and poor children', in Bradshaw, J. (ed) *The Well-Being of Children in the UK*, London, Save the Children.

Bradshaw, J. (2005) 'Child poverty and deprivation', in Bradshaw, J. and Mayhew, E. (eds) *The Well-Being of Children in the UK* (2nd edition), London, Save the Children.

Bradshaw, J. and Finch, N. (2001) *Real Poverty*, PSE Working Paper, York, University of York.

Bradshaw, J. and Finch, N. (2003) 'Overlaps in dimensions of poverty', *Journal of Social Policy*, vol 32, no 4, pp 513-25.

Bradshaw, J. and Mayhew, E. (eds) (2005) *The Well-Being of Children in the UK* (2nd edition), London, Save the Children.

Bradshaw, J. and Williams, J. (2000) 'Adult poverty in Britain', in Gordon, D., Adelman, L., Ashworth, K., Bradshaw, J., Levitas, R., Middleton, S., Pantazis, C., Patsios, D., Payne, S., Townsend, P. and Williams, J. (eds) *Poverty and Social Exclusion in Britain*, York, Joseph Rowntree Foundation.

Bradshaw, J., Hoelscher, P. and Richardson, D. (2007a) 'An index of child well-being in the European Union', *Social Indicators Research*, vol 80, no 1, pp 133-77.

Bradshaw, J., Middleton, S., Townsend, P. and Gordon, D. (1998) 'Proposal to the Joseph Rowntree Foundation for a survey of poverty and social exclusion in Britain', Unpublished paper.

Bradshaw, J., Mitchell, D. and Morgan, J. (1987) 'Evaluating adequacy: the potential of budget standards', *Journal of Social Policy*, vol 16, no 2, pp 165-81.

Bradshaw, J., Richardson, D. and Ritakallio, V-M. (2007b) 'Child poverty and child well-being in Europe', *Journal of Children's Services*, vol 2, no 1, pp 18-36.

Bradshaw, J., Williams, J., Levitas, R., Pantazis, C., Patsios, D., Townsend, P., Gordon, D. and Middleton, S. (2000) 'The relationship between poverty and social exclusion in Britain', Paper presented to the 26th General Conference of the International Association for Research in Income and Wealth, Cracow, Poland, 27 August to 2 September.

Bramley, G. (1997) 'Poverty and local public services', in Gordon, D. and Pantazis, C. (eds) *Breadline Britain in the 1990s*, Aldershot, Ashgate.

Brannen, J. (1999) 'Children and agency in academic and public policy discourses', in White, K. J. (ed) *Children and Social Exclusion: Towards an Understanding and Practice that is More Inclusive*, London, NCVCCO.

Braye, S. (2000) 'Participation and involvement in social care', in Kemshall, H. and Littlechild, R. (eds) *User Involvement and Participation in Social Care: Research Informing Practice*, London, Jessica Kingsley Publishers.

Brock, D. (1993) 'Quality of life measures in healthcare and medical ethics', in Nussbaum, M. C. and Sen, A. (eds) *The Quality of Life*, Oxford, Clarendon Press.

Brooks, R. (1996) 'EuroQol: the current state of play', *Health Policy*, vol 37, no 1, pp 53-72.

Brown, I., Renwick, R. and Nagler, M. (1996) 'The centrality of quality of life in health promotion and rehabilitation', in Renwick, R., Brown, I. and Nagler, M. (eds) (1996) *Quality of Life in Health Promotion and Rehabilitation: Conceptual Approaches, Issues, and Applications*, Thousand Oaks, CA, Sage Publications.

Brown, L. (2002) *The Role of Family Group Conferences in Child Protection*, Bath, University of Bath.

Brown, L. and Smith, J. (1997) 'The extent and location of "children in need" in Gloucestershire: a socio-demographic analysis', Unpublished paper, Gloucestershire Social Services.

Bru, E., Murberg, T. A. and Stephens, P. (2001) 'Social support, negative life events and pupil misbehaviour among Norwegian adolescents', *Journal of Adolescence*, vol 24, no 6, pp 715-27.

Bryman, A. and Cramer, D. (1997) *Quantitative Data Analysis with SPSS for Windows: A Guide for Social Scientists*, London, Routledge.

Buchanan, A. (2007) 'Including the socially excluded: the impact of government policy on vulnerable families and children in need', *British Journal of Social Work*, vol 37, no 2, pp 187-207.

Bugra, A. and Irzik, G. (1999) 'Human needs, consumption and social policy', *Economics and Philosophy*, vol 15, no 2, pp 187-208.

Buhmann, B., Rainwater, L., Schmaus, G. and Smeeding, T. M. (1988) 'Equivalence scales, well-being, inequality and poverty: sensitivity estimates across ten countries using the Luxembourg Income Survey database', *The Review of Income and Wealth*, June, pp 115-41.

Bullock, R., Gooch, D. and Little, M. (1998) *Children Going Home: The Re-Unification of Families*, Aldershot, Ashgate.

Bullock, R., Little, M. and Millham, S. (1994) 'Assessing the quality of life for children in local authority care or accommodation', *Journal of Adolescence*, vol 17, no 1, pp 29-40.

Burchardt, T. (2000) 'Social exclusion: concepts and evidence', in Gordon, D. and Townsend, P. (eds) *Breadline Europe: The Measurement of Poverty*, Bristol, The Policy Press.

Burchardt, T. (2006) 'Happiness and social policy: barking up the right tree in the wrong neck of the woods', in Bauld, L., Clarke, K. and Maltby, T. (eds) *Social Policy Review 18*, Bristol, The Policy Press, pp 145-64.

Burchardt, T., Le Grand, J. and Piachaud, D. (1999) 'Social exclusion in Britain 1991-1995', *Social Policy and Administration*, vol 33, no 3, pp 227-44.

Buxton, M. (1992) 'Are we satisfied with QALYs? What are the conceptual and empirical uncertainties and what must we do to make them more generally useful?', in Hopkins, A. (ed) *Measures of the Quality of Life: And the Uses to Which Such Measures may be Put*, London, Royal College of Physicians of London.

Bynner, J. (1998) 'What are the causes of social exclusion affecting young children?', in HM Treasury (eds) *Cross-Departmental Review of Provision for Young Children: Supporting Papers (Volume 1)*, London, HM Treasury.

Bynner, J. (2001) 'Childhood risks and protective factors in social exclusion', *Children and Society*, vol 15, no 5, pp 285-301.

Byrne, D. (1999) *Social Exclusion*, Buckingham, Open University Press.

Cainkar, L. and Abunimah, A. (1998) 'Palestinian refugees in Jordan', Unpublished paper, Chicago, IL, Chapin Hall Center for Children.

Calman, K. C. (1984) 'Quality of life in cancer patients: an hypothesis', *Journal of Medical Ethics*, vol 10, no 3, pp 124-27.

Campbell, A., Converse, P. E. and Rodgers, W. L. (1976) *The Quality of American Life*, New York, Russell Sage.

Campbell, T. (1983) *The Left and Rights*, London, Routledge.

Carr-Hill, R. A., Dixon, P., Mannion, R., Rice, N., Rudat, K., Sinclair, R. and Smith, P. C. (1997) *A Model of the Determinants of Expenditure on Children's Personal Social Services*, York, Centre for Health Economics.

Casas, F. (1997) 'Children's rights and children's quality of life; conceptual and practical issues', *Social Indicators Research*, vol 42, no 3, pp 283-98.

Castel, R. (1991) 'De l'indigence à l'exclusion, la désaffiliation. Précarité du travail et vulnérabilité relationelle', in Donzelot, J. (ed) *Face à l'Exclusion: Le Modèle Français*, Paris, PUF. [Cited in Martin, 1996, p 386]

CDC (Centers for Disease Control and Prevention) (1998) *Measuring Violence-Related Attitudes, Beliefs and Behaviours among Youths: A Compendium of Assessment Tools*, Atlanta, US Department of Health and Human Services.

Chaskin, R. (2006) 'Family support as community-based practice: considering a community capacity framework for family support provision', in Dolan, P., Canavan, J. and Pinkerton, J. (eds) *Family Support as Reflective Practice*, London, Jessica Kingsley Publishers.

Cheetham, J. and Fuller, R. (1998) 'Social exclusion and social work: policy, practice and research', in Barry, M. and Hallett, C. (eds) *Social Exclusion and Social Work: Issues of Theory, Policy and Practice*, Lyme Regis, Russell House Publishing.

Church, C. (2000) 'Poverty and sustainable development', in Seymour, J. (ed) *UK Human Development Report*, London, United Nations Environment and Development UK Committee.

Citro, C. F. and Michael, R. T. (1995) *Measuring Poverty: A New Approach*, Washington, DC, National Research Council, National Academy Press.

Clark, A. E. and Oswald, A. J. (1995) 'Satisfaction and comparison income', Unpublished paper, London School of Economics and Political Science.

Cohen, G. A. (1993) 'Equality of what? On welfare, goods and capability', in Nussbaum, M. C. and Sen, A. (eds) *The Quality of Life*, Oxford, Clarendon Press.

Colton, M., Drury, C. and Williams, M. (1995) 'Children in need: definition, identification and support', *British Journal of Social Work*, vol 25, no 6, pp 711-728.

Commins, P. (1995) 'Social exclusion in the context of the European Union's Third Poverty Programme', *Druzboslovne Razprave*, vol 11, no 19-20, pp 137-50.

Cooper, A., Hetherington, R., Baistow, K., Pitts, J. and Spriggs, A. (1995) *Positive Child Protection: The View from Abroad*, Lyme Regis, Russell House.

Cooper, D. M. (1998) 'More law and more rights: will children benefit?', *Child and Family Social Work*, vol 3, no 2, pp 77-86.

Corden, A. and Duffy, K. (1998) 'Human dignity and social exclusion', in Sykes, R. and Alcock, P. (eds) *Developments in European Social Policy: Convergence and Diversity*, Bristol, The Policy Press.

Corsaro, W. (1996) *The Sociology of Childhood*, Thousand Oaks, CA, Pine Forge Press.

Cranston, M. (1967) 'Human rights, real and supposed', in Raphael, D. D. (ed) *Political Theory and the Rights of Man*, London, Macmillan.

CSO (Central Statistical Office) (1994) *Social Focus on Children*, London, HMSO.

Cullingford, C. (1999) *The Causes of Exclusion: Home, School and the Development of Young Criminals*, London, Kogan Page.

Cummins, R. A. (1997) *Comprehensive Quality of Life Scale – School Version (Grades 7-12), 5th Edition (ComQoL-S5)*, Melbourne, Deakin University School of Psychology.

Cummins, R. A. and Lau, A. L. D. (2005) *Personal Well-Being Index – School Children: Draft Manual* (3rd edition), Melbourne, Deakin University School of Psychology.

Cummins, R. A. and Lau, A. L. D. (2006) 'Using health and subjective well-being for quality of life measurement: a review', in Bauld, L., Clarke, K. and Maltby, T. (eds) *Social Policy Review 18*, Bristol, The Policy Press.

Currie, J. (1995) *Welfare and the Well-Being of Children*, Chur, Switzerland, Harwood.

Dale-Risk, K. (2001) 'Human rights for children: not yet fully grown', *Representing Children*, vol 13, no 4, pp 260-72.

Daly, C. (1999) 'Social exclusion and the needs and rights of children: a conflict or a resolution?', in White, K. J. (ed) *Children and Social Exclusion: Towards an Understanding and Practice that is More Inclusive*, London, NCVCCO.

Daniel, P. and Ivatts, J. (1998) *Children and Social Policy*, London, Macmillan.

Dartington Social Research Unit (1999) *Matching Needs and Services* (2nd edition), Dartington, Dartington Academic Press.

Dartington-i (2007) *Development Work to Inform Strategy and Service Design: An examination of the needs of children referred to Early Years, Education, Social Services, Youth Offending Services and Connexions in Leeds,* Report submitted to Leeds Children and Young People's Strategic Partnership.

Dasgupta, P. (1993) *An Inquiry into Well-Being and Destitution*, Oxford, Oxford University Press.

Day, H. and Jankey, S. G. (1996) 'Lessons from the literature: toward a holistic model of quality of life', in Renwick, R., Brown, I. and Nagler, M. (eds) *Quality of Life in Health Promotion and Rehabilitation: Conceptual Approaches, Issues, and Applications*, Thousand Oaks, CA, Sage Publications.

DCMS (Department for Culture, Media and Sport) (2006) *Time for Play: Encouraging Greater Play Opportunities for Children and Young People*, www.everychildmatters. gov.uk/resources-and-practice/IG00154/ [Accessed 30 August 2007]

Deeming, C. (2005) 'Minimum income standards: how might budget standards be set for the UK?', *Journal of Social Policy*, vol 34, no 4, pp 1-18.

DEFRA (Department for Environment, Food and Rural Affairs) (2004) *Quality of Life Counts*, London, National Statistics.

de Gaulejac, V. and Taboada Leonetti, I. (1994) *La lutte des places*, Paris, Desclée de Brouwer/EPI. [Cited in Strobel, 1996, pp 179-80]

DeHart, G. B., Sroufe, L. A. and Cooper, R. G. (2004) *Child Development: Its Nature and Course* (5th edition), New York, McGraw-Hill.

Deleeck, H., van den Bosch, K. and de Lathouwer, L. (eds) (1992) *Poverty and the Adequacy of Social Security in the EC*, Aldershot, EUROPASS Research Consortium/Avebury.

Deleeck, H., de Lathouwer, L. and van den Bosch, K. (1988) *Social Indicators of Social Security: A Comparative Analysis of Five Countries*, Antwerp, Centre for Social Policy.

Dennis, N. and Erdos, G. (2000) *Families without Fatherhood* (3rd edition), London, Civitas: Institute for the Study of Civil Society.

Desai, M. (1986) 'Drawing the line: on defining the poverty threshold', in Golding, P. (ed) *Excluding the Poor*, London, CPAG.

DETR (Department for the Environment, Transport and the Regions) (1999a) *A Better Quality of Life: A Strategy for Sustainable Development for the UK*, London, The Stationery Office.

DETR (1999b) *Quality of Life Counts: Indicators for a Strategy for Sustainable Development for the UK: A Baseline Assessment*, London, The Stationery Office.

de Vaus, D. A. (1996) *Surveys in Social Research* (4th edition), London, UCL Press.

DfES (Department for Education and Skills) (2003) *Every Child Matters*, Cm 5860, London, The Stationery Office.

DfES (2006a) *Common Assessment Framework for Children and Young People: Managers' Guide*, London, DfES.

DfES (2006b) *Common Assessment Framework for Children and Young People: Practitioners' Guide*, London, DfES.

DfES and National Statistics (2006) *Children in Need in England: Results of a Survey of Activity and Expenditure as Reported by Local Authority Social Services' Children and Families Teams for a Survey Week in February 2005: Local Authority Tables and Further National Analysis*, www.dfes.gov.uk/rsgateway/DB/VOL/v000647/vweb02-2006.pdf [Accessed 16 November 2006]

DH (Department of Health) (1995) *Child Protection: Messages from Research*, London, HMSO.

DH (2000) *Children in Need in England: First Results of a Survey of Activity and Expenditure as Reported by Local Authority Social Services' Children and Families Teams for a Survey Week in February 2000*, London, DH.

DH (2001a) *The Children Act Report 2000*, London, DH.

DH (2001b) *Children Act 1989 Then and Now: Messages from Research*, London, The Stationery Office.

DH (2001c) *Research Governance Framework for Health and Social Care*, London, Department of Health Publications.

DH, DfEE (Department for Education and Employment) and Home Office (2000) *Framework for the Assessment of Children in Need and their Families*, London, The Stationery Office.

Di Blasi, Z., Harkness, E., Ernst, E., Georgiou, A. and Kleijnen, J. (2001) 'Influence of context effects on health outcomes: a systematic review', *The Lancet*, vol 357, issue 9258, 10 March, pp 757-62.

Donnelly, J. (1999) 'Human rights, democracy and development', *Human Rights Quarterly*, vol 21, no 3, pp 608-32.

Donnison, D. (1982) *The Politics of Poverty*, Oxford, Martin Robertson.

Doraid, M. (1997) *Analytical Tools for Human Development* (3rd edition), New York, UNDP, Human Development Report Office.

Dorling, D. and Simpson, L. (1998) *Statistics in Society*, London, Arnold.

Dorling, D. and Thomas, B. (2004) *People and Places: A 2001 Census Atlas of the UK*, Bristol, The Policy Press.

Downes, C. (1990) 'Security and autonomy: criteria for judging the quality of care offered to adolescents in time-limited placements', in Baldwin, S., Godfrey, C. and Propper, C. (eds) *Quality of Life: Perspectives and Policies*, London, Routledge.

Doyal, L. and Gough, I. (1991) *A Theory of Human Need*, Basingstoke, Macmillan.

Drew, S. (2000) *Children and the Human Rights Act 1998*, London, Save the Children.

Drewnowski, J. (1974) *On Measuring and Planning the Quality of Life*, The Hague, Mouton.

Drèze, J. and Sen, A. (1989) *Hunger and Public Action*, Oxford, Clarendon Press.

DSS (Department of Social Security) (1999) *Opportunity for All: Tackling Poverty and Social exclusion. Indicators of Success: Definitions, Data and Baseline Information*, London, DSS.

Duffy, K. (1998) 'Combating social exclusion and promoting social integartion in the European Union', in Oppenheim, C. (ed) *An Inclusive Society: Strategies for Tackling Poverty*, London, IPPR.

Dworetzky, J. P. (1996) *Introduction to Child Development*, St Paul, Minneapolis, MN, West Publishers.

Dworkin, R. (1978) *Taking Rights Seriously*, London, Duckworth.

DWP (Department for Work and Pensions) (2005) *Opportunity for All: Seventh Annual Report 2005*, London, TSO.

DWP (2006) *Households Below Average Income 2004/05*, London, DWP.

EC (European Commission) (1994) *Social Europe: Towards a Europe of Solidarity – Combating Social Exclusion*, DGV, Brussels, Commission of the European Communities, Supplement 4/93.

Eekelaar, J. and Dingwall, R. (1990) *The Reform of Child Care Law: A Practical Guide to the Children Act 1989*, London, Routledge.

Eiser, C., Mohay, H. and Morse, R. (2000a) 'The measurement of quality of life in young children', *Child: Care, Health and Development*, vol 26, no 5, pp 401-13.

Eiser, C., Vance, Y. H. and Seamark, D. (2000b) 'The development of a theoretically driven generic measure of quality of life for children aged 6-12 years: a preliminary report', *Child: Care, Health and Development*, vol 26, no 6, pp 445-56.

Ennew, J. (2002) 'Outside childhood: street children's rights', in Franklin, B. (ed) *The New Handbook of Children's Rights: Comparative Policy and Practice*, London, Routledge.

Ennew, J. and Miljeteig, P. (1996) 'Indicators for children's rights: progress report on a project', *International Journal of Children's Rights*, vol 4, no 3, pp 213-36.

Esping-Andersen, G. (1990) *The Three Worlds of Welfare Capitalism*, Cambridge, Polity Press.

Etzioni, A. (1997) *The New Golden Rule: Community and Morality in a Democratic Society*, London, Profile Books.

Euvrard, F. and Prelis, A. (1994) 'La lutte contre la pauvreté dans la construction européene', *Recherche et Prévision*, vol 38. [Cited in Strobel, 1996, p 179]

Evans, M. and Scarborough, J. (2006) *Can Current Policy End Child Poverty in Britain by 2020?*, York, Joseph Rowntree Foundation.

Evans, M., Paugam, S. and Prélis, J.A. (1995) *Chunnel Vision: Poverty, Social Exclusion and the Debate on Social Welfare in France and Britain*, Discussion Paper WSP 115, London, London School of Economics and Political Science.

Fahmy, E. (2006) 'Youth, poverty and social exclusion', in Pantazis, C., Gordon, D. and Levitas, R. (eds) *Poverty and Social Exclusion in Britain: The Millennium Survey*, Bristol, The Policy Press.

Farquhar, M. (1995) 'Elderly people's definitions of quality of life', *Social Science and Medicine*, vol 41, no 10, pp 1439-46.

Farson, R. (1978) *Birthrights*, Harmondsworth, Penguin.

Feher, F., Heller, A. and Markus, G. (1983) *Dictatorship Over Needs: An Analysis of Soviet Societies*, Oxford, Blackwell.

Ferrera, M., Matsaganis, M. and Sacchi, S. (2002) 'Open coordination against poverty: the new EU "social inclusion process"', *Journal of European Social Policy*, vol 12, no 3, pp 227-39.

Field, A. (2000) *Discovering Statistics using SPSS for Windows*, London, Sage Publications.

Figueroa, A., Altamirano, T. and Sulmont, D. (1995) 'Social exclusion and social inequality in Peru', in Rodgers, G., Gore, C. and Figueiredo, J. B. (eds) *Social Exclusion: Rhetoric, Reality, Responses*, Geneva, International Institute for Labour Studies.

Fisher, T. and Bramley, G. (2006) 'Social exclusion and local services', in Pantazis, C., Gordon, D. and Levitas, R. (eds) *Poverty and Social Exclusion in Britain: The Millennium Survey*, Bristol, The Policy Press.

Fitzpatrick, R. (1996) 'Alternative approaches to the assessment of health-related quality of life', in Offer, A. (ed) *In Pursuit of the Quality of Life*, Oxford, Oxford University Press.

Foreman, A. (1996) 'Health needs assessment', in Percy-Smith, J. (ed) *Needs Assessments in Public Policy*, Buckingham, Open University Press.

Fox-Harding, L. (1991) *Perspectives in Childcare Policy*, London, Longman.

Franklin, B. (1989) 'Children's rights: developments and prospects', *Children and Society*, vol 3, no 1, pp 50-66.

Franklin, B. (ed) (2002) *The New Handbook of Children's Rights: Comparative Policy and Practice*, London, Routledge.

Freeman, M. (1995) 'Children's rights in a land of rites', in Franklin, B. (ed) *The Handbook of Children's Rights: Comparative Policy and Practice*, London, Routledge.

Freeman, M. D. A. (1983) *The Rights and the Wrongs of Children*, London, Frances Pinter.

Freire, P. (1970) *The Pedagogy of the Oppressed*, London, Penguin.

Frey, B. and Stutzer, A. (2002) *Happiness and Economics: How the Economy and Institutions Afford Well-Being*, Princeton, NJ, Princeton University Press.

Friedmann, J. (1996) 'Rethinking poverty: empowerment and citizen rights', *International Social Science Journal*, vol 148, no 2, pp 161-72.

Fuentes, N. and Rojas, M. (2000) 'Economic theory and social well-being: Mexico', Paper presented at the Third Conference of the International Society for Quality of Life Studies, Girona, Spain, 20-22 July.

Funk, B. A., Huebner, E. S. and Valois, R. F. (2006) 'Reliability and validity of a Brief Life Satisfaction Scale with a high school sample', *Journal of Happiness Studies*, vol 7, no 1, pp 41-54.

Furstenberg, F. F. and Hughes, M. E. (1997) 'The influence of neighbourhoods on children's development: a theoretical perspective and a research agenda', in Hauser, R. M., Brown, B. V. and Prosser, W. R. (eds) *Indicators of Children's Well-Being*, New York, Russell Sage Foundation.

Garbarino, J. and Kostelny, K. (1992) 'Child maltreatment as a community problem', *Child Abuse and Neglect*, vol 16, no 4, pp 455-64.

Gewirth, A. (1978) *Reason and Morality*, Chicago, IL, University of Chicago Press.

Gewirth, A. (1982) *Human Rights: Essays on Justification and Applications*, Chicago, IL, University of Chicago Press.

Ghate, D. and Hazel, N. (2002) *Parenting in Poor Environments: Stress, Support and Coping*, London, Jessica Kingsley Publishers.

Giddens, A. (1998) *The Third Way: The Renewal of Social Democracy*, Cambridge, Polity Press.

Gilbert, D. (2006) *Stumbling on Happiness: Why the Future Won't Feel the Way You Think It Will*, London, HarperCollins.

Glendon, M. A. (1991) *Rights Talk*, New York, Free Press.

Glennerster, H., Lupton, R., Noden, P. and Power, A. (1999) *Poverty, Social Exclusion and Neighbourhood: Studying the Area Bases of Social Exclusion*, CASE Paper 22, London, Centre for the Analysis of Social Exclusion, London School of Economics and Political Science.

Godfrey, C. and Powell, M. (1990) 'The relationship between individual choice and government policy in the decision to consume hazardous goods', in Baldwin, S., Godfrey, C. and Propper, C. (eds) *Quality of Life: Perspectives and Policies*, London, Routledge.

Golding, P. (ed) (1986) *Excluding the Poor*, London, CPAG.

Goode, J., Callender, C. and Lister, R. (1998) *Purse or Wallet? Gender Inequalities and Income Distribution within Families on Benefits*, London, Policy Studies Institute.

Goodin, R. E. (1988) *Reasons for Welfare: The Political Theory of the Welfare State*, Princeton, NJ, Princeton University Press.

Goodin, R. E. (1990) 'Relative needs', in Ware, A. and Goodin, R. E. (eds) *Needs and Welfare*, London, Sage Publications.

Gordon, D. (2000a) 'Measuring absolute and overall poverty', in Gordon, D. and Townsend, P. (eds) *Breadline Europe: The Measurement of Poverty*, Bristol, The Policy Press.

Gordon, D. (2000b) 'Inequalities in income, wealth and standard of living in Britain', in Gordon, D. and Pantazis, C. (eds) *Tackling Inequalities: Where are we Now and What Should be Done?*, Bristol, The Policy Press.

Gordon, D. (2006) 'The concept and measurement of poverty', in Pantazis, C., Gordon, D. and Levitas, R. (eds) *Poverty and Social Exclusion in Britain: The Millennium Survey*, Bristol, The Policy Press.

Gordon, D. and Forrest, R. (1995) *People and Places 2: Social and Economic Distinctions in England*, Bristol, SAUS, University of Bristol.

Gordon, D. and Loughran, F. (1997) 'Child poverty and needs based allocation', *Research, Policy and Planning*, vol 15, no 3, pp 28-38.

Gordon, D. and Pantazis, C. (1997) 'Measuring poverty in Britain in the 1990s', in Gordon, D. and Pantazis, C. (eds) *Breadline Britain in the 1990s*, Aldershot, Ashgate.

Gordon, D. and Spicker, P. (eds) (1999) *The International Glossary on Poverty*, London, Zed Books.

Gordon, D., Adelman, L., Ashworth, K., Bradshaw, J., Levitas, R., Middleton, S., Pantazis, C., Patsios, D., Payne, S., Townsend, P. and Williams, J. (2000) *Poverty and Social Exclusion in Britain*, York, Joseph Rowntree Foundation.

Gore, C. and Figueiredo, J. B. (eds) (1997) *Social Exclusion and Anti-Poverty Policy: A Debate*, Research Series 110, Geneva, International Institute of Labour Studies.

Gough, I. (2000) 'The needs of capital and the needs of people', in Gough, I., *Global Capital, Human Needs and Social Policies: Selected Essays 1994-1999*, Houndmills, Palgrave.

Gough, I. and Thomas, T. (1994) 'Need satisfaction and welfare outcomes: theory and explanations', *Social Policy and Administration*, vol 28, no 1, pp 33-56.

Graham, P., Stevenson, J. and Flynn, D. (1997) 'A new measure of health-related quality of life for children: preliminary findings', *Psychology and Health*, vol 12, no 5, pp 655-65.

Green, H., McGinnity, A., Meltzer, H., Ford, T. and Goodman, R. (2005) *Mental Health of Children and Young People in Britain, 2004*, Basingstoke, Palgrave Macmillan.

Greenspoon, P. J. and Saklofske, D. H. (2001) 'Toward and integration of subjective well-being and psychopathology', *Social Indicators Research*, vol 54, no 1, pp 81–108.

Guldberg, H. (2000) 'Child protection and the precautionary principle', in Morris, J. (ed) *Rethinking Risk and the Precautionary Principle*, Oxford, Butterworth-Heineman.

Haidt, J. (2006) *The Happiness Hypothesis*, New York, Basic Books.

Hall, C. (2000) *Organisation and Outcome in Personal Social Services for Children and Families*, Report submitted to the Department of Health, Dartington, Dartington Social Research Unit.

Hamlin, A. (1993) 'Welfare', in Goodin, R. E. and Pettitt, P. (eds) *A Companion to Contemporary Political Philosophy*, Oxford, Blackwell Publishers.

Hammarberg, T. (1995) 'Preface', in Franklin, B. (ed) *The Handbook of Children's Rights: Comparative Policy and Practice*, London, Routledge.

Harwin, J. and Forrester, D. (1999) 'Measuring child rights around the world: the potential of global indicators to monitor the UN Convention on the Rights of the Child', *Representing Children*, vol 12, no 2, pp 121–35.

Hendrick, H. (ed) (2005) *Child Welfare and Social Policy: An Essential Reader*, Bristol, The Policy Press.

Hester, M. and Pearson, C. (1997) 'Domestic violence and child contact arrangements: children's right to safety', in John, M. (ed) *A Charge against Society: The Child's Right to Protection*, London, Jessica Kingsley Publishers.

Hill, M. and Tisdall, K. (1997) *Children and Society*, London, Longman.

Hill, M., Davis, J., Prout, A. and Tisdall, K. (2004) 'Moving the participation agenda forward', *Children & Society*, vol 18, no 2, pp 77–96.

Hill, M. S. and Jenkins, S. P. (1999) *Poverty among British Children: Chronic or Transitory?*, Working Paper 1999-23, Colchester, Institute for Social and Economic Research.

Hill, P. (2002) 'Adjustment disorders', in Rutter, M. and Taylor, E. (eds) *Child and Adolescent Psychiatry* (4th edition), Oxford, Blackwell.

Hillman, M. (ed) (1993) *Children, Transport and the Quality of Life*, London, Policy Studies Institute.

Hills, J. (1999) 'Social exclusion in the UK: the state of current research', Paper presented to the Statistics Users Council/CEIES Joint Conference on Social Exclusion Statistics, London, 22 November.

Hills, J. (2002) 'Does a focus on "social exclusion" change the policy response?', in Hills, J., Le Grand, J. and Piachaud, D. (eds) *Understanding Social Exclusion*, Oxford, Oxford University Press.

Hills, J., Piachaud, D. and Le Grand, J. (eds) (2006) *Understanding Social Exclusion*, Oxford, Oxford University Press.

Hirsch, D. (2006) *What Will it Take to End Child Poverty? Firing on All Cylinders*, York, Joseph Rowntree Foundation.

Hirst, J. (1999) 'Reading the Human Rights Act', *Community Care*, 2-8 December, pp 20-22.

HM Government (2006) *Reaching Out: An Action Plan on Social Exclusion*, London, Cabinet Office.

HM Treasury (2002) *Opportunity and Security for All: Investing in an Enterprising, Fairer Britain. New Public Spending Plans 2003-2006*, London, HM Treasury.

Hobcraft, J. (1998) *Intergenerational and Life-Course Transmission of Social Exclusion: Influences of Child Poverty, Family Disruption, and Contact with the Police*. CASEpaper 15, London School of Economics, ESRC Centre for the Analysis of Social Exclusion.

Hobcraft, J. and Kiernan, K. (2001) 'Childhood poverty, early motherhood and adult social exclusion', *British Journal of Sociology*, vol 52, no 3, pp 495-517.

Holt, J. (1974) *Escape from Childhood: The Needs and Rights of Children*, Harmondsworth, Penguin.

Hopkins, A. (1992) 'Editor's introduction', in Hopkins, A. (ed) *Measures of the Quality of Life: And the Uses to Which Such Measures may be Put*, London, Royal College of Physicians of London.

Howarth, C., Kenway, P., Palmer, G. and Street, C. (1998) *Monitoring Poverty and Social Exclusion: Labour's Inheritance*, York, Joseph Rowntree Foundation.

Hunt, S. and McKenna, S. (1992) 'Do we need measures other than QALYs?', in Hopkins, A. (ed) *Measures of the Quality of Life: And the Uses to Which Such Measures may be Put*, London, Royal College of Physicians of London.

Huppert, F. A. (2005) 'Positive mental health in individuals and populations', in Huppert, F. A., Baylis, N. and Keverne, B. (eds) *The Science of Well-Being*, Oxford, Oxford University Press.

Huppert, F. A., Baylis, N. and Keverne, B. (eds) (2005) *The Science of Well-Being*, Oxford, Oxford University Press.

Huston, A. C. (ed) (1991) *Children in Poverty: Child Development and Public Policy*, Cambridge, Cambridge University Press.

Hyams-Parish, A. (1996) *Banished to the Exclusion Zone: School Exclusions and the Law from the Viewpoint of the Child*, Colchester, The Children's Legal Centre, University of Essex.

ICPQOL (Independent Commission on Population and Quality of Life) (1996) *Caring for the Future: Making the Next Decades Provide a Life Worth Living*, Oxford, Oxford University Press.

Ignatieff, M. (1984) *The Needs of Strangers*, New York, Viking.

Illich, I. (1999) 'Needs', in Sachs, W. (ed) *The Development Dictionary: A Guide to Knowledge as Power*, London, Zed Books.

Jack, G. (2000) 'Ecological influences on parenting and child development', *British Journal of Social Work*, vol 30, no 6, pp 703-20.

Jack, G. (2002) 'Ecological perspectives in assessing children and families', in Horwath, J. (ed) *The Child's World: Assessing Children in Need, the Reader*, London, Jessica Kingsley Publishers.

Jack, G. and Jordan, B. (1999) 'Social capital and child welfare', *Children and Society*, vol 13, no 4, pp 242-56.

Jackson, C. (1985) *Who Will Take Our Children? The Story of the Evacuation in Britain 1939-1945*, London, Methuen.

Jackson, T., Marks, N., Ralls, J. and Stymme, S. (1997) *Sustainable Economic Welfare in the UK 1950-1996*, London, New Economics Foundation.

James, A. and Prout, A. (eds) (1997) *Constructing and Reconstructing Childhood: Contemporary Issues in the Sociological Study of Childhood* (2nd edition), London, Falmer.

James, A., Jenks, C. and Prout, A. (1998) *Theorising Childhood*, London, Polity Press.

James, O. (2007) *Affluenza*, London, Vermilion.

Jarman, B. (1983) 'Identification of underprivileged areas', *British Medical Journal*, vol 286, pp 1705-9.

Jeffs, T. (2002) 'Schooling, education and children's rights', in Franklin, B. (ed) *The New Handbook of Children's Rights: Comparative Policy and Practice*, London, Routledge.

John, M. (ed) (1996a) *Children in Our Charge: The Child's Right to Resources*, London, Jessica Kingsley Publishers.

John, M. (ed) (1996b) *Children in Charge: The Child's Right to a Fair Hearing*, London, Jessica Kingsley Publishers.

John, M. (ed) (1997) *A Charge Against Society: The Child's Right to Protection*, London, Jessica Kingsley Publishers.

John, M. (2003) *Children's Rights and Power: Charging Up for a New Century*, London: Jessica Kingsley Publishers.

Johnson, R. and Sawbridge, P. (2004) 'Family placements: matching needs and services', in White, V. and Harris, J. (eds) *Developing Good Practice in Children's Services*, London, Jessica Kingsley Publishers.

Jones, M. and Basser-Marks, L.-A. (1997) 'Beyond the Convention on the Rights of the Child: the rights of children with disabilities in international law', *International Journal of Children's Rights*, vol 5, no 2, pp 177-92.

Jordan, B. (1996) *A Theory of Poverty and Social Exclusion*, Cambridge, Polity Press.

Jordan, B. (2006a) 'Well-being: the next revolution in children's services?', *Journal of Children's Services*, vol 1, no 1, pp 41-50.

Jordan, B. (2006b) *Rewarding Company, Enriching Life: The Economics of Relationships and Well-Being*, www.billjordan.co.uk [Accessed 6 December 2006]

Jordan, B. with Jordan, C. (2000) *Social Work and the Third Way: Tough Love as Social Policy*, London, Sage Publications.

Joseph, K. and Sumption, J. (1979) *Equality*, London, John Murray.

Kahneman, D., Diener, E. and Schwartz, N. (eds) (1999) *Well-Being: The Foundations of Hedonic Psychology*, New York, Russell Sage Foundation.

Kangas, O. and Ritakallio, V. M. (1995) *Different Methods – Different Results? Approaches to Multidimensional Poverty*, Helsinki, National Research and Development Centre for Welfare and Health.

Kaufman Kantor, G. and Jasinski, J. L. (1998) 'Dynamics and risk factors in partner violence', in Jasinski, J. L. and Williams, L. M. (eds) *Partner Violence: A Comprehensive Review of 20 Years of Research*, Thousand Oaks, CA, Sage Publications.

Kellmer-Pringle, M. (1974) *The Needs of Children*, London, Hutchinson.

Kempson, E., Bryson, A. and Rowlingson, K. (1994) *Hard Times? How Poor Families Make Ends Meet*, London, Policy Studies Institute.

Kemshall, H. and Littlechild, R. (eds) (2000) *User Involvement and Participation in Social Care: Research Informing Practice*, London, Jessica Kingsley Publishers.

Kendrick, A. (2005) 'Social exclusion and social inclusion: themes and issues in residential child care', in Crimmens, D. and Milligan, I. (eds) *Facing Forward: Residential Child Care in the 21st Century*, Lyme Regis, Russell House Publishing.

Kennedy, H. (2000) 'Foreword', in Klug, F., *Values for a Godless Age: The story of the United Kingdom's New Bill of Rights*, London, Penguin.

Kent, G. (1997) 'Realising international children's rights through implementation of national law', *International Journal of Children's Rights*, vol 5, no 4, pp 439-56.

Kenway, P. and Rahman, M. (2000) *Mapping Disadvantage: Young People who Need Help in England and Wales*, London, The Prince's Trust.

Keyes, C. L. M. (2005) 'Mental illness and/or mental health? Investigating axioms of the complete state model of health', *Journal of Consulting and Clinical Psychology*, vol 73, no 3, pp 539-48.

Kilkelly, U. (1999) *The Child and the European Convention on Human Rights*, Aldershot, Ashgate.

Kilkelly, U. (2006) 'Operationalising children's rights: lessons from research', *Journal of Children's Services*, vol 1, no 4, pp 36-47.

Kirby, P., Lanyon, C., Cronin, K. and Sinclair, R. (2003) *Building a Culture of Participation: Involving Children and Young People in Policy, Service Planning, Delivery and Evaluation*, London, DfES.

Klug, F. (2000) *Values for a Godless Age: The story of the United Kingdom's New Bill of Rights*, London, Penguin.

Knox, P. L. (1975) *Social Well-Being: A Spatial Perspective*, London, Open University Press.

Kolvin, I., Miller, F. J. W., Scott, D. M., Gatzanis, S. R. M. and Fleeting, M. (1990) *Continuities of Deprivation? The Newcastle 1000 Family Study*, Aldershot, Avebury.

Kroll, B. (2000) 'Not intruding, not colluding: process and practice in a contact centre', *Children and Society*, vol 14, no 3, pp 182-93.

Krooshof, T., Prins, M. and Janssen, J. (2000) 'Youth subcultures in the Netherlands and their changing function for social identity', Paper presented to the Third Conference of the International Society for Quality of Life Studies, Girona, Spain, 20-22 July.

Lambert, R. and Millham, S. (1968) *The Hothouse Society*, London, Weidenfeld and Nicolson.

Land, K., Lamb, V. L. and Kahler Mustillo, S. (2000) 'Child well-being in the United States 1975-1997: some findings from a new index', Paper presented to the Third Conference of the International Society for Quality of Life Studies, Girona, Spain, 20-22 July.

Lane, R. E. (1996) 'Quality of life and quality of persons: a new role for government?', in Offer, A. (ed) *In Pursuit of the Quality of Life*, Oxford, Oxford University Press.

Lane, R. E. (2000) *The Loss of Happiness in Market Democracies*, New Haven, CT, Yale University Press.

Lansdown, G. (1998) 'The rights of disabled children', *International Journal of Children's Rights*, vol 6, no 2, pp 221-7.

Lansdown, G. and Newell, P. (1994) *UK Agenda for Children: A Systematic Analysis of the Extent to which Law, Policy and Practice in the UK Complies with the Principles and Standards Contained in the UN Convention on the Rights of the Child*, London, Children's Rights Development Unit.

Layard, R. (2003) 'Income and Happiness: Rethinking Economic Policy', Unpublished paper, London, London School of Economics and Political Science.

Layard, R. (2005) *Happiness: Lessons from a New Science*, London, Allen Lane.

Layte, R., Nolan, B. and Whelan, C. (2000) 'Poverty and affluence in Ireland: a comparison of income and deprivation approaches to the measurement of poverty', in Gordon, D. and Townsend, P. (eds) *Breadline Europe: The Measurement of Poverty*, Bristol, The Policy Press.

Leach, P. (1994) *Children First: What We Must Do – And Are Not Doing – For Our Children Today*, London, Michael Joseph.

Ledogar, R. J. (1993) 'Implementing the Convention on the Rights of the Child through National Programmes for Action for Children', *International Journal of Children's Rights*, vol 1, no 3-4, pp 377-91.

Lee, P. and Murie, A. (1997) *Poverty, Housing Tenure and Social Exclusion*, Bristol, The Policy Press.

Leisering, L. and Walker, R. (1998) 'New realities: the dynamics of modernity', in Leisering, L. and Walker, R. (eds) *The Dynamics of Modern Society: Poverty, Policy and Welfare*, Bristol, The Policy Press.

Lenoir, R. (1974) *Les Exclus: Un Francais sur Dix*, Paris, Editions du Seuil. [Cited in Martin, 1996, p 383]

Lessof, C. and Jowell, R. (1999) 'Measuring social exclusion', Paper presented to the Statistics Users Council/CEIES Joint Conference on Social Exclusion Statistics, London, 22 November.

Levitas, R. (1996) 'The concept of social exclusion and the new Durkheimian hegemony', *Critical Social Policy*, vol 16, no 46, pp 5-20.

Levitas, R. (1998) *The Inclusive Society? Social Exclusion and New Labour*, Basingstoke, Macmillan.

Levitas, R. (2000) 'What is social exclusion?', in Gordon, D. and Townsend, P. (eds) *Breadline Europe: The Measurement of Poverty*, Bristol, The Policy Press.

Levitas, R. (2006) 'The concept and measurement of social exclusion', in Pantazis, C., Gordon, D. and Levitas, R. (eds) *Poverty and Social Exclusion in Britain: The Millennium Survey*, Bristol, The Policy Press.

Levitas, R., Pantazis, C., Patsios, D. and Townsend, P. (2000) 'Social exclusion in Britain', in Gordon, D., Adelman, L., Ashworth, K., Bradshaw, L., Levitas, R., Middleton, S., Pantazis, C., Patsios, D., Payne, S., Townsend P. and Williams, J. (eds) *Poverty and Social Exclusion in Britain*, York, Joseph Rowntree Foundation.

Lister, R. (1990) *The Exclusive Society: Citizenship and the Poor*, London, Child Poverty Action Group.

Lister, R. (1997) *Citizenship: Feminist Perspectives*, Basingstoke, Macmillan.

Lister, R. (2004) *Poverty*, Cambridge, Polity Press.

Little, M. (2002) 'The law concerning services for children with social and psychological problems', in Rutter, M. and Taylor, E. (eds) *Child and Adolescent Psychiatry* (4th edition), Oxford, Blackwell.

Little, M. and Kelly, S. (1995) *A Life Without Problems?*, Aldershot, Arena.

Little, M. and Madge, J. (1998) 'Inter-agency assessment of need in child protection', Unpublished report submitted to the NHS R&D Executive, Dartington, Dartington Social Research Unit.

Little, M. and Mount, K. (1999) *Prevention and Early Intervention with Children in Need*, Aldershot, Ashgate.

Little, M., Axford, N. and Morpeth, L. (2002) *Aggregating Data: Better Management Information and Planning in Children's Services*, Dartington, Warren House Press.

Little, M., Axford, N. and Morpeth, L. (2003) *Threshold: Determining the Extent of Impairment to Children's Development*, Dartington, Warren House Press.

Little, M., Kohm, A. and Thompson, R. (2005) 'The impact of residential placement on child development: research and policy implication', *International Journal of Social Welfare*, vol 14, no 3, pp 200-9.

Little, M., Madge, J., Mount, K., Ryan, M. and Tunnard, J. (1999) *Matching Needs and Services* (2nd edition), Dartington, Dartington Academic Press.

Littlewood, P. (1999) 'Schooling, exclusion and self-exclusion', in Littlewood, P., Glorieux, I., Herkommer, S. and Jonsson, I. (eds) *Social Exclusion in Europe: Problems and Paradigms*, Aldershot, Ashgate.

Lloyd, E. (2006) 'Children, poverty and social exclusion', in Pantazis, C., Gordon, D. and Levitas, R. (eds) *Poverty and Social Exclusion in Britain: The Millennium Survey*, Bristol, The Policy Press.

Long, A. (1994) 'Assessing health and social outcomes', in Popay, J. and Williams, G. (eds) *Researching the People's Health*, London, Routledge.

Lowndes, V., Pratchett, L. and Stoker, G. (2006) *Locality Matters: Making Participation Count in Local Politics*, London, Institute for Public Policy Research.

Lupton, R. and Powers, A. (2002) 'Social exclusion and neighbourhoods', in Hills, J., Le Grand, J. and Piachaud, D. (eds) *Understanding Social Exclusion*, Oxford, Oxford University Press.

Lyon, C. and Parton, N. (1995) 'Children's rights and the Children Act 1989', in Franklin, B. (ed) *The Handbook of Children's Rights: Comparative Policy and Practice*, London, Routledge.

McAuley, C., Pecora, P. J. and Rose, W. (eds) (2006) *Enhancing the Well-Being of Children and Families through Effective Interventions: International Evidence for Practice*, London, Jessica Kingsley Publishers.

McCormack, S. J. and Richard, J. (1974) 'To save or let die: the dilemma of modern medicine', *Journal of the American Medical Association*, vol 229, no 2, pp 172-6.

MacDonald, R. (1997a) 'Dangerous youth and the dangerous class', in MacDonald, R. (ed) *Youth, the 'Underclass' and Social Exclusion*, London, Routledge.

MacDonald, R. (ed) (1997b) *Youth, the 'Underclass' and Social Exclusion*, London, Routledge.

MacDonald, R. and Marsh, J. (2005) *Disconnected Youth? Growing Up in Britain's Poor Neighbourhoods*, Basingstoke, Palgrave Macmillan.

MacGillivray, A. and Zadek, S. (1995) *Accounting for Change: Indicators for Sustainable Development*, London, New Economics Foundation.

MacGregor, S. (1981) *The Politics of Poverty*, London, Longman.

Mack, J. and Lansley, S. (1985) *Poor Britain*, London, George Allen and Unwin.

Marks, N. and Shah, H. (2005) 'A well-being manifesto for a flourishing society', in Huppert, F. A., Baylis, N. and Keverne, B. (eds) *The Science of Well-Being*, Oxford, Oxford University Press.

Marshall, T. H. (1950) *Citizenship and Social Class (and Other Essays)*, Cambridge, Cambridge University Press.

Martin, C. (1996) 'French review article: the debate in France over "social exclusion"', *Social Policy and Administration*, vol 30, no 4, pp 382-92.

Martin, P. (2005) *Making Happy People: The Nature of Happiness and its Origins in Childhood*, London, Fourth Estate.

Maslow, A. (1943) 'A theory of human motivation', *Psychological Review*, vol 50, pp 370-96.

Mason, J. and Fattore, T. (eds) (2005) *Children Taken Seriously: In Theory, Policy and Practice*, London, Jessica Kingsley Publishers.

Mayall, B. (2002) *Towards a Sociology for Childhood: Thinking from Children's Lives*, Buckingham, Open University Press.

Mayes, D. G. (2002) 'Social exclusion and macro–economic policy in Europe: a problem of dynamic and spatial change', *Journal of European Social Policy*, vol 12, no 3, pp 195-209.

Mejer, L. (2000) 'Social exclusion in the EU member states', *Statistics in Focus, Population and Social Conditions* 1/2000, Luxembourg, Eurostat.

Melamid, E. and Brodbar, G. (2003) 'Matching Needs and Services: an assessment tool for community-based service systems', *Child Welfare*, vol 82, no 4, pp 397-412.

Messu, M. (1993) 'Dérégulation et régulation sociales: contribution à l'analyse sociologique des politiques sociales', *Cahier de Recherches* 51, CREDOC. [Cited in Strobel, 1996, p 174]

Messu, M. (1994) 'Pauvreté et exclusion en France', in Merrien, F.-X. (ed) *Face à la Pauvreté*, Paris, L'Atelier. [Cited in Procacci, 1996, p 12]

Michalos, A. C. (1986) 'Job satisfaction, marital satisfaction, and the quality of life: a review and a preview', in Andrews, F. M. (ed) *Research on the Quality of Life*, Ann Arbor, MI, Institute for Social Research.

Micklewright, J. (2002) 'Social exclusion and children: a European view for a US debate', in Kahn, A. J. and Kamerman, S. B. (eds) *Beyond Child Poverty: The Social Exclusion of Children*, New York, The Institute for Child and Family Policy, Columbia University.

Micklewright, J. and Stewart, K. (1999) *Is Child Welfare Converging in the European Union?*, Innocenti Occasional Papers, Economic and Social Policy Series 69, Florence, UNICEF International Child Development Centre.

Middleton, S., Ashworth, K. and Braithwaite, I. (1997) *Small Fortunes: Spending on Children, Childhood Poverty and Parental Sacrifice*, York, Joseph Rowntree Foundation.

Miller, D. (1976) *Social Justice*, Oxford, Clarendon Press.

Miller, D. (1999) *Principles of Social Justice*, Cambridge, MA, Harvard University Press.

Mills, G. G. and Davies, M. (1999) 'The marginal child: a study of socially disaffiliated children in the South Pacific', *International Journal of Children's Rights*, vol 7, no 3, pp 239-58.

Mingione, E. (1997) 'Enterprise and exclusion', in Christie, I. and Perry, H. (eds) *The Wealth and Poverty of Networks: Tackling Social Exclusion*, London, Demos.

Mittler, P. (2000) *Working towards Inclusive Education: Social Contexts*, London, Fulton.

Mizen, P., Bolton, A. and Pole, C. (1999) 'School age workers: the paid employment of children in Britain', *Work, Employment and Society*, vol 13, no 3, pp 423-38.

Moore, M., Sixsmith, J. and Knowles, K. (1996) *Children's Reflections on Family Life*, London, Falmer Press.

Morrow, V. M. (2000) '"Dirty looks" and "trampy places" in young people's accounts of community and neighbourhood: implications for health inequalities', *Critical Public Health*, vol 10, no 2, pp 141-52.

Muffels, R., Berghman, J. and Dirven, H.-J. (1992) 'A multi-method approach to monitor the evolution of poverty', *Journal of European Social Policy*, vol 2, no 3, pp 193-213.

Muldoon, M. F., Barger, S. D., Flory, J. D. and Manuck, S. B. (1998) 'What are quality of life measurements measuring?', *British Medical Journal*, vol 316, no 7130, pp 542-5.

Mulkay, M., Ashmore, M. and Pinch, T. (1987) 'Measuring the quality of life: a sociological invention concerning the application of economics to healthcare', *Sociology*, vol 21, no 4, pp 541–64.

Murie, A. (2000) 'How can we end inequalities in housing?', in Gordon, D. and Pantazis, C. (eds) *Tackling Inequalities: Where are We Now and What can be Done?*, Bristol, The Policy Press.

Murray, C. (1990) 'The British underclass', *The Public Interest*, vol 99, pp 4–28.

Najman, J. M. and Levine, S. (1981) 'Evaluating the impact of medical care and technologies on the quality of life: a review and critique', *Social Science and Medicine*, vol 15F, pp 107–15.

National Statistics/DEFRA (Department for Environment, Food and Rural Affairs) (2006) *Sustainable Development Indicators in Your Pocket: An Update of the UK Government Strategy Indicators*, London, DEFRA.

Nettle, D. (2005) *Happiness: The Science Behind your Smile*, Oxford, Oxford University Press.

Nickel, J. W. (1987) *Making Sense of Human Rights: Philosophical Reflections on the Universal Declaration of Human Rights*, Berkeley, CA, University of California Press.

Nkrumah, F. K. (1992) *The Quality of Child Life and Health: An Indictment against Society?*, Accra, Ghana Universities Press.

Norberg-Hodge, H. (1996) 'The pressure to modernise and globalise', in Mander, J. and Goldsmith, E. (eds) *The Case against the Global Economy (and for a Turn Toward the Local)*, San Francisco, CA, Sierra Club Books.

Nozick, R. (1974) *Anarchy, State and Utopia*, Oxford, Blackwell.

Nussbaum, A. C. (1993) 'Non-relative virtues: an Aristotelian approach', in Nussbaum, M. C. and Sen, A. (eds) *The Quality of Life*, Oxford, Clarendon Press.

Nussbaum, A. C. and Sen, A. (1993) 'Introduction', in Nussbaum, M. C. and Sen, A. (eds) *The Quality of Life*, Oxford, Clarendon Press.

Nussbaum, M. (1995) 'Human capabilities, female human-beings', in Nussbaum, M. and Glover, J. (eds) *Women, Culture and Development: A Study of Human Capabilities*, Oxford, Clarendon Press.

OECD (Organisation for Economic Co-operation and Development) (1976) *Public Expenditure on Income Maintenance Programmes*, Paris, OECD.

Offer, A. (1996) 'Introduction', in Offer, A. (ed) *In Pursuit of the Quality of Life*, Oxford, Oxford University Press.

Offer, A. (2006) *The Challenge of Affluence: Self-Control and Well-Being in the United States and Britain since 1950*, Oxford, Oxford University Press.

Oldfield, N. and Yu, A. C. S. (1993) *The Cost of a Child: Living Standards for the 1990s*, London, CPAG.

Oliver, M. and Barnes, C. (1998) *Disabled People and Social Policy: From Exclusion to Inclusion*, London, Longman.

ONS (Office for National Statistics) (1997) *Social Trends 27*, London, The Stationery Office.

ONS (1998) *Social Trends 28*, London, The Stationery Office.

ONS (2000) *Social Inequalities 2000 Edition*, London, The Stationery Office.

Oppenheim, C. (1998) 'An overview of poverty and social exclusion', in Oppenheim, C. (ed) *An Inclusive Society: Strategies for Tackling Poverty*, London, IPPR.

Orshansky, M. (1965) 'Counting the poor: another look at the poverty profile', *Social Security Bulletin*, June, pp 3-29.

Orshansky, M. (1969) 'How poverty is measured', *Monthly Labor Review*, no 92, pp 37-41.

Osberg, L. (2002) *Trends in Poverty: The UK in International Perspective – How Rates Mislead and Intensity Matters*, Working Paper 2002-10, Colchester, Institute for Social and Economic Research.

Oyen, E. (1999) 'Introducing the glossary', in Gordon, D. and Spicker, P. (eds) *The International Glossary on Poverty*, London, Zed Books.

Packman, J. (1968) *Child Care: Needs and Numbers*, London, Allen and Unwin.

Palmer, G., MacInnes, T. and Kenway, P. (2006) *Monitoring Poverty and Social Exclusion in the UK 2006*, York, Joseph Rowntree Foundation.

Palmer, G., Rahman, M. and Kenway, P. (2002) *Monitoring Poverty and Social Exclusion 2002*, York, Joseph Rowntree Foundation.

Pantazis, C. and Gordon, D. (1997) 'Poverty and health', in Gordon, D. and Pantazis, C. (eds) *Breadline Britain in the 1990s*, Aldershot, Ashgate.

Pantazis, C., Gordon, D. and Levitas, R. (eds) (2006) *Poverty and Social Exclusion in Britain: The Millennium Survey*, Bristol, The Policy Press.

Papadopoulos, T. (2000) *Welfare Support for the Unemployed: A Comparative Analysis of Social Policy Responses to Unemployment in Twelve EU Member States*, Aldershot, Ashgate.

Parker, H. (ed) (1999) *Low Cost But Acceptable: A Minimum Income Standard for the UK: Families with Children*, Bristol, The Policy Press.

Parker, R. (1990) *Away from Home: A History of Childcare*, Barkingside, Barnardo's.

Parsons, C. (1999) *Education, Exclusion and Citizenship*, London, Routledge.

Parton, N. (1991) *Governing the Family: Child Care, Child Protection and the State*, Basingstoke, Macmillan.

Paugam, S. (1995) 'The spiral of precariousness', in Room, G. (ed) *Beyond the Threshold: The Measurement and Analysis of Social Exclusion*, Bristol, The Policy Press.

Paugam, S. (1996a) 'Poverty and social disqualification: a comparative analysis of cumulative social disadvantage in Europe', *Journal of European Social Policy*, vol 6, no 4, pp 287-303.

Paugam, S. (1996b) *A New Social Contract? Poverty and Social Exclusion: A Sociological View*, EUI Working Papers 96/37, Florence, European University Institute.

Payne, S. (2006) 'Mental health, poverty and social exclusion', in Pantazis, C., Gordon, D. and Levitas, R. (eds) *Poverty and Social Exclusion in Britain: The Millennium Survey*, Bristol, The Policy Press.

Percy-Smith, J. (1996) 'Introduction: assessing needs – theory and practice', in Percy-Smith, J. (ed) *Needs Assessments in Public Policy*, Buckingham, Open University Press.

Percy-Smith, J. (ed) (2000a) *Policy Responses to Social Exclusion: Towards Inclusion?*, Buckingham, Open University Press.

Percy-Smith, J. (2000b) 'Introduction: the contours of social exclusion', in Percy-Smith, J. (ed) *Policy Responses to Social Exclusion: Towards Inclusion?*, Buckingham, Open University Press.

Percy-Smith, J. and Sanderson, I. (1992) *Understanding Local Needs*, London, IPPR.

Pettitt, B. (ed) (1998) *Children and Work in the UK: Reassessing the Issues*, London, CPAG.

Phillips, M. (1996) *All Must Have Prizes*, London, Little Brown and Co.

Piachaud, D. (1979) *The Cost of a Child*, London, CPAG.

Piachaud, D. (1981) 'Peter Townsend and the Holy Grail', *New Society*, 10 September, pp 419–21.

Pinker, R. (1999) 'Do poverty definitions matter?', in Gordon, D. and Spicker, P. (eds) *The International Glossary on Poverty*, London, Zed Books.

Pinney, A. (2005) *Disabled Children in Residential Placements*, London, Department for Education and Skills.

Plant, R. (1990) Untitled essay, in Institute of Economic Affairs (ed) *Citizenship and Rights in Thatcher's Britain: Two Views*, London, Institute of Economic Affairs.

Plant, R. (1991) *Modern Political Thought*, Oxford, Blackwell.

Plant, R., Lesser, H. and Taylor-Gooby, P. (1980) *Political Philosophy and Social Welfare: Essays on the Normative Basis of Welfare Provision*, London, Routledge and Kegan Paul.

Pollard, E. L. and Rosenberg, M. L. (2003) 'The strengths-based approach to child well-being: let's begin with the end in mind', in Bornstein, M. H., Davidson, L., Keyes, C. L. M. and Moore, K. A. (eds) *Well-Being: Positive Development Across the Life-Course*, Mahwah, NJ, Lawrence Erlbaum Associates.

Ponton, L. E. (1997) *The Romance of Risk: Why Teenagers Do the Things they Do*, Oxford, Basic Books.

Porteous, D. (1996) 'Methodologies for needs assessment', in Percy-Smith, J. (ed) *Needs Assessments in Public Policy*, Buckingham, Open University Press.

Preston-Shoot, M. and Wigley, V. (2005) 'Mapping the needs of children in need', *British Journal of Social Work*, vol 35, no 2, pp 255-75.

Price Cohen, C. and Wolthius, A. (1995) 'Committee on the Rights of the Child: eighth session reports of states parties', *International Journal of Children's Rights*, vol 3, no 2, pp 263-9.

Procacci, G. (1996) *Against Exclusion: The Poor and the Social Sciences*, EUI Working Paper RSC 96/41, Florence, Robert Schuman Centre, European University Institute.

Pullinger, J. and Matheson, J. (1999) 'Social exclusion: availability and plans for official statistics', Paper presented to the Statistics Users Council/CEIES Joint Conference on Social Exclusion Statistics, London, 22 November.

Purdy, L. M. (1992) *In their Best Interest? The Case against Equal Rights for Children*, Ithaca, NY, Cornell University Press.

Quilgars, D. and Wallace, A. (2002) 'The environment and children', in Bradshaw, J. (ed) *The Well-Being of Children in the UK*, London, Save the Children.

Qvortrup, J. (1994) 'Childhood matters: an introduction', in Qvortrup, J., Bardy, M., Sgritta, G. and Wintersberger, H. (eds) *Childhood Matters: Social Theory, Practice and Politics*, Aldershot, Avebury Press.

Rabiee, P., Sloper, P. and Beresford, B. (2005) 'Desired outcomes for children and young people with complex health care needs and children who do not use speech for communication', *Health and Social Care in the Community*, vol 13, no 5, pp 478-87.

Rahnema, M. (1999) 'Poverty', in Sachs, W. (ed) *The Development Dictionary: A Guide to Knowledge as Power*, London, Zed Books.

Raphael, D. (1996a) 'Defining quality of life: eleven debates concerning its measurement', in Renwick, R., Brown, I. and Nagler, M. (eds) *Quality of Life in Health Promotion and Rehabilitation: Conceptual Approaches, Issues, and Applications*, Thousand Oaks, CA, Sage Publications.

Raphael, D. (1996b) 'Quality of life and adolescent health', in Renwick, R., Brown, I. and Nagler, M. (eds) *Quality of Life in Health Promotion and Rehabilitation: Conceptual Approaches, Issues, and Applications*, Thousand Oaks, CA, Sage Publications.

Ravens-Sieberer, U., Gosch, A., Rajmil, L., Erhart, M., Bruil, J., Duer, W., Auquier, P., Power, M., Abel, T., Czemy, L., Mazur, J., Czimbalmos, A., Tountas, Y., Hagquist, C., Kilroe, J. and European KIDSCREEN Group (2005) 'KIDSCREEN-52 quality of life measure for children and adolescents', *Expert Review of Pharmacoeconomics and Outcomes Research*, vol 5, no 3, pp 353-64.

Rawls, J. (1971) *A Theory of Justice*, Cambridge, MA, Harvard University Press.

RBKC (Royal Borough of Kensington and Chelsea) (1993) *Children and Families: Census 91*, London, RBKC Corporate Research and Information Group.

Renwick, R. and Brown, I. (1996) 'The Centre for Health Promotion's conceptual approach to quality of life: being, belonging, and becoming', in Renwick, R., Brown, I. and Nagler, M. (eds) (1996) *Quality of Life in Health Promotion and Rehabilitation: Conceptual Approaches, Issues, and Applications*, Thousand Oaks, CA, Sage Publications.

Renwick, R., Brown, I. and Nagler, M. (eds) (1996) *Quality of Life in Health Promotion and Rehabilitation: Conceptual Approaches, Issues, and Applications*, Thousand Oaks, CA, Sage Publications.

Rhoden, N. K. (1985) 'Treatment dilemmas for imperiled newborns: why quality of life counts', *Southern California Law Review*, vol 58, no 6, pp 1283-347.

Ridge, T. (1998) 'The impact of social exclusion on children and young people "looked after" by local authorities: a child-centred study of social exclusion, friendship and social integration', MSc dissertation, University of Bath.

Ridge, T. (2002) *Childhood Poverty and Social Exclusion: From a Child's Perspective*, Bristol, The Policy Press.

Ridge, T. (2005) 'Supporting children? The impact of child support policies on children's well-being in the UK and Australia', *Journal of Social Policy*, vol 34, no 1, pp 121-42.

Ridge, T. and Millar, J. (2000) 'Excluding children: autonomy, friendship and the experience of the care system', *Social Policy and Administration*, vol 34, no 2, pp 160-75.

Ringen, S. (1987) *The Possibility of Politics*, Oxford, Clarendon Press.

Ringen, S. (1988) 'Direct and indirect measures of poverty', *Journal of Social Policy*, vol 17, no 3, pp 351-65.

Ringen, S. (1995) 'Well-being, measurement and preferences', *Acta Sociologica*, vol 38, no 1, pp 3-15.

Roach, J. L. and Roach, J. K. (eds) (1972) *Poverty: Selected Readings*, Harmondsworth, Penguin Books.

Robinson, P. and Oppenheim, C. (1998) *Social Exclusion Indicators: A Submission to the Social Exclusion Unit*, London, IPPR.

Roche, J. (2001) 'Quality of life for children', in Foley, P., Roche, J. and Tucker, S. (eds) *Children in Society: Theory, Policy and Practice*, Basingstoke, Palgrave.

Roche, J. and Tucker, S. (2003) 'Extending the social exclusion debate: an exploration of the family lives of young carers and young people with ME', *Childhood*, vol 10, no 4, pp 439-56.

Roche, M. (1995) 'Citizenship and modernity', *British Journal of Sociology*, vol 46, no 4, pp 715-33.

Rogerson, R. J. (1995) 'Environmental and health-related quality of life: conceptual and methodological similarities', *Social Science and Medicine*, vol 41, no 10, pp 1373-82.

Roker, D. (1998) *Worth More Than This: Young People Growing Up in Poverty*, Brighton, Trust for the Study of Adolescence.

Roll, J. (1992) *Understanding Poverty: A Guide to the Concepts and Measures*, Occasional Paper 15, London, The Family Policy Studies Centre.

Room, G. (1995) 'Poverty and social exclusion: the new European agenda for policy and research', in Room, G. (ed) *Beyond the Threshold: The Measurement and Analysis of Social Exclusion*, Bristol, The Policy Press.

Room, G. (1999) 'Social exclusion, solidarity and the challenge of globalisation', *International Journal of Social Welfare*, vol 8, no 3, pp 166-74.

Room, G. (2000) 'Trajectories of social exclusion: the wider context in the third and first worlds', in Gordon, D. and Townsend, P. (eds) *Breadline Europe: The Measurement of Poverty*, Bristol, The Policy Press.

Room, G. et al (eds) (1992) *Observatory on National Policies to Combat Social Exclusion: Second Annual Report*, Report to the Commission of the European Communities, Lille, European Economic Interest Group 'Animation and Research'.

Rosenberg, M. (1965) *Society and the Adolescent Self Image*, Princeton, NJ, Princeton University Press.

Rosenfeld, M. (1989) *Emergence from Extreme Poverty*, Paris, Science and Service Fourth World Publication.

Rosser, R. M. and Watts, V. C. (1972) 'The measurement of hospital output', *International Journal of Hospital Epidemiology*, vol 1, no 4, pp 361-8.

Rowlands, J. (1997) 'A better way to define needs', *Children's Services News*, July, p 4.

Rowntree, B. S. (1901) *Poverty: A Study of Town Life*, London, Macmillan.

Rowntree, B. S. and Lavers, G. (1951) *Poverty and the Welfare State: A Third Social Survey of York Dealing only with Economic Questions*, London, Longman.

Rubin, Z. (1980) *Children's Friendships*, London, Fontana.

Runciman, W. G. (1966) *Relative Deprivation and Social Justice: A Study of Attitudes to Social Inequality in Twentieth Century England*, London, Penguin.

Rutter, M. (1989) 'Pathways from childhood to adult life', *Journal of Child Psychology and Psychiatry*, vol 30, no 1, pp 23-51.

Rutter, M. (1999) 'Psychosocial adversity and child psychopathology', *British Journal of Psychiatry*, vol 174, no 6, pp 480-93.

Rutter, M., Giller, H. and Hagell, A. (1998) *Antisocial Behaviour by Young People*, Cambridge, Cambridge University Press.

Rutter, M., Tizard, J. and Whitmore, K. (1970) *Education, Health and Behaviour*, London, Longman.

Saporiti, A. (1999) 'Statistics on childhood', in Verhellen, E. (ed) *Understanding Children's Rights: Collected Papers Presented at the Fourth International Interdisciplinary Course on Children's Rights*, December, Ghent, Belgium, University of Ghent.

Saraceno, C. (1997) 'The importance of social exclusion (commentary on chapter 10)', in Beck, W., van der Maesen, L. and Walker, A. (eds) *The Social Quality of Europe*, Bristol, The Policy Press.

Scanlon, T. (1993) 'Value, desire, and quality of life', in Nussbaum, M. C. and Sen, A. (eds) *The Quality of Life*, Oxford, Clarendon Press.

Schimmel, N. (2006) 'Freedom and autonomy of street children', *International Journal of Children's Rights*, vol 14, no 3, pp 211-34.

Schluter, M. and Lee, D. (1993) *The R Factor*, London, Hodder & Stoughton.

Schluter, M. and Lee, D. (eds) (2002) *The R Option: Building Relationships as a Better Way of Life*, Cambridge, The Relationships Foundation.

Schoch, R. (2006) *The Secrets of Happiness*, London, Profile Books.

Scott, J. (1994) *Poverty and Wealth: Citizenship, Deprivation and Privilege*, London, Longman.

Scott, J. and Ward, H. (eds) (2005) *Safeguarding and Promoting the Well-Being of Children, Families and Communities*, London, Jessica Kingsley Publishers.

Seabrook, J. (1999) 'Basic needs', *Resurgence*, vol 193, pp 38-9.

Seligman, M. E. P. (2005) 'Positive psychology, positive prevention and positive therapy', in Snyder, C. R. and Lopez, S. J. (eds) *Handbook of Positive Psychology*, Oxford, Oxford University Press.

Sen, A. (1981) *Poverty and Famines: An Essay on Entitlement and Deprivation*, Oxford, Clarendon Press.

Sen, A. (1982) *Choice, Welfare and Measurement*, Oxford, Blackwell.

Sen, A. (1983) 'Poor, relatively speaking', *Oxford Economic Papers*, vol 35, no 2, pp 135-69.

Sen, A. (1985a) 'A sociological approach to the measurement of poverty: a reply to Professor Peter Townsend', *Oxford Economic Papers*, vol 37, no 4, pp 669-76.

Sen, A. (1985b) 'Rights and capabilities', in Honderich, T. (ed) *Morality and Objectivity*, London, Routledge and Kegan Paul.

Sen, A. (1993) 'Capability and well-being', in Nussbaum, M. C. and Sen, A. (eds) *The Quality of Life*, Oxford, Clarendon Press.

Sen, A. (1999) *Development as Freedom*, New York, Anchor Books.

Sen, A. (2000) *Social Exclusion: Concept, Application, and Scrutiny*, Social Development Papers 1, Manila (Philippines), Asian Development Bank.

SEU (Social Exclusion Unit) (1997) *Social Exclusion Unit*, London, Cabinet Office.

SEU (1998a) *Bringing Britain Together: A National Strategy for Neighbourhood Renewal*, Cm 4045, London, The Stationery Office.

SEU (1998b) *Truancy and School Exclusion*, Cm 3957, London, The Stationery Office.

SEU (1998c) *Rough Sleeping*, Cm 4008, London, The Stationery Office.

SEU (1999a) *Teenage Pregnancy*, Cm 4342, London, The Stationery Office.

SEU (1999b) *Bridging the Gap: New Opportunities for 16–18 year-olds Not in Education, Employment or Training*, Cm 4405, London, The Stationery Office.

SEU (2002) *Young Runaways*, London, SEU.

Sharma, N. (2002) *Still Missing Out? Ending Poverty and Social Exclusion: Messages to Government from Families with Disabled Children*, Basildon, Barnardo's Publications.

Sheppard, M. (2006) *Social Work and Social Exclusion: The Idea of Practice*, Aldershot, Ashgate.

Silver, H. (1994) 'Social exclusion and social solidarity: three paradigms', *International Labour Review*, vol 133, no 5-6, pp 531-78.

Sinclair, I. and Gibbs, I. (1998) *Children's Homes: A Study in Diversity*, Chichester, Wiley.

Sinclair, R. (1996) 'Children and young people's participation in decision-making: the legal framework in social services and education', in Hill, M. and Aldgate, J. (eds) *Child Welfare Services: Developments in Law, Policy, Practice and Research*, London, Jessica Kingsley.

Sinclair, R. (1999) *The Language of Need: Social Workers Describing the Needs of Children*, London, Department of Health.

Sinclair, R. and Carr–Hill, R. A. (1996) *The Categorisation of Children in Need*, London, National Children's Bureau.

Skevington, S. M. and Gillison, F. B. (2006) 'Assessing children's quality of life in health and social services: meeting challenges and adding value', *Journal of Children's Services*, vol 1, no 2, pp 41-50.

Slevin, M. L., Plant, H., Lynch, D., Drinkwater, J. and Gregory, W. M. (1988) 'Who should measure quality of life, the doctor or the patient?, *British Journal of Cancer*, vol 57, pp 109-12.

Smith, C. (1997) 'Children's rights: have carers abandoned values?', *Children and Society*, vol 11, no 1, pp 3-15.

Smith, D. M. (1977) *Human Geography: A Welfare Approach*, London, Edward Arnold.

Smith, G. (1980) *Social Need: Policy, Practice and Research*, London, Routledge and Kegan Paul.

Social Exclusion Taskforce (2007) *Reaching Out: Think Family. Analysis and Themes from the Families at Risk Review*, London, Cabinet Office.

Soper, K. (1993) 'A theory of human need', *New Left Review*, vol I/197, pp 113-28.

SPC (Social Protection Committee) (2001) *Report on Indicators in the Field of Poverty and Social Exclusion, October 2001*, Employment and Social Policy Council Document No. 13509/01, Brussels, European Commission.

Spicker, P. (1999) 'Definitions of poverty: eleven clusters of meaning', in Gordon, D. and Spicker, P. (eds) *The International Glossary on Poverty*, London, Zed Books.

Spieth, L. E. and Harris, C.V. (1996) 'Assessment of health–related quality of life in children and adolescents: an integrative review', *Journal of Paediatric Psychology*, vol 21, no 2, pp 175-93.

SRA (Social Research Association) (2002) *Ethical Guidelines*, London, SRA.

Stewart, A. (1995) 'Two conceptions of citizenship', *British Journal of Sociology*, vol 46, no 1, pp 63-78.

Stewart, F. (1996) 'Basic needs, capabilities, and human development', in Offer, A. (ed) *In Pursuit of the Quality of Life*, Oxford, Oxford University Press.

Streeten, P., Javed Burki, S., Ul Haq, M., Hicks, N. and Stewart, F. (1981) *First Things First: Meeting Basic Human Needs in Developing Countries*, New York, Oxford University Press for the World Bank.

Strobel, P. (1996) 'From poverty to social exclusion: a wage–earning society or a society of human rights?', *International Social Science Journal*, vol 148, no 2, pp 173-90.

Tao, J. and Drover, G. (1997) 'Chinese and western notions of need', *Critical Social Policy*, vol 17, no 50, pp 5-25.

Taylor, K. (2005) 'Understanding communities today: using Matching Needs and Services to assess community needs and design community-based services', *Child Welfare*, vol 84, no 2, pp 251-264.

Thomas, N. (2002) *Children, Family and the State: Decision-Making and Child Participation*, Bristol, The Policy Press.

Thomas, N. and O'Kane, C. (2000) 'Discovering what children think: connections between research and practice', *British Journal of Social Work*, vol 30, no 6, pp 819-35.

Touraine, A. (1991) 'Face à l'exclusion', *Esprit*, vol 141, pp 7-13. [Cited in Abrahamson, 1997, p 4]

Townsend, P. (1979) *Poverty in the UK*, Harmondsworth, Penguin.

Townsend, P. (1985) 'A sociological approach to the measurement of poverty: a rejoinder to Professor Amartya Sen', *Oxford Economic Papers*, vol 37, no 4, pp 659-68.

Townsend, P. (1993) *The International Analysis of Poverty*, Milton Keynes, Harvester Wheatsheaf.

Townsend, P. and Gordon, D. (2000) 'Introduction: the measurement of poverty in Europe', in Gordon, D. and Townsend, P. (eds) *Breadline Europe: The Measurement of Poverty*, Bristol, The Policy Press.

Toynbee, P. (2003) *Hard Work: Life in Low-Pay Britain*, London, Bloomsbury.

Tsakloglou, P. and Papadopoulos, F. (2002) 'Aggregate level and determining factors of social exclusion in twelve European Countries', *Journal of European Social Policy*, vol 12, no 3, pp 211-25.

Tunnard, J. (2002) 'Matching Needs and Services: emerging themes from its application in different social care settings', in Ward, H. and Rose, W. (eds) *Approaches to Needs Assessment in Children's Services*, London, Jessica Kingsley Publishers.

Twine, F. (1994) *Citizenship and Social Rights: The Interdependence of Self and Society*, London, Sage Publications.

UN (United Nations) (1995) *The World Summit for Social Development. The Copenhagen Declaration and Programme of Action*, New York, UN.

UNDP (United Nations Development Programme) (1991) *Human Development Report*, New York, UNDP.

UNICEF (United Nations Children's Fund) (1998) *Indicators for Global Monitoring of Children's Rights: Summary Report and Background Papers*, International meeting 9-12 February, Geneva, Switzerland, New York, UNICEF Division of Evaluation, Policy and Planning.

Vafea, A., Lemou, M. and Houndoumadi, A. (2000) 'An intervention program to promote the quality of life among urban minority children in Athens, Greece', Paper presented to the Third Conference of the International Society for Quality of Life Studies, Girona, Spain, 20-22 July.

Van Bueren, G. (1995) *The International Law on the Rights of the Child*, Dordrecht, Martinus Nijhoff Publishers/Save the Children.

van Praag, B., Hagenaars, A. and van Weeren, J. (1980) *Poverty in Europe*, Report to the Commission of the EC, Leyden, University of Leyden.

Vance, Y. H., Morse, R. C., Jenney, M. E. and Eiser, C. (2001) 'Issues in measuring quality of life in childhood cancer: measures, proxies, and parental mental health', *Journal of Child Psychology and Psychiatry*, vol 42, no 5, pp 661-7.

Veit-Wilson, J. (1986) 'Paradigms of poverty: a rehabilitation of B. S. Rowntree', *Journal of Social Policy*, vol 15, no 1, pp 66-99.

Veit-Wilson, J. (1987) 'Consensual approaches to poverty lines and social security', *Journal of Social Policy*, vol 16, no 2, pp 183-211.

Veit-Wilson, J. (1998) *Setting Adequacy Standards: How Governments Define Minimum Incomes*, Bristol, The Policy Press.

Verhellen, E. (1999) 'The Convention on the Rights of the Child', in Colla, H. E., Gabriel, T., Millham, S., Muller-Teusler, S. and Winkler, M. (eds) *Handbook of Residential and Foster Care in Europe*, Kriftel, Germany, Luchterhand.

Waldfogel, J. (2006) *What Children Need*, Cambridge, MA, Harvard University Press.

Waldron, J. (1984) 'Introduction', in Waldron, J. (ed) *Theories of Rights*, Oxford, Oxford University Press.

Waldron, J. (1993) 'Rights', in Goodin, R. E. and Pettitt, P. (eds) *A Companion to Contemporary Political Philosophy*, Oxford, Blackwell Publishers.

Walker, R. (1987) 'Consensual approaches to the definition of poverty: towards an alternative methodology', *Journal of Social Policy*, vol 16, no 2, pp 213-26.

Walker, R. (1995) 'The dynamics of poverty and social exclusion', in Room, G. (ed) *Beyond the Threshold: The Measurement and Analysis of Social Exclusion*, Bristol, The Policy Press.

Wallace, M. and Denham, C. (1996) *The ONS Classification of Local and Health Authorities of Great Britain*, London, HMSO.

Ward, H. and Peel, M. (2002) 'An inter-agency approach to needs assessment', in Ward, H. and Rose, W. (eds) *Approaches to Needs Assessment in Children's Services*, London, Jessica Kingsley Publishers.

Ware, A. and Goodin, R. E. (1990) 'Introduction', in Ware, A. and Goodin, R. E. (eds) *Needs and Welfare*, London, Sage Publications.

Warnock, M. (1998) *An Intelligent Person's Guide to Ethics*, London, Duckworth.

Wedge, P. and Essen, J. (1982) *Children in Adversity*, London, Pan Books.

West, D. J. and Farrington, D. P. (1973) *Who Becomes Delinquent?*, London, Heinemann.

Whelan, B. J. and Whelan, C. T. (1995) 'In what sense is poverty multidimensional?', in Room, G. (ed) *Beyond the Threshold: The Measurement and Analysis of Social Exclusion*, Bristol, The Policy Press.

White, K. J. (1999) 'Introduction', in White, K. J. (ed) *Children and Social Exclusion: Towards an Understanding and Practice that is More Inclusive*, London, NCVCCO.

WHO (World Health Organization) (1948) *World Health Organization Constitution, Basis Documents*, Geneva, WHO.

WHO (1993) *International Classification of Diseases – 10th Edition (ICD-10)*, Geneva, WHO.

WHOQOL Group (World Health Organization Quality of Life Group) (1993) *Measuring Quality of Life: The Development of the World Health Organization Quality of Life Instrument (WHOQOL)*, Geneva, WHO.

Widdows, J. (1997) *A Special Need for Inclusion: Children with Disabilities, their Families and Everyday Life*, London, The Children's Society.

Wiggins, D. (1985) 'Claims of need', in Honderich, T. (ed) *Morality and Objectivity*, London, Routledge and Kegan Paul.

Williams, A. and Kind, P. (1992) 'The present state of play about QALYs', in Hopkins, A. (ed) (1992) *Measures of the Quality of Life: And the Uses to Which Such Measures may be Put*, London, Royal College of Physicians of London.

Williams, F. (1998) 'Agency and structure revisited: rethinking poverty and social exclusion', in Barry, M. and Hallett, C. (eds) *Social Exclusion and Social Work: Issues of Theory, Policy and Practice*, Lyme Regis, Russell House Publishing.

Williamson, H. (1997) 'Status zer0 youth and the "underclass": some considerations', MacDonald, R. (ed) *Youth, the 'Underclass' and Social Exclusion*, London, Routledge.

Wilson, W. J. (1987) *The Truly Disadvantaged: The Inner City, the Underclass and Public Policy*, Chicago, IL, University of Chicago Press.

Woodhead, M. (1997) 'Psychology and the construction of children's needs', in James, A. and Prout, A. (eds) *Constructing and Reconstructing Childhood: Contemporary Issues in the Sociological Study of Childhood*, London, The Falmer Press.

Wresinski, J. (1994) *Chronic Poverty and Lack of Basic Security*, Paris, Economic and Social Council.

Wringe, C. A. (1981) *Children's Rights: A Philosophical Study*, London, Routledge and Kegan Paul.

Yépez del Castillo, I. (1994) 'A comparative approach to social exclusion: lessons from France and Belgium', *International Labour Review*, vol 133, no 5-6, pp 613-33.

Young, J. (1999) *The Exclusive Society: Social Exclusion, Crime and Difference in Late Modernity*, London, Sage Publications.

Zielinski, D. S. and Bradshaw, C. P. (2006) 'Ecological influences on the sequelae of child maltreatment: a review of the literature', *Child Maltreatment*, vol 11, no 1, pp 49-62.

Index

Page references for notes are followed by n

Well-being
In search of a good life?
Beverley A. Searle

"Beverley Searle's research is a key benchmark study on the state of well-being. It is essential reading for all those interested in a better understanding of subjective well-being and in the measurement of it at a national level." **Professor Jonathan Bradshaw, Department of Social Policy and Social Work, University of York**

HB £55.00 US$99.00 **ISBN** 978 1 86134 887 6 240 x 172mm 208 pages January 2008

Welfare and well-being
Social value in public policy
Bill Jordan

"This is a reasoned yet passionate critique of contract and public choice theory and charts a way forward for a progressive social policy." **Professor Ian Gough, Department of Social and Policy Sciences, University of Bath**

PB £22.50 US$39.95 **ISBN** 978 1 84742 080 0
HB £65.00 US$110.00 **ISBN** 978 1 84742 081 7 234 x 156mm 224 pages tbc October 2008

To order copies of these publications or any other Policy Press titles please visit **www.policypress.org.uk** or contact:

In the UK and Europe:
Marston Book Services, PO Box 269,
Abingdon, Oxon, OX14 4YN, UK
Tel: +44 (0)1235 465500
Fax: +44 (0)1235 465556
Email: direct.orders@marston.co.uk

In the USA and Canada:
ISBS, 920 NE 58th Street, Suite 300,
Portland, OR 97213-3786, USA
Tel: +1 800 944 6190
(toll free)
Fax: +1 503 280 8832
Email: info@isbs.com

In Australia and New Zealand:
DA Information Services,
648 Whitehorse Road Mitcham,
Victoria 3132, Australia
Tel: +61 (3) 9210 7777
Fax: +61 (3) 9210 7788
E-mail: service@dadirect.com.au